Praise for *Straight to Hell*

"Shots are drunk, nether parts are exposed and rubbed against food, bread rolls are hurled, drugs are inhaled and prostitutes paid. It's Bertie Wooster's Drones Club via the darker corners of Edward St. Aubyn and Bret Easton Ellis."

—*Wall Street Journal*

"Beyond the shock factor, it's the humour in the book that stands out . . . [LeFevre] flinches from nothing: the Herculean inappropriateness of trading-floor antics, the hookers, the cocaine . . . This book is going to annoy and offend a lot of people, with good reason. It is a vicious, vacuous, caustic world he illuminates. But it would be a shameful waste if we didn't have LeFevre to find the humour in it all."

—*Euromoney* (UK)

"LeFevre's workplace anecdotes include tales of nastiness, sabotage, favoritism, sexism, racism, expense-account padding, and legally questionable collusion."   —*New Yorker*

"There's no question that [LeFevre] knows his way around the business, and it's a dirty one. There's collusion, competition, nepotism, and a whole lot of reprehensible stuff going on in the business side, and it's fascinating . . . A great read."

—*Business Insider*

"In some memoirs, the author tries to pull back the curtain to provide a glimpse into a particular time and place, but LeFevre attempts to rip the drapes right off. He gives a naked look at how business in the world of finance is conducted. LeFevre . . . doesn't shy away from witnessing and partaking in some of the seedier antics . . . You may not like LeFevre's tact, but he knows what he's talking about."   —Turney Duff, CNBC

STRAIGHT TO HELL

STRAIGHT TO HELL

True Tales of Deviance, Debauchery, and Billion-Dollar Deals

JOHN LEFEVRE

Grove Press

New York

Published simultaneously in Canada
Printed in the United States of America

ISBN 978-0-8021-2521-7
eISBN 978-0-8021-9208-0

Grove Press
an imprint of Grove Atlantic
154 West 14th Street
New York, NY 10011

groveatlantic.com

16 17 18 19   10 9 8 7 6 5 4 3 2

To my wife and children.
I wrote this for you, on the condition that you never read it.

Contents

Author's Note

"**G**oldman fucking Sachs. Ever heard of it?"
It was the perfect inaugural tweet. *Ever heard of it?* is such a common (and irritating) banker phrase that it had become its own joke, like when one banker says, "Nice tie. Brooks Brothers?" and the other banker dismisses him with, "Charvet. Ever heard of it?" I've always made fun of this mentality by adding "Ever heard of it?" after any kind of shameless place or name-dropping.

Just a few hours earlier, I had been in a bar in Hong Kong with a group of friends, all of whom were finance guys. Although markets had recovered from the bowels of the financial crisis, the summer of 2011 was still a tumultuous time.

The Occupy movement was just starting to gain momentum; people were still angry. Despite the housing collapse, the ensuing crisis, and subsequent bailouts, not a single banker had been held criminally responsible. Bonuses had remained relatively intact and the equity markets had come roaring back from the lows of 2009. The fact that most people hadn't benefited from the market recovery, and that income inequality was breaking through generational highs, only further fanned the flames of anger and resentment. One friend of mine joked about how his wife had been nearly heckled out of a Manhattan doctor's office after being overheard telling the receptionist that their insurance was provided by Goldman Sachs. Anti–Wall Street sentiment was rampant. "Fucking plebes."

Earlier that day, I had seen a *Daily Mail* story about an anonymous Twitter account (@CondeElevator) that hilariously chronicled the most ridiculous conversations overheard in the elevators of the infamous Condé Nast building. *Holy shit, I thought. If people are so intrigued by this kind of banality, I cannot imagine what they would think if they heard the outrageous things bankers say and do.* Despite all of the vilification and negative attention, most people still had no idea what Wall Street culture was really like. In the drunken haze of that subsequent evening, @GSElevator was born—"Things heard in the Goldman Sachs elevators do not stay in the Goldman Sachs elevators. Email me what you hear." The premise was simple—to illuminate Wall Street culture in an entertaining and insightful way.

I chose Goldman Sachs because of their position as public enemy #1, and people's fascination with "vampire squids" and the absurdity of Lloyd Blankfein claiming to be "doing God's work." More specifically, in having recently gone through the arduous process of being offered the prestigious job of Head of Asia Debt Syndicate at Goldman Sachs (a hiring that was deemed newsworthy by Bloomberg and others), I found their culture to be an amplified version of broader banking culture. I kept the construct of elevators simply as an homage to the original Condé Naste feed, but made it clear that it was never literally about conversations overheard in elevators at Goldman Sachs.

Over the days that followed, I got mentions in the the *Daily Mail*, on Gawker, at *ZeroHedge*, in the *New York Post*, and elsewhere. I had friends calling and accusing me of being the source, or culprit, depending on their point of view. I had other friends being accused themselves. I even had an ex-girlfriend (the Warden) telling anyone who would listen that it was me. All of a sudden, a silly, drunken, inside joke had run out of control, jeopardizing my identity and my livelihood and threatening to impact me and my friends.

So when the *New York Times* reached out asking for an interview, of course I lied to them. Because, who gives a fuck? It was a bullshit Twitter account with 2,000 followers. More important, my personal details were irrelevant. @GSElevator is not even a real person; it's the concentrated reflection of a culture and a mentality, the aggregation of "every banker." Getting focused on me the person misses the point. More to the point, as a "submit what you hear" platform, @GSElevator does work at Goldman Sachs, and JPMorgan, and Morgan Stanley, and everywhere else. But who gives a shit? What mattered more was that the authenticity of my voice ruffled feathers and captivated people around the world and across the spectrum.

I had no idea where the Twitter account would take me, but I did know that I had been collecting stories (the inane and insane) over the course of my career in banking. I joined the fixed-income desk of Salomon Brothers immediately out of college.* Starting in the wake of the dot-com bubble bursting and working through the financial crisis, across three continents, I enjoyed a colorful career during a turbulent and defining period in the history of financial markets and our society in general.

---

*I say Salomon as opposed to Citigroup or Salomon Smith Barney because the legal entity that employed me was technically Salomon Brothers International, and also to reflect the fact that the culture within fixed income was still very different than the rest of the bank.

As "one of the most prolific syndicate managers in Asia," I saw it all. I worked intimately with investment banking and sales and trading, corporate and sovereign clients, and asset managers and hedge funds. I did deals with every bank on Wall Street—directing traffic at Wall Street's epicenter: the bond syndicate desk.

Once I left Hong Kong, I was less worried about my identity coming out. I started tweeting about specific details and events that made my identity obvious to a large number of people within the capital markets community. I wasn't subtle—in an article I wrote for *Business Insider*, I recommended a haircut by Sammy at the Mandarin Oriental in Hong Kong. He's so old and shaky that it had always been a running joke of mine to send visiting colleagues his way for a straight-razor shave.

Once I made the decision to write a book, I knew that my identity wouldn't remain the terribly kept secret that it was. In fact, I was counting on it. Revealing myself was the only way for me to speak candidly and credibly about the vantage point from which I have observed and enjoyed my outrageous experiences.

This book isn't an indictment of any particular firm, some kind of exposé, or a moralistic tale of redemption. Rather, my objective is to unapologetically showcase the true soul of Wall Street in a way that hasn't been done before. No epiphanies. No apologies. No fucks given.

Many of the names, some of the characteristics and descriptions of people, and other minor details have been changed in order to protect people's identities. It's not my intention to be mean-spirited or inadvertently impact people's careers or personal lives, and many of the people mentioned in this book are still my close friends to this day. As it relates to the people I don't give a shit about, fortunately for them, the lawyers made me change those names too.

STRAIGHT TO HELL

If you can only be good at one thing, be good at lying . . . because if you're good at lying, you're good at everything.

Every year, children learn a valuable life lesson: Santa loves rich kids more.

Sometimes, I will apologize for farting even when I didn't just so people think mine don't stink.

My garbage disposal eats better than 99% of the world.

Statistically speaking, you shouldn't worry about what your first wife's mother looks like.

Windows on the World

"**E**xcuse me, another round of Bloodys, please?"

It's August 2001, and I'm hanging out at Windows on the World, at the top of Tower One of the World Trade Center, with a few of my fellow new analyst classmates. It's only 9:30 A.M., but we don't really care. Most of my drinking companions are either European or well connected; everyone else is far too cautious to skip out on training. They're all across the street in the auditorium of 7 World Trade, diligently taking notes about financial accounting, bond math, or whatever.

I'm not worried about skipping class; I was there first thing to put my name on the sign-in sheet, and I've got a promise from a friendly classmate that he'll text me if there's any kind of impromptu roll call. So far, that text hasn't come, but I keep a pack of Marlboro Lights in my pocket just in case I need an alibi for the time it takes me to make it down two elevators and back across the street.

Besides, it should be time to celebrate. We've made it. Wall Street, the pinnacle, some might argue, for any ambitious and accomplished college graduate looking to enter the workforce. I don't recall the precise statistics, but we're reminded on a daily basis how fortunate we are—the firm received something like 25,000 applications for roughly 350 spots globally.

Gazing out the window on the 107th floor, I feel confident, even invincible. It wasn't always that way. During my interview with Lazard Frères, a prestigious boutique investment bank and one of the last true partnerships on Wall Street, I almost passed out from vertigo staring out the window from the mere fifty-seventh floor of 30 Rockefeller Plaza. Then, after a final-round interview superday with Bear Stearns, I inadvertently sent a thank-you email to the head of emerging markets, telling him how much I wanted to work for JPMorgan. During a Goldman Sachs interview, some asshole asked me who, living or dead, I would most like to have dinner with. I guess he wasn't particularly impressed that I named Tupac Shakur ahead of Marcus Aurelius or Alexander Hamilton. Still, despite these hiccups, in the end, I wanted to do fixed income, and for that, there was arguably no better place to be than Salomon Brothers, with the recently added platform and balance sheet of Citigroup behind it.

There's only one slight problem: my analyst class is the largest in the history of investment banking. We were hired based on quotas set in mid-2000, before it was evident that the dot-com party was over. Nowhere is this more painfully clear than in the European TMT team (telecom, media, and technology), which hired forty first-year analysts. On the first day of training, those analysts were informed that there were now only seven available spots, leaving them scrambling to find a new team before the end of training or be out of a job.

With the exception of TMT, most analysts aren't assigned or invited to join a specific team until near the end of training.

Having received an offer after my internship in debt capital markets the previous summer, I already know I have a bid from that group if I want it. But for most of the analysts, the real competition is just beginning. It turns out that landing a coveted Wall Street job isn't the finish line; it's the starting block. You wouldn't know it looking at the flushed faces around our table at Windows on the World, surrounded by Brooklyn Lager empties and half-chewed celery sticks.

Later that afternoon, we are given the first of many ominous warnings.

"Let this be a reminder to all of you. Not only are you required to attend all training sessions, you are expected to act in a professional manner and take them seriously. Additionally, next Tuesday, we will have our first exam—accounting. In all likelihood, the bottom 10% will be let go."

A posh-sounding British kid, one of my drinking buddies, raises his hand. "But I studied classics at Oxford? This doesn't seem fair." Apparently, it's not all shits and giggles.

"What do you think the training is for? I'm sure you'll do fine."

This doesn't faze me at all; I studied finance and economics. Other than learning how to use Excel without a mouse, I don't really need the training.

It turns out that HR is not bluffing. The day after the first exam, the results are posted on two large bulletin boards in the back of the auditorium. In a lazy attempt at privacy, one board lists each person's name along with a random numerical code next to it. The second board has each person's code listed in numerical order with their exam result next to it.

Obviously, the first thing everybody does is look up their own scores—I passed with flying colors. After that, we all spend the next ten minutes indiscreetly running back and forth between the two boards gossiping and checking the results of our friends and adversaries. HR makes no attempt to provide summary statistics or clarity on the results, leaving those who had not fared well to fester in uncertainty while awaiting formal confirmation of their fate. That night, the bottom 10% is notified with a simple note under the door of their temporary corporate housing apartments. We are all a bit envious of the people who no longer have a roommate.

There's a certain nonchalance and indifference about the firm's approach to this process that we all find both disconcerting and thrilling. The next week, it happens again after the financial math exam. Same drill—the bottom 10% is let go. Again, I have nothing to worry about. There's blood in the water now, and I have to admit, the process is somewhat exhilarating.

I do feel bad for some of these kids. I just hope they saved their Barneys receipts. Pathetically, one kid even tries selling his new watch before he leaves town. But what the fuck am I going to do with a Movado?

With the exams out of the way, and the deadweight gone, everything settles down as the emphasis of training shifts to things like PowerPoint, Excel, financial modeling, and presentation skills. We are each assigned a cubicle on a spare floor in 7 World Trade to work on group projects and individual homework assignments.

The homework assignments are a joke. Five minutes before class, I'll jump on my computer, go to the shared drive, and find a copy of someone else's completed assignment. With a name change and a quick scan of the document to make sure the answers are sensible, I print it out and head off to class. Many of the kids in my class, particularly the ones I associate with, do this as well.

One day, our HR point person steps up in front of us in the auditorium. "I'd just like to inform you that we've had to let go eight of your classmates for copying homework assignments."

A few of my classmates—many of whom wouldn't last—look at each other, appalled that anyone could be capable of cheating, while the rest of us look at each other in relief that we hadn't also been caught, highlighting the age-old battle between the front-of-the-class and the back-of-the-class mentalities.

From that day forward, I am more careful. Instead of five minutes before class, I'll come in ten minutes early. Then I'll add my own personal touch on the formatting, rephrase some of the answers, and even make a couple of intentionally unique mistakes.

Again, within a week, four more people are fired for stealing homework. This time, it turns out that some of our more spiteful classmates had started sabotaging files in the drive, even creating fake files with all incorrect answers. As we see it, if you're dumb enough to get caught cheating, you probably don't belong on Wall Street.

We celebrate by skipping training the following day for a liquid breakfast up in the sky followed by lunch at Peter Luger.

After that, things start to settle down again. HR reassures us that, barring any further disciplinary issues, all the cuts have been made. The rest of training is spent rather uneventfully in the auditorium or, for a select group of us, across the street. Our evenings are spent doing team-building exercises, bowling at Lucky Strike, and getting drunk on Hudson River cruises. I'm not one for name tags and meet and greets, but there is certainly a business case to be made for getting to know all the kids in my class.

For the final day of training, the firm puts on a celebratory pep rally in the auditorium of 388 Greenwich Street.

Bigwigs like Mark Simonian (global head of TMT), Sir Deryck Maughan (chairman and former CEO of Salomon Brothers), Michael Klein (head of investment banking), and Tom Maheras (head of fixed income) each deliver rousing speeches about how there's no firm in the world they'd rather work for and no better place for us to start our careers.

Now we feel like we've made it—all 272 of us who remain. Having arrived late, I'm stuck in the back with a middle seat that will make it impossible to slip out unnoticed. Shortly after we begin, a kid I sort of know a few rows in front of me gets up and tries to make an exit. Man, he's got balls. Mid-speech, he's shuffling across, forcing people to stand up in order to make way for him to pass.

"Excuse me. Sorry. Pardon me." It's like being in a movie theater except that the room is fully lit, and he's interrupting a Master of the Universe who is busy onstage talking about his favorite thing—himself.

Ten minutes later, the kid walks back down the aisle of the auditorium. This time, he looks red-faced and teary-eyed. "Excuse. Sorry. Pardon me," he repeats over and over as he makes his way back to his seat. Holy shit, did his mom just die? What the fuck happened? Once he gets to his seat, instead of sitting, he reaches down, grabs his signature Salomon Smith Barney blue-and-green canvas duffel bag, and turns back around. His blotchy red face turns completely scarlet and the puffy eyes unload a waterfall of tears. "Excuse me. Sorry. Pard—ah—ah uh ah uh." He can't even get the words out without whimpering. His efforts to muffle the sound of his sobbing almost make him hyperventilate. It's disgusting. And then, just like that, he's gone.

Meanwhile, onstage, Sir Deryck Maughan is wrapping up his speech. "Congratulations on being a member of the analyst class of 2001, the most qualified class in our storied history."

Five minutes later, another analyst gets up and walks out. A few minutes pass, and then she comes back, collects her purse and canvas bag, and leaves, looking rather more stoic than the first guy, but still stunned. Now a few people in the back are starting to suspect something is quite obviously wrong. As she walks out, from my vantage point, I can see her mouth to a friend, "I just got fired." Most people from the middle of the room forward are still unaware of what's happening behind them.

Five minutes later, another guy gets up and starts to walk out. He doesn't appear to realize that he's about to get shit-canned. Someone from the back shouts out, *"Dude*, just bring your stuff with you," which is good for more than a few laughs.

Finally, between the disruption and the whispers working their way around the room, people start to figure out what's happening. An Asian girl sitting next to me, whom I had never spoken to before, says, "Shit. I got a notice under my door to see HR this morning at ten fifteen A.M. That's in ten minutes. I assumed it was regarding the team I would be assigned to. But clearly not." And with that, she gets up, says, "It's been real, y'all," to no one in particular, and walks out.

Confirmation of the news, and the meaning of the HR notices, has now spread across the entire analyst class. At this point, all the people who had received an HR notice get up and start walking out.

Back onstage, Michael Klein doesn't skip a beat. He assures us that we can all be just like him one day.

I later find out that the first kid who got fired begged HR to go back into the auditorium to collect his bag for him and spare him the tearful walk of shame. They refused. No worries; I hear he's a successful broker now.

Don't apologize for being late with a Starbucks latte in your hand.

If someone asks you a question and you don't know the answer, belittle them. It's better to be an asshole than look stupid.

It's okay to trade the possibility of your 80s and 90s for more guaranteed fun in your 20s and 30s.

Don't wear shoes memorable enough to be recognized under a bathroom stall.

Advice for a daughter depends almost entirely on how attractive she is.

A Felonious Mentality

"Y̲ou may have escaped from this situation unscathed, but in my eyes, you are nothing but a weasel." My adviser, Mr. Cobb, has just burst into my dorm room to share this uplifting gem with me.

He looks at me (my head studiously buried in a textbook), glances over at my stereo (classical music playing softly), and then just rolls his eyes. Had I not been fourteen years old, he probably would have made the jerk-off hand motion.

In all fairness, his presumption isn't too far off. Just two minutes earlier, I had recognized the sound of his not insubstantial weight coming up the stairs, quickly turned off the game of Maelstrom I was playing on my McIntosh, flipped open my chemistry book, and switched from Dr. Dre's *The Chronic* to the Vivaldi's *Four Seasons* CD I stole from my mom.

"Mr. Cobb, coming from you, I think I'll take that as a compliment."

Fuck him. As my fourth form (tenth grade) adviser, he's supposed to be my ally, my father figure away from home, the guy in my corner, and a guiding presence during these crucial, character-building early teenage years. Instead, he has looked for every opportunity to pick me off. And at this point, there's nothing I can do to change his opinion of me.

I've just experienced my first major run-in with the Choate Rosemary Hall authorities. Coming back from class a few days earlier, I had decided to grab a seat in the dormitory common room and hang out with some friends. The chair I chose immediately collapsed from my rather underwhelming weight. I looked down to discover that someone had broken off the leg and then reattached it in a way that made it appear structurally sound; it was a booby trap.

Admittedly, my reaction was rather juvenile. I picked up the chair and repeatedly smashed it into the ground until it splintered and broke apart, leaving the room strewn with shards of jagged wood and pieces of foamy cushion.

That night, at our weekly dorm meeting, our housemaster, Mr. Gadua (whom we had nicknamed "The Gimp"), inquired about the broken chair. "I need the person who broke the chair to come forward." Of course, no one said a word.

The next day, I received a meeting request from my dean; someone must have ratted me out. I'm getting sent before the judicial committee. Not only am I facing a charge for breaking the chair, I'm also accused of a much more serious honor code violation for lying to The Gimp. Boarding schools tend to get sanctimonious and self-righteous when it comes to issues of honor.

My first instinct was to argue that I broke the chair in order to prevent other people from being injured. But that wouldn't absolve me from the honor code violation. So I decided to keep my argument simple. "In my mind, as it relates to a chair, it is impossible to break something that is already broken. So when The Gimp asked us about the chair, I did not step forward, because I genuinely do not know who broke the chair." Case dismissed.

Even at this impressionable age, I knew that I wanted to go to Wall Street. I had never really enjoyed obeying authority figures, especially the idiotic ones like Mr. Cobb or The Gimp. Besides the influence of watching the movie *Wall Street* on basic cable and reading *Liar's Poker* (and then *Den of Thieves*, *The Predator's Ball*, and *Barbarians at the Gate*), my fascination with Wall Street really crystallized during my first year at boarding school. I became captivated by financial markets, the men who mastered them, and the tangible benefits that came with it.

This was only reinforced when all the parents came down from places like Greenwich for parents' weekend. The Wall Street dads were the cool dads with the sports cars and a propensity for profanity. They'd tell our dean we were spending the weekend with them in Connecticut, only to let us disappear into New York City, where we'd take down a suite at the Waldorf Astoria and use the concierge desk to get us into places like Scores and Au Bar. This is when I internalized the number one rule of life: "Rules are for the obedience of fools and the guidance of wise men."

From my experience, Wall Street generally attracts people with a certain mentality. It then takes those people, breaks them down, and molds them to suit its singular purpose— making money. Priorities are relative. Concepts of wealth are relative. Expectations and standards of hard work and intelligence are relative. Morality and deviance are relative. Wall Street operates in its own reality. Assimilate or die.

In its own way, boarding school was great preparation for investment banking. Not only were the Wall Street dads different, so were their kids. They had a much more evolved perspective, at a much earlier age, than the rest of us—a certain confidence, a kill-or-be-killed mind-set, even a felonious streak when it came to authority. They were the kids in the dorms who somehow managed to get a doctor's note that allowed them to have a refrigerator in their room. (It turns out every investment banker knows at least one doctor who owes him a favor. Where else were we supposed to get the Ritalin?) Their parents not only let them break rules they didn't think should apply to them, but encouraged and abetted them. Boarding students can't have cars on campus? No problem, just keep it in the parking lot at the public library in town. Students aren't allowed to have cell phones (it's the mid-1990s)? Be smart; just don't get caught. Let scholarship kids, or worse, do-gooder types follow the rules. Then come talk to me in twenty years.

They make little attempt to operate within the framework of a "meritocracy" unless it suits them. Can't break 1300 on the SATs because you're a moron? No problem. Get diagnosed "learning disabled" and then take all standardized tests untimed. One friend and classmate got an 1100 on his SATs, which, despite his being a legacy applicant, obviously wasn't going to get him into Penn. A doctor's note later, he was retaking the test untimed. Instead of spending four hours in a gymnasium with strict proctors looming over him like the rest of us, he had an entire week in a private classroom with minimal supervision, allowing him to covertly save vocabulary words, analogies, and math problems in his TI-82 calculator so that he could correct any mistakes the following day. A 1400 on the retake, which is still embarrassing under the circumstances—that's like only netting $50K on a an insider trading scheme—got him off the Penn wait list, and now he works for a hedge fund in London and drives a Ferrari. Granted, he bought it used for less than the price of a BMW 5-series and works in a mid-office capacity, but none of that registers with his Facebook friends. He was born on third base and scored on a wild pitch, but at least he can convince his friends (and himself) that he hit a triple and stole home. The ends justify the means; that's an important concept to understand if you want to be successful on Wall Street, and is one that boarding school taught me well.

Being a young, naive kid from Texas, it took some time for me to grasp this mentality, but I caught up pretty quickly. By junior year, I was the one with the Sega Genesis and TV hidden in my closet on top of my minifridge.

I also learned other key trading-floor skills: bullying, hazing, and the art of a great prank. One night, a kid who lives across the hall from me leaves his room to go take a shower; he's one of these dopes who showers at night right before lights-out in order to save time in the morning.

Shower pranks are fairly standard. Someone will steal their towel, or lock them out of their own room, or both. That's boring. It's happened to this kid so many times that he practically showers with one hand on his towel.

Knowing that we are both studying for the same calculus exam at 8 A.M. the next morning, I go into his room, take his calculus textbook and binder full of notes, stuff them into his closet, and then lock the closet door by looping his Kryptonite bicycle lock through the door handles and leaving the key inside.

Then, for good measure, I also lock him out of his room.

He thinks that's the joke—that someone has locked him out of his room while he was in the shower. No big deal. He walks downstairs in his towel and asks the housemaster to come up and let him in using the master key.

It's only about fifteen minutes later, presumably when he sits down to study, that he realizes that his books are missing and there's a Kryptonite lock on his closet.

Now he has to go back downstairs and explain the situation to our housemaster, who has to call campus security, which then has to summon someone from the maintenance department to come up and physically saw off his closet door, a process that eats up two hours of prime study time.

Although they had their suspicions, no one was ever able to determine who the culprit/mastermind was. I'm pretty sure I beat him on that calculus test. My transformation from a young, naive kid from Texas was coming along.

I was usually on some form of restriction or probation, and always under a cloud of suspicion. But I was developing an appreciation for absurdity and an ability to adapt quickly to the situation at hand. The two come together one memorable spring weekend afternoon. I am sitting in my room, which faces away from the quad and out across the parking lot to the junior varsity tennis courts. The parking lot is surprisingly full, as are each of the courts, with players and spectators. There are more parents than on a typical boarding school sports Saturday, which means it's a home match against a nearby day school.

I'm a decent tennis player, but I never bothered playing in school. Being on the golf team was way more fun. With a dozen or so guys and only one coach, it was impossible for him to supervise all of us. Along with a few friends, our objective was always to play well enough to make the team and then never well enough to qualify for the top seven who would travel on match day for the tournaments.

A few times a week, we'd bus over to the Farms Country Club and play nine holes. Coach DeMarco would watch everyone tee off and then play his way up through each pairing so that he could watch and assess all of us fairly. We always made sure to be among the last few groups off the tee. Once our coach played a hole with us, we had six or seven uninterrupted holes to drink the beers we had stashed in our golf bags—and then throw the empties away on the eighth hole.

So here I am idling in my room having intentionally missed the golf tournament. For whatever reason, I decide to amuse myself by placing my speakers facing out my open windows and in the direction of the tennis courts. Snoop Dogg's *Doggystyle*. Track 7. Volume up. Play.

Snoop kicks off "Lodi Dodi" with a gentle reminder to his detractors that they are welcome to fellate him. The sound is felt and heard with immediate effect. Most of the spectators instantly turn and face the dormitories looking for the source of the disruption. I crank up the volume almost to the point of blowing my Kenwood speakers.

All match play soon grinds to a halt; I'm not sure if it's because the music is so distracting, or if they simply can't hear each other recite the score. That's when I see the tennis coach, Mr. Goodyear, frantically scanning the windows. This guy is so stiff that he wears bow ties on weekends. He drops his clipboard and breaks into a full sprint toward the dorm complex.

Fuck. What I've just done is petulant, immature, and, worst of all, indefensible in its stupidity. I probably only have about thirty seconds to figure a way out of this.

I dive away from the windows, strip naked, grab my towel, and sprint out and down the hallway toward the showers, leaving the music blaring and making sure to lock my door on my way out. I stay in the shower long enough for my heart rate to normalize, and then dry off and head back to my room.

Mr. Bowtie waits at my door. He's hounding one of the security guys, who is fumbling through his massive key chain trying to find the master key for our dorm. Goodyear sees me coming toward them and screams, "Is this your room? Open the damn door."

"It's not locked. I never lock my door." I'm cool and relaxed. With the speakers facing out the window, we can hear each other perfectly, although the walls and floors are shaking like we're backstage at a concert. As soon as they get in, Goodyear goes right for the plug.

I'm quick to point out that this has all the markings of an ill-conceived prank—someone has clearly taken advantage of the fact that I trustingly left my door unlocked while I was in the shower. "I don't know who could've done this, but everyone pranks everyone around here." Bowtie slinks off disappointed; he'll have to wait another day to bring me down. Unbelievably, the security guy winks at me; he knows who's boss.

One of my most important life lessons came senior year: Two different English teachers have tasked my housemate and me with the identical essay assignment on *Beowulf*. What starts out as innocent and sincere brainstorming quickly escalates to us staring over a laptop crystallizing our ideas together. We sit there for the next couple of hours, casually talking and taking turns typing. The end result is phenomenal.

A week later, I get another summons from my dean; once again, I'm being sent before the judicial committee, this time charged with cheating, an offense punishable by suspension. If you get suspended during your senior year, you have to inform the colleges that you're applying to—basically I'm fucked.

The verdict comes back with a unanimous 5–0 vote in favor of probation for my codefendant and a 5–0 vote in favor of suspension for me. He is a two-sport varsity athlete and I'm an underachieving scumbag whose own adviser failed to support him at the hearing.

There's no justice in this world—a valuable lesson to learn at a young age, especially if you want to end up on Wall Street. I've seen some of the best traders and sales guys get fired at the expense of worthless assholes. Who you know is as important as what you do and how you are perceived is more important than any reality.

Knowing that the dean of students, who is also my English teacher from the previous year, has a soft spot for me, I take the unusual step of appealing the unanimous decision. I make a compelling argument that this is simply an instance of unauthorized collaboration, as opposed to outright cheating. The following day, my suspension is overturned, making me the first and only case in Choate history (that I know of) where a unanimous judicial committee decision has been overturned.

There was a time when we sent the undesirables to islands. Now you have to buy an island just to get away from them.

Sure, I'll shave my head if my wife gets cancer, but I'm not going to quit drinking just because she's pregnant.

The only thing more impressive than my accomplishments is my résumé.

If there's a hot chick behind me at the ATM, I'll always leave my receipt in the machine so she can see the balance.

Only Neanderthals resort to violence. I prefer crushing one's spirit, hope, or ego.

Ode to
Liar's Poker

In *Liar's Poker*, Michael Lewis makes reference to the "suitcase goof," which, as he recollects, started innocuously in 1982 with one trader putting pink lace panties in another trader's weekend bag, and then gradually escalated until entire contents of suitcases were being replaced with soggy toilet paper.

All of our bosses in fixed income—Paul Young, Phil Bennett, Jim Forese, Mike Corbat, Mark Watson, and Jeremy Amias, and our ultimate boss, Tom Maheras—worked their way up through the *Liar's Poker* era of Salomon Brothers from the early 1980s through the Treasury scandal of the early 1990s. Not only do they embody that now-infamous culture, but all the junior bankers go out of their way to embrace and emulate it as well. As analysts, we would sit around over beers after work and share second- and thirdhand stories. "Hey, did you hear what happened at the MDs' off-site?"

Of course, we had all heard the story. Ed Bowman hired a helicopter and some former SAS soldiers as actors to swoop in and stage a mock kidnapping of Mahir Haddad during the middle of an outdoor team-building exercise. That would have been hilarious had it not been for the fact that Mahir had grown up in war-torn Beirut and had seen close friends and family kidnapped or killed; he was not amused.

Mahir extracted his revenge on the Dino Ferrari that Ed had obnoxiously driven to the off-site, covering it in toothpaste and inadvertently destroying the original paint job in the process. For fear of further escalation, Tom Maheras was brought in to forge a truce and temper the culture of aggressive and mean-spirited trading-floor antics and office pranks.

However, the goofs continued. Just as I was finding my feet on the trading floor, Rick Goldberg, the global head of ████████████, set the benchmark with a suitcase prank that quickly became the stuff of Salomon Brothers legend.

On a trading floor, it's not uncommon for people who are traveling to leave their suitcases right next to their desks. It's not that they are necessarily afraid of being victimized if they let their bags out of their sight; it's simply a logistical function of the closets being so far away.

One day, this New Jersey guido-made-good, Vinny Funaro, comes in with a small Samsonite travel bag. He's off to Montreal for a bachelor party weekend. Goldberg immediately pulls aside one of the analysts and whips out a hundred-dollar bill. "Okay, here's what I'm going to need you to do. Go down and find the nearest restaurant supply store, or God knows what, and buy me a big, metal, industrial spatula. Can you handle that?" The analyst nods confidently. This was typical Goldberg, getting his foot in the door before dropping the hammer. "Good. Then I'm going to need you to also pick up some dirty magazines. I want raunchy, hard-core porn, as much as you can carry. And it has to be gay."

"Fuck you," the analyst shoots back. "I'm not doing that."

There is no such thing as a hierarchy in times like this.

So Goldberg pulls out two more hundred-dollar bills and says, "How about now?"

The kid nods and grabs the money.

"Okay, but for that kind of money, it better be some raunchy shit. Fisting, bukakke. Don't hold back."

The analyst comes back about an hour later. "Sorry, the porn was easy; the spatula took fucking forever." With that, they wait for Funaro to leave his desk. As soon as he's off the floor, Goldberg kicks into action with clinical precision. He takes the spatula, bends it into the shape of a gun, and places it at the bottom of Funaro's suitcase. On top of that, he crafts an intricate nest of pornographic magazines, and then proceeds to construct a sandwich of clothing and gay porn, alternating layers all the way up to the top—where he neatly applies a final layer of clothing, restoring the bag back to its original appearance.

"Say a word and I'll kill you." He emphasizes the point, not that he has to; everyone knows where their bread is buttered. And with that, they all watch a short time later as Funaro heads out early to catch his flight and get a head start on his long weekend.

On the following Monday morning, it doesn't take long for shit to hit the fan. Before he even sits down, Funaro starts losing it. "Which one of you fucksticks did it? Come on, I know Goldberg put you up to it." He knows no one has the balls to carry out a stunt like that without the order from up top, but he can't do anything to his boss; all he can do is take it out on the analysts.

Everyone just stares at their screens in silence, trying not to crack up. "Do you fucktards understand what happened to me? My friend from grade school is getting married. A lot of these guys I haven't seen in years. They aren't bankers or Wall

Street guys. They're firefighters, cops, and blue-collar guys. You think they understand this shit?"

The gag could not have worked more perfectly. Going through airport security, the gun-shaped spatula set off all kinds of alarms. The TSA agent immediately pulled him aside and asked to inspect the contents of his bag, which of course got no objection on Funaro's part. The latex-glove-clad agent then started slowly dissecting the sandwich of clothing and hard-core porn, holding each magazine up in the air as if it were radioactive. Meanwhile, the entire bachelor party, having already cleared security, stood there watching this spectacle unfold, asking each other the same questions.

Once security reached the spatula, it became clear that this was someone's sick idea of a joke. However, it also became clear that this passenger had not "packed the bag himself," nor was he "familiar with all of its contents," which triggered an entirely new wave of security protocols. So Funaro and his entire troupe of guidos got held up for another twenty minutes and almost missed their flight. To this day, he has no idea who the culprit was.

When I get to London, it really strikes me how the guys in New York treat us like second-class citizens, as if London is some satellite office. Given the respective sizes of the US and European bond markets, the New York desk generally does more deals in a day than we do in a week. They treat us accordingly, coming through every few months under the guise of "helping" us educate and pitch European clients on targeting US investors. We all know that these trips are an excuse for them to live it up in London, Paris, and Madrid for a week. Of these people, Mike Benton is particularly odious. He's one

of those Americans who immediately adopts the British vernacular with words like "bloody," "mate," and "cheers." He
even treats my boss like a tour guide: "Is there a quicker way
to Savile Row without taking the bloody tube?"

One day, he comes back to the office and proudly announces
to everyone in earshot that he just came back from having
a mold of his feet done for custom-made John Lobb shoes.
"Bloody expensive at two thousand quid."

I'm not sure if he thought it would be faster or if he was
just too cheap to pay for shipping, but he arranges to have the
shoes delivered to our office so that we can interoffice them
to him for free in the internal overnight pouch. He asks Chris
Nichols, also a managing director, to handle it for him.

"Sure, I'll have Alan [his analyst] send them across when
they arrive."

"Cheers, mate."

Like clockwork, the shoes arrive six weeks later, in a shoe
box that is neatly wrapped in durable brown wrapping paper.
Chris, the custodian of the shoes, is traveling on business when
the package arrives, so our shared desk assistant casually leaves
the package on his desk.

This just so happens to coincide with a day when I am working late into the night. Other than Kamal Meraj, a friend and
fellow analyst, the trading floor is completely deserted. As
we're walking out, I can't help but notice the package just
sitting there. I fill Kamal in on the backstory and relay what
a complete douchebag Mike Benton is; we both decide this is
too good an opportunity to pass up.

We delicately unwrap the box, taking great care to make
sure the tape doesn't tear the packaging. Inside a smart-looking
pouch, we find a work of art. It's like I'm holding a pair of
Fabergé eggs. I should be wearing gloves.

We take the real shoes and carefully place them back inside their pouch and into a shopping bag. I hide the shopping bag in the bottom of one of the desk's seldom-used communal filing cabinets, where old pitch books, deal folders, and offering prospectuses go to die. We know they'll be safe there, and it's a location that can never be traced back to us.

Then I take some bright red, hand-painted, wooden Dutch clogs, which I have just stolen from underneath a desk where the Holland coverage team sits, and stuff them into the John Lobb box. They're perfect; they even have a colorful cartoonish windmill painted across the vamp and toe cap of each shoe. From there, we surgically wrap the box back up in the original packaging and tape and put it back on the desk.

The next day, the package is gone, presumably courtesy of the desk assistant. I'll never know exactly what happened when Mike Benton received that parcel on the New York trading floor. I'd like to think that, consistent with his insufferable personality, he made a huge production of opening the box, having spent the last six weeks telling everyone around him how much he paid for "the best shoes in the world." His face must have been brighter than those clogs.

A few days after the package is shipped, Chris, the managing director and shoe custodian, is back in the office. I watch him take a phone call, in which his emotions vacillate between anger and fits of almost uncontrollable laughter. He hangs up and gathers our attention.

"So, that was Mike. You're not going to believe what happened to him." He then proceeds to tell the story of how in place of his £2,000 handcrafted, bespoke John Lobb shoes, he received bright red wooden clogs. He was so blinded with rage that it didn't even occur to him that it might be a prank. Instead, he immediately called John Lobb and went so ballistic that they simply apologized profusely and said they would immediately get to work making him a new pair free of charge.

Ready for my victory lap, I quietly make my way over to the filing cabinet for the big reveal. The only problem is that the shoes aren't there. I check both cabinets on either side. There is no mistaking it; the shoes are gone. So I simply slink away back to my seat and never make mention of it again. I can only assume one of the late-night janitors pulled an "Andy Dufresne."

My favorite suitcase goof of all happened during my last summer in London. On a quiet Friday, one of the associates, Chico, shows up to work wheeling one of those quintessential Tumi carry-on suitcases. Next to the blue-and-green duffel bags, it's the standard-issue investment banker travel accoutrement.

We call him Chico because that's the name I gave him. Technically speaking, since we're close in rank and on the same desk, he is a rival in that we quietly compete for the attention and praise of our mutual superiors. Hence, my first order of business when I moved to the desk was to assign him a dismissive and belittling nickname, which worked to great effect as "Chico" was quickly adopted by most people on the floor.

Chico is one of those guys who really tries hard to play the part of a "Salomon guy." Even after Salomon Smith Barney is completely integrated into Citigroup, he insists on still saying "Salomon" when he answers the phone. He keeps a copy of *Liar's Poker* in his drawer and loves nothing more than exalting gossip and tales of Salomon Brothers lore. "Hey, did you hear Mark Watson's wife bought him an Aston Martin, and he didn't even notice the money missing from his account?" Yeah, Chico, we've heard you tell that story. "Hey, did you hear Melanie

Czarra bought two town houses in Fulham and knocked them together?" Yeah, Chico, you told us.

Chico even tries claiming that he was "on the horn" buying oil futures as the second plane was hitting the World Trade Center on 9/11, as if we don't know that he still lives at home with his parents.

On this quiet summer day, Chico is quick to inform us that he has a nice, civilized weekend planned in the English countryside. His big goofy grin is unable to contain his excitement; it's his first weekend away with the new girlfriend and they're going down to Devon to meet her family.

During lunchtime, I notice that Chico's computer is asleep. Typically, it's a point of pride to run downstairs and pick up a quick sandwich and be back at your desk before your computer falls asleep, which is about a ten-minute window. During the summer lull, a sleeping computer can quickly be construed as a long lunch or "cheeky" trip to the pub. That piece of shit has the nerve to take a long lunch on a Friday when he is already leaving early to catch his train? Fuck him; I'm gonna make him pay for that. Not only will I get to teach him a painful lesson, I'll also improve my own stature and notoriety on the floor.

It just so happens that I have a few old boxes obstructing my legroom, filled with unread bond prospectuses for long-since-priced deals. I expeditiously, but not at all subtly, remove all the contents of Chico's suitcase and replace them with an equal weight of Greece and Poland bond prospectuses. I'm not a total animal; instead of throwing his original contents away (which I should do because apparently Chico still shops at T.M.Lewin, a shitty version of Brooks Brothers), I place them into a trash bag and hide them in the coat closet—not where I hid the disappearing John Lobbs.

At this point, what I've done is hardly a secret. Not only are a few of my colleagues complicit, they're accessories, having helped me temper my exuberance in loading the bag, thus making sure it wasn't unnaturally heavy. Part of me expects some kindhearted soul to pull Chico aside and give him a heads-up, or slyly suggest that he look inside his luggage. Nope. Nathan. Nada.

Two o'clock comes and Chico cheerfully says his good-byes and heads off to catch his train. People keep looking around, waiting for someone else to say or do something. Nothing. There are some sheepish looks, a few long stares, and a slight whiff of sympathy, but for the most part, people are just trying not to laugh. Finally, he's gone; a giant collective exhale fills the row, followed by uproarious laughter.

"You really should have said something," one guy laments, mostly to alleviate his own guilt. Too late for that.

The head of the desk, a well-regarded transplant from the New York office, stands up, points down to his own Tumi suitcase next to his seat, and says, "Now, I know I don't even have to check inside my suitcase. You can't be that fucking stupid." And with that, we all have one final laugh and get back to work.

It took us many months to find out exactly what happened next, but Chico would later say that it was the single most humiliating experience of his entire life.

This flashy young investment banker with a double first from Cambridge meets his posh girlfriend at Paddington Station, where they are off to meet her family in the countryside for a weekend full of long walks, trips to the pub, and tennis on the family's estate. Unsurprisingly, the trains run late and they are stretched to make it in time for the formal family dinner. A few quick introductions and then it's off upstairs to change. It's like Downton fucking Abbey.

This is when Chico opens his bag for the first time. The words he later uses to describe the feeling are "horror" and "disbelief." It's early evening and there isn't a store for miles; he'll have no choice but to explain to everyone that he is the victim of a horrendous prank.

Worse than the inconvenience and the humiliation of having to borrow clothing is the implication, and the manner in which the prank is interpreted by a potential father-in-law on whom he is trying to make a good first impression. The only logical conclusion for Chico's girlfriend and her parents to draw is that he must not receive a great deal of respect in the office. Who would want their daughter to date the office bitch?

They broke up a few months later, and frankly, I don't blame her. To this day, when somebody messes with another person, it's not uncommon for us to say, "Man, you just got Chico'd."

I want a girlfriend strong and independent enough to change a flat tire, and hot enough that she never has to.

If I had a time machine, I probably wouldn't even use it.

My 7 is your 9, bro.

If I get a message with a typo, I'll analyze the letter placement on the keyboard to assess if it's justified or not.

You should have to earn access to the "Reply All" function on email.

The Parental Visit

At the end of my first year as an analyst, I'm feeling pretty good about myself. Performance reviews have come back and I'm ranked at the top of my class. At this point in my career, it actually doesn't matter if I get a bonus of $50,000 or $100,000. The most important thing is being told that no one else in my class is ranked higher or paid better. The money is also nice, but it's not like I have student loans to worry about.

My rabbi (mentor) balks when I tell him I'm going to invest my bonus in a diversified equity portfolio so that I am better positioned to buy an apartment the following year. "Why the fuck are you going to worry about trying to save money now? Why struggle to save one dollar today when it'll be easy for you to save ten in just a couple of years? Spend that cash. Believe in yourself, baby."

It makes so much sense that I convince a few of my analyst class friends to go to Saint-Tropez the following month, with the sole purpose of spending our entire bonuses in five days. That assignment turns out to be significantly easier than we had anticipated.

Within a few months, I am back to living paycheck to paycheck. I have a nice apartment overlooking the Thames, but otherwise my expenses shouldn't be unmanageable. In theory, I shouldn't even have time to spend my money fast enough; I'm in the office late into the evening at least five days a week.

Working late (after 8 P.M.) also allows me to take advantage of the company's generous dinner allowance (£20) and free car service home. Even if we finish earlier, most of the analysts will usually go out for drinks or sometimes hit the gym before coming back, ordering food, and taking a car home. My go-to is takeout from Nobu's sister restaurant in Canary Wharf, which I pick up on my way home. I am addicted to the rock shrimp salad, the hamachi sashimi with jalapeño and ponzu sauce, and the black cod with miso. My spend is usually closer to £40, so I just add another analyst's name on the receipt and expense it as dinner for two. I don't feel bad about it; it's what we are taught by the older analysts. And I'm not even that bad; the M&A analysts are far more brazen.

Once we are issued BlackBerrys around 2002, and we're able to check emails anywhere at any time, there is nothing that chains young bankers to their desks. This isn't really true for us on the trading floor; I typically need to be in front of my Bloomberg terminal, manning the dealerboard, and within earshot of the trading and syndicate desks. But the M&A analysts don't give a shit, especially if their direct superiors are out of the office. Many of them start going to movies in the middle of the day, and if they get an urgent call or important email, it's no different from if they had been at Starbucks or just having a cigarette. Then they'll go back to the theater the next day to pick up where they left off and finish the movie.

Investment banking analysts are like prisoners; the smallest acts of insubordination give us an incredible amount of joy and help us endure the generally stressful existence of being a banking analyst.

Most of our free time and expendable income is spent partying at places like Home House, Tramp, and Annabel's. When we get bored with London, we go to Paris or Stockholm. Because of the hours and company we keep, it becomes incredibly easy to get wrapped up in the culture. At this point, the only friends I have in London are fellow banking analysts and colleagues. Everyone else doesn't get it: the lifestyle, the long hours and canceled plans, the binge drinking, and the nihilistic sense of humor. I don't think any of them have ever woken up from a blackout on a subway car and gone direct to office still wearing last night's tuxedo, only to be showered with praise. How could they understand? And they certainly don't have the disposable income—although it doesn't always feel limitless at the rate I spend it.

At the end of my second year, I once again land at the top of my class. Saint-Tropez is even more decadent, a week in a duplex at the Hotel Byblos overlooking the pool. Our days are spent trying to keep up at Nikki Beach and Le Club 55 followed by nights at VIP Room and Les Caves du Roy. It's impossible not to have a great time, but all the same, a week in the south of France is a jarring reminder of just how much wealth exists in the world, and that in the universe of people who actually matter, investment bankers are still close to the bottom.

Shortly after my Saint-Tropez tan has faded away, I am back to struggling to make ends meet. Banking has given me a very distorted view of money, priorities, and what I deserve or feel that I am entitled to. Despite my paycheck, I feel poor. This detached sense of reality, combined with my increasingly selective social circles and a blindingly aspirational culture, has created a lifestyle as precarious as any middle-class one. The numbers are just bigger.

No matter, toward the end of my third and final year as an analyst, I am once again expecting to be at the top of my class in rank and bonus. So, I take my new girlfriend on a quick vacation to Jumby Bay in Antigua. If we break up before the summer, I'll still be able to make the annual pilgrimage to Saint-Tropez after I get my bonus.

We spend our days sailing, snorkeling, and rotating between the beach bar, the pool bar, and the spa. Our nights alternate between mellow evenings ordering room service because we're too lazy to put clothes on and drunken trips to a nearby casino, which has a dangerous policy of allowing us to charge chips back to our hotel.

After a gluttonous and glorious week on the beach, reality strikes in the form of a monster hotel bill of just over $25,000, including $12,000 in charges from the casino. The credit card I had used to make the reservation is declined. I try another one—declined. I then embarrassingly call and check the available balances on all of my cards; even if I split it up, I'm not going to get to $25K.

Asking my girlfriend for help isn't an option. It's not that I'd be embarrassed—after all, she was the drunken asshole who had spent four hours playing roulette—but I know that her only credit card has a picture of Hello Kitty on it. Plus, she's currently in the gift shop adding to the tab in real time.

It's a no-brainer. I'll pay with the company card, and then simply call and pay it back before the statement comes due. It's not terribly uncommon for someone to use a corporate card for small ticket items or dinners that don't end up being reimbursed. But I have never heard of anyone doing it for an entire vacation. We're still living in the wake of Enron and WorldCom, so job security is a constant concern irrespective of my performance reviews and class rank. As they say in Japan, "The nail that sticks out gets hammered down." I really don't want to do anything to tarnish my reputation, but right now, I have no other options.

"I'm sorry, sir. Unfortunately, we do not accept Diners Club." I think he's amused that I even have a Diners card. All employees were forced to trade in their American Express cards a few years earlier when Sandy Weill decided to buy Diners Club.

The great *Wall Street* line comes to mind: "I'm tapped out, Marv." There's only one option left. I have no choice but to suck up my pride and call my parents, whom I hadn't even informed of my extravagant vacation plans, given their opinion of my propensity for living beyond my means.

They are remarkably graceful and immediately offer up their credit card details, which makes me feel like a fifteen-year-old again—at boarding school trying to order something from the Patagonia catalog. They bail me out, but I know I'm not going to hear the end of this. Thankfully, my third-year analyst bonus is only a few weeks away, so by the time their lecture finally comes around, I'll be flush again.

The following week, I attempt to reassure my mother that everything is fine. She knows how much money I make and how little time I have to spend it. She's heard about the pressures and stresses associated with being a young banker. She's seen how my career path has amplified my id, or as I like to say on our weekly phone calls when she asks me what I've been up to, "Just workin' and gadaboutin'." But the last time she visited me in London, she conflated my head cold with a possible drug problem.

"No, Mom. Of course I don't do cocaine."

The only way I can think to placate her concern is to invite her to London, particularly now that my new apartment is nice enough that she can stay with me. She jumps on the invitation without hesitation. Two hours later, I get an email with her flight confirmation; she's arriving that following Thursday, coincidentally the day after my planned house-warming party. Thank Christ. I don't really want her meeting my friends or cramping my style.

For a twenty-four-year-old kid, my new apartment is pretty sweet—two bedrooms, split-level, a block removed from King's Road and just two blocks from Sloane Square.

The day before my party, my boss gets a call from Imperial Tobacco informing us that we've been short-listed for their upcoming Eurobond benchmark. We've been asked to make a final presentation to them in person the following morning. It's a prestigious, must-win mandate for us and one we expect to be fiercely contested over by the banks.

I've been tasked with putting together the presentation—a few pages outlining European bond market conditions, a review of our credentials as the number one bond house in the world, and then our specific recommendations for Imperial Tobacco, which I hash out with our syndicate desk. By the time I've got everything together, my boss is gone for the day; he's an old-school banker who came to Salomon via Schroders, which means 5 P.M. is martini time.

Normally, he simply trusts me to coordinate the inputs and put the presentation together without fucking up, but this is an important pitch. I fax it over to his house that evening for him to mark up any changes and fax back. I don't mind; it's always good to cover your ass.

Typically, I'd send the presentation upstairs to the printer and then have it couriered over to his house a few hours later, but my boss has another idea.

"I'm not waiting up while these get printed." That means he's probably had too many cocktails. "You hang on to them and then bring them with you in the morning. You wrote the presentation; might as well come to the meeting. We're taking the express train from Paddington at eight A.M. sharp."

Fuck. I had not counted on attending. I have my party tonight and my mother arriving tomorrow morning on the red-eye from Houston.

By the time the printer gets my presentations done, I'm already two hours late to my own party. When I walk in, there are twenty or so friends and colleagues packed into my living room. The entire place reeks of weed. Apparently, my girlfriend has started the party without me.

Perfect. This is exactly what I need to come home to. I just busted my ass all day on a last-minute fire drill, have to suffer through an early-morning meeting tomorrow, and then I'm hosting my mother for an entire week—primarily because she's worried that I am spiraling out of control.

I take a hit and grab a drink. We spend the next few hours drinking and smoking and having a blast.

The next morning, my three alarm clocks earn their keep. It's 7:30 A.M.; I have to be at Paddington Station in thirty minutes. It's nearly five kilometers away, which would take at least fifteen minutes, even in light traffic.

My apartment is a fucking mess. Thank God my Polish housekeeper is coming to clean before my mom arrives.

Five minutes later, I'm showered, suited, and headed out the door. My girlfriend is still passed out in bed. I stop to leave my key in my mailbox for my mom and then sprint toward King's Road, presentations in hand. There's another suit on my corner ahead of me, waving down the only available taxi in all directions, so I throw out a "Sorry, it's an emergency," and offer him a twenty-pound note. He lets me take the cab.

At 7:55 A.M., I get a text from my boss: "We're standing adjacent platform twelve."

At 8:00 A.M., I receive another text: "Boarding train. John, I am getting rather concerned."

Finally, my cab pulls up in front of Paddington Station. I respond back, "Am here. See you on train," and then jump out and race toward the concourse. As I come up toward platform twelve, I see the train starting to ease its way into motion. I think I can still make it. If I don't, there is a strong likelihood that I will be fired.

That's when one of those bluecoats sees me barreling toward the moving train. He steps in front of me. "This train is departed." He looks prepared to stop me with physical force.

"Can't miss this train." I'm sprinting right at him. I head fake to one side and then make a striding leap around him, then jump onto the last car just as the doors close, at 8:02 A.M.

At 8:03 A.M., another text from my boss: "Sitting car one. You better be on this train. It's the only express." I'm so far back that it takes me a solid ten minutes to work my way up to the front, which must have been an eternity for my boss. But all is forgiven; we devote the next forty-five minutes to reviewing the presentation and outlining our pitch, and then spend the remainder of the journey in silence.

A short cab ride later, we're at the client's office, waiting patiently in a conference room for them to show up. I'm so proud of myself for pulling this off that I've forgotten how terribly hungover I am. I might still be a little bit drunk.

My phone vibrates. Unknown caller. I ignore it.

A minute later, my phone rings again. I ignore it.

My boss is perplexed. "We probably have another minute or two in case you need to answer that."

It vibrates a third time. It could be someone from the office who didn't know I was out for a meeting. I answer it.

"What the fuck is wrong with you?" It's my dad. I guess my mom's plane landed an hour early.

I can't acknowledge in front of my colleagues what's happening.

"Yes, this is he." I respond with unrelated, innocuous banter. I'm just hoping my colleagues can't hear the screaming on the other end.

My dad doesn't stop. "Your mother has just flown ten hours to see you and this is how you show your appreciation, by having her walk into a filthy crack house?" Fuck, I guess this means the maid hasn't shown up yet. She's fired.

"Uh-huh. Understood." I have to cup my ear to prevent his fury from spilling out into the conference room.

He's not finished. "What? What are you saying?"

"Okay. Got it. Just in a meeting right now." Meanwhile the finance director of Imperial Tobacco and his team are starting to walk into the conference room. "That makes sense. Thanks for letting me know." And then I hang up, quickly turn my phone off, and wipe my sweaty hand on my suit pants just in time to shake hands with the client.

The meeting goes great. My boss lets me do a considerable amount of talking. The client basically tells us that we are in the deal with two other to-be-determined banks. I get a "nicely done" from my boss as we're heading back to the train station.

I explain to him that the phone call I had received had been from my landlord about a leak in my flat and that instead of heading back to the office with him, I'd have to go home and sort it out with the plumber.

When I arrive home, my mom is still in a state of shock.

The Polish maid never showed up. My girlfriend's idea of cleaning up before she left was simply to open all the windows and air the apartment out.

As it is emotionally relayed to me, my mom walked into my apartment. The two French doors leading to the balcony were wide open and swinging in the breeze that was being channeled through the living room and out the gaping bay windows on the opposite side, leaving the oversized curtains dancing eerily on both ends—not exactly the welcome my mother had been expecting.

Vodka, tequila, and wine bottles, empty glasses and beer cans, are on nearly every horizontal service. On my dining table sits the remnants of a 2 A.M. trip to Al-Dar II, the local Lebanese kebab shop. I don't even have any recollection of that, but apparently we put together quite a buffet-style feast in the middle of my living room. Amidst the stinky remnants of lamb and baba ghanoush is one of my degenerate friends' idea of an art project: greasy kebab sticks on a canvas of hummus, lined up to form a swastika.

The silver Asprey wine filter my parents had given me is now being used to hold marijuana seeds and stems that we had separated out. My pretentious collection of stolen hotel ashtrays is filled with joints, cigarettes, and cigar butts. One of them, inexplicably, has a wad of bloodstained Kleenex. For good measure, there's even an upside-down plate with traces of white powder on it. Honestly, it wasn't mine.

This is apparently how I greet my mom on her trip across the world just to make sure that I have my life under control.

There's nothing I can say. I can't blame my maid for not showing up, because my mom would just be appalled that I would ever consider leaving a mess like this for her in the first place. I can't tell her that I just helped win an important mandate for a €750 million bond deal, because she'd be even more concerned that this is how I spent the night before an important meeting.

"Wanna get some food?" Fuck, I hope she won't get mad if I order wine at lunch.

When can we stop calling them hipsters and go back to calling them pussies?

A guy came up to me at the gym and asked me what event I was training so hard for. Life, motherfucker.

If I ever "check in" somewhere on Facebook, it'll be Mt. Everest, Mars, or Kate Upton's bedroom. Not Chili's happy hour.

I leave the Hamptons on Sundays so that my family doesn't have to.

If your bachelor party revolves around a big steak dinner and a strip club, count me out. I did that last night.

The Handover

My move from London to Hong Kong is highly improbable. At the end of my first year in London, they ask me to think about moving to Asia. My simple response to my boss is: "Fuck no."

First of all, I can't fathom moving to Asia; I've never even been there. More important, every single person I know in the Hong Kong office hates it; they complain of tyrannical bosses, a rigid hierarchy, and never-ending hundred-hour workweeks. It's not uncommon for me to get frantic calls from one of my capital markets counterparts in Asia at all hours of the day and night, begging and pleading for help on some US$ or Eurobond pitch book they're working on.

There's no way I'm moving to Asia. Some of the Brits do it because Hong Kong retains many of the creature comforts of having been a formidable British colony, and has the added benefit of a 15% income tax rate compared with the 50% effective rate we enjoy in London. Others move, as people did to any of the satellites during the colonial era, to find opportunities unafforded to them at home. Or, simply put, they have experienced varying degrees of failure and, as a "Square Mile Reject," are looking for a fresh start—hence the well-trod acronym FILTH, or Failed In London, Try Hong Kong. This antiquated, colonial throwback notion is less relevant now given the surge of talent flocking to the region in the face of robust economic growth in Asia following the crisis of 1997. Nonetheless, an element of that FILTH stigma remains.

Fast-forward a few years, and my rabbi, Paul Young, the head of European syndicate, is also running the team in Asia. Now that the region is growing up, he wants to have one of "his guys" on the ground out there. This time it might be different; I am a little bit more senior than when I had previously been approached, and now I've got a legitimate sponsor in my rabbi.

Paul Young is an imposing figure on the London trading floor; "legendary" would be too strong a word, if for no other reason than he had only recently moved across from New York, but he's revered as an old-school Salomon Brothers guy, tough but fair. This is the same guy who convinced me not to save any of my bonuses as an analyst.

He is also an infamous low-talker; no one can hear a word he says outside of five feet. It's genius; he knows everybody has to listen to him, so by speaking softly, it requires they lean in like a bunch of little schoolkids. And that's exactly how he wants it. God forbid anyone ever says, "I'm sorry, Paul, what did you say?" He'll just stare at them like they're an idiot.

I once had to go to New York with Paul for a meeting, so we decided (he asked me) to share a car from Canary Wharf to Heathrow Airport. It was a junior banker's dream—airtime and exposure with senior management. I did not at all expect to sit next to him on the plane, but when we arrived at the airport, out of sheer politeness, I said, "Hey, Paul, where are you sitting?"

"Concorde, baby. See you in New York." Then, he walked away.

So when Paul asks me to move to Hong Kong, he isn't asking; he's telling. Nonetheless, moving to Asia is a big decision. I had just settled into my elegant flat off King's Road and I had finally secured Chelsea FC season tickets in the Matthew Harding Lower section at Stamford Bridge. I am also in a relationship that has recently become quite serious.

Despite all of these reservations, Paul convinces me to go there the following week for an exploratory trip. I'm on the Friday night British Airways flight to Hong Kong and, twelve hours later, in a taxi on my way to the Grand Hyatt. Flying in for the weekend will give me a better sense of a city that has always been very much an enigma to me. Would I like it? Would I be comfortable as a minority in a distinctly foreign country? Could I see myself having a viable career and making a life for myself? Most important, would I be happy? Those are the smart questions, and I have three days to find the answers.

The summer in London is essentially just a handful of nice days a year. By comparison, Hong Kong is a tropical island. Having failed to do any meaningful due diligence, I do not realize that I have arrived in the middle of the rainy typhoon season. As my luck would have it, a storm has just blown through town, taking with it all the pollution and humidity, leaving clear blue skies and a gentle island breeze. I just assume this is how it is all the time.

My first order of business is to head down to the pool, with its palm trees, sweeping views of Victoria Harbor, and extravagant seafood buffet. This is my first experience with the service-orientated nature of Asian hospitality—and it's fucking fantastic. Before I even realize that I want another drink, there's a guy pouring one for me. Every time I make a trip back to the buffet line, some lackey is waiting at my table with a fresh ramekin of melted butter just in case I decided to pick up another lobster tail—which of course I do.

I have been in Hong Kong for all of two hours, but as far as urban financial hubs go, this is paradise—blue skies, a poolside seafood buffet at a five-star hotel overlooking a harbor of boats zipping by with electrifying purpose.

I don't take off my bathrobe or swim trunks for the entire weekend, other than a quick trip to pick up a new Blancpain and to meet a friend from college for drinks in Lan Kwai Fong, or LKF, Hong Kong's famous *gweilo*-orientated dining and drinking district.

If I move at all, it's just to get from the pool area to the spa area, where my first order of business is to dial up the trifecta—simultaneous pedicure, manicure, and face and scalp massage. Later that day, I take it up a notch with the one-hundred-minute "four hands" full body massage. It's sensory overload. The next day, after too many cocktails and too much sun, I sleep through my entire massage. Good thing there's a pretty easy solution for that. When they wake me up, I just tell them to start over.

I am hooked. I don't even need to see the office or meet the people. But of course, I can't just say that. People will question my judgment and my priorities if I flippantly decide to throw my career on a completely different track and move around the world on the basis of two days in a hotel. I need the firm to think that I am doing them a huge favor and making a sacrifice by moving.

My uneventful day in the Hong Kong office is simply a box-ticking exercise. I'm heading back to London without really having sought the answers to many of the questions I came with, but I don't really care. Hong Kong is an exotic seductress.

I call Paul from the airport. "Well, it's a long way from my family. I have a girlfriend, and as you know, we have been thinking about moving to New York. I'm just not so sure that this is the right move for me."

"What the fuck? Call you back." *Click.* I'm not too alarmed. On the trading floor, rules of etiquette are completely different. It's not at all uncommon for someone to hang up on you and mean nothing by it.

I check in with British Airways and breeze through immigration. I have just enough time to have some food and try to get drunk in the lounge, grab a forty-five-minute massage, and then peruse the terminal for a thoughtless gift for my girlfriend back in London—I know now there's no real point in investing further in the relationship.

As I'm paying for the cheapest Hermès H bracelet I can find, my phone rings. It's Paul. I continue to play my bluff. "Well, I'm in the airport. Gotta tell you. It looks great in terms of career, but personally, I just don't know about being so far away from my family, not to mention the issue of my girlfriend. And living in China."

"Don't be a pussy. It's Hong Kong, not China. And chicks there love white dudes with cash."

Even though I'm sold on the move, I want them to sweat it out a little bit. One of the things I have learned is that if the firm thinks they're doing me a favor, then I'm totally fucked. As long as it looks like I'm making the sacrifices, then hopefully, they will take better care of me at bonus time.

"I hear you, but . . ." I try to ease the conversation into an agreement with one last feign of reluctance.

"But what? What the fuck? Do me a favor before you get on the plane. Go to a newsagent and buy a stack of Asian porn. Learn to love it, baby. You can find yourself five new girlfriends." And that was it.

The Hong Kong to London flight has to be one of the best trips in the world. You can have dinner, plenty of drinks, and even a massage before getting on a midnight flight. And then you can have a few more drinks, watch an entire movie, and then pass out for ten-plus hours. Next thing you know, it's 5 A.M. in London, and you wake up feeling well rested and refreshed.

I stop at Starbucks on my way home, thinking it's probably better to break the news to my girlfriend with a latte and a cinnamon roll. I was moving to Hong Kong, and I wasn't ready for her to drop everything and join me there as some *tai tai* (the colloquial Cantonese term for a wealthy married woman who does not work), spending her time booking restaurants, taking yoga lessons, and planning exotic weekend trips.

Leaving London wasn't terribly difficult. Don't get me wrong, it's one of the great cities in the world. But it takes an incredible amount of money to enjoy London in perpetuity the way that London should be enjoyed. And being just another banker doesn't exactly cut it when you are surrounded by RAVs (Russians, Arabs, and Villains) who view London as the place to go if you want to buy respectability.

Britain is a country that, since World War II, has been on a managed decline. The men live vicariously through their favorite soccer team, celebrating its success with "a few pints" and commiserating over its failings with "a few pints." And the women—walking muffin tops. Yet they stride around with a terribly misplaced sense of entitlement.

Even their TV shows are emblematic of their mediocre mentality. *EastEnders* and *Coronation Street* are all about fat, dumb, ugly, poor people. And there begins the vicious cycle of complacent underachievers. Maybe I'm biased because, despite being born in England, I grew up in the US. At least our equivalent TV shows are full of good-looking rich people doing big business deals and dating glamorous women. I wouldn't mind my kids growing up wanting to be J. R. Ewing, but who the fuck wants to be a pub landlord in Essex?

I love London, but I'm looking forward to the change of scenery.

I move to Hong Kong in the fall of 2004. I check myself into the Mandarin Oriental hotel, which will be my home for the next month, or until I find a more permanent place to live.

My tour guide and mentor in Hong Kong is Dennis Lipton, the head of hedge fund sales. He is Mr. Perfect—the handsome all-American lacrosse star in college who joins the Morgan Stanley sales desk in New York, before moving across to Salomon Brothers and rising to the rank of apartment on Central Park West and beach house in Nantucket. He's the guy at the black-tie charity functions that every older woman wants to introduce to her daughter. He moved to Hong Kong in the wake of the Asian crisis of the late 1990s to ride the wave of growth in hedge funds investing in the region. His housing allowance alone is $15,000 a month (in 2004 dollars), which gets him a house on the Peak, the most prestigious and expensive area of Hong Kong. His kids' school fees are paid for and the firm even throws in a country-club membership. With two maids, a nanny, and a full-time driver, life in Asia is good for Lipton.

Despite having it all, Lipton is in the process of moving back to New York. While I am not replacing him, our roles are so intertwined that we decide to overlap, with me shadowing him for a few months. The firm wants him to introduce me to most of his key clients to ensure better continuity while it looks for a formal replacement for him.

On my first Monday, he tells me to meet him at 6 P.M. at the Lobster Bar in the Shangri-La hotel so that he can introduce me to one of his best clients. By the time I get there, he's already pretty lit—drinking by himself.

"Here, you're gonna need this." He hands me a piece of paper before I can even sit down. "It's Joe's cell number. You're going to need to get to know Joe. He's our dealer."

I had heard about people on Wall Street doing drugs, but up until that point, it hadn't been that big of a deal. Of course, as analysts, we'd sometimes get together and smoke some weed, but only occasionally would we come in contact with anything harder. It was all rather discreet—a far cry from having a virtual stranger tell me having a reliable drug dealer on speed dial is an important part of client coverage.

Joe, as I quickly find out, is the go-to drug dealer for expats. He operates with impunity around Hong Kong's Central and Mid-Levels Districts and is so brazen that he'll have one of his associates make midday deliveries in a not-too-subtle souped-up Toyota Supra right in front of our office.

We pound drinks at the Shangri-La for about three hours. Charlie, one of the new sales associates, has joined us, but still no client.

"Okay, we gotta roll," Lipton declares, even though his glass is still full. "Change of plans, we're meeting Trainwreck at Vegas."

"'Trainwreck at Vegas'?" I'm confused.

"Dude. It's only one of our best clients. And probably gonna be one of your best friends in Hong Kong after I leave. Let's go." Lipton is definitely amped up on something.

This is not how I am accustomed to getting to know new colleagues or meeting clients. I'm not going to let him treat me like his bitch. "Go ahead, man. My drink's full and Charlie hasn't even got his yet. We'll meet you there in a half hour."

"Okay. Text me. My wife's in town so I'm on the clock." He bolts without thinking twice about his bar tab.

Thirty minutes later, I'm calling Lipton from a cab, asking him to pass his phone to the nearest Chinese person so that they can give directions to our driver. Finally, we pull up to some nondescript office building somewhere between Wan Chai and Causeway Bay. We get out and take the elevator up to a floor where there is nothing but a single black door with a speakeasy-type slot.

I ring the bell. A woman's face appears.

"Hi. We're here with Dennis Lipton."

"No, I am sorry." She closes the window.

I try again. "Denn-iss Liip-tonn. Our friend. Here. We with him." Although the firm is providing me with Chinese lessons, right now I speak only two languages: English and louder, slower English.

That does the trick. She opens the door and motions for us to follow her down a long, poorly lit corridor. It reminds me of a hotel hallway, with doors running along both sides, each of which presumably leads to a private room. Finally, we reach our destination.

Lipton is sitting on the couch. His pants are around his ankles. Some chick is on her knees, blowing him. And some other chick is standing on the couch, completely naked, with her knees slightly pressed against his shoulders, her pussy in his face. And there he is, our head of hedge fund sales, who makes more than a million bucks a year, married with kids, sitting there, eating out some prostitute.

"Dude," I shout to announce our entrance, otherwise at a loss for words.

"Yo. Yo. Yo," he shouts, twisting his neck back so that he can make eye contact. Upon seeing my obvious discomfort, he yells, "What? Pussy's pussy."

I survey the room. There's Lipton and two other white guys, one of whom I presume to be Trainwreck. They each have a girl on their lap; of course Dennis has two. There's another girl in a cocktail dress singing karaoke in front of a big-screen projection TV, disco ball spinning above her head, and about four other girls sitting around an adjacent table, drinking and playing a dice version of Liar's Poker.

In front of Lipton is a table with several elaborate and exotic fruit plates. Next to the fruit is a pile of cocaine.

After a quick nod of acknowledgment in lieu of the traditional handshake and business card introduction, Charlie and I pour ourselves the drink du jour—Johnnie Walker and iced green tea—and sit with the girls playing dice.

I won't lie; we're having a blast.

Lipton finishes, recharges with a quick bump, and then joins us at the table. "Dude. Sorry, man. I gotta bounce. Fuckin' curfew." He's still buckling his pants and buttoning his shirt. "Yo, I need you to do me a solid and grab this. I don't have enough cash and my wife checks all my statements."

"No sweat. I got this." What else can I say?

"Is my shirt tucked in? Bitch gets suspicious if my shirt's disheveled." Never mind the smell of pussy on his breath.

We stayed with Trainwreck and his hedge fund buddy and had a great time until the night faded into a blur. The next morning—a Tuesday—it's only really when I find my pants, and a few credit card receipts, that I began to piece the night back together. Total receipts for the night, including the Shan-gri-La bar tab, came in at HK$21,000, or around US$2,700.

I realized a very important thing that had eluded me during my exploratory trip a few months prior: that Lipton was leaving Hong Kong, not because of the opportunity in New York, but because he had a coke problem and his wife was threatening to divorce him.

It's a good thing that I wasn't moving here with a wife or a coke problem.

The age-of-consent laws should be different for Asian chicks. Sometimes, I can't tell if they're 14 or 40.

Coasters are for people who need to put their drink down.

Money can't buy happiness but it solves 95% of the problems that make you unhappy.

Whenever someone asks how I'm doing, I usually just lie and say "good," even though I'm doing a lot better than that.

Some people assume I am quiet, boring, or shy without ever realizing that I just don't like them.

I'll Call You on Your Cell

In simple terms, the bond syndicate desk is the bridge between the issuer clients who need money and the investor clients who have money to invest. Hence, it is uniquely positioned above the Chinese Wall—the invisible wall between investment banking and debt capital markets (the private side) and sales and trading (the public side). The Chinese Wall is designed to prevent confidential and material nonpublic information from entering the public domain, even within the same firm.

When it comes to sourcing new deals, my job as a syndicate manager is to provide market intelligence and make strategic recommendations to the bankers and their clients regarding their capital market needs. This advice is based on my evaluation of credit market conditions, prevailing investor sentiment, risk appetite, etc. I work intimately with sales and trading and with their clients, such as asset managers and hedge funds, in order to formulate these market views.

Once we are mandated on a deal, I work directly with the issuer client to plan and implement the appropriate deal strategy—expected pricing, investor marketing requirements (the amount of work we'll need to do in order to sell the deal, as dictated by the familiarity of the investor base with this issuer and the complexity of the structure), and the execution timetable. Once the deal is announced publicly, I work with the investors to guide and control the entire execution process and their participation in it—from book building through pricing. It is my responsibility to determine the price of each new bond deal and to allocate the bonds to the investors of my choosing. It can be a powerful position, and is one that requires an ability to weigh many risks and unknowns. Being able to prioritize among several important layers and conflicting interests is a must.

There's a reason that Michael Lewis referred to syndicate managers as the "omniscient, omnipotent, omnivorous Presence" on the trading floor. Our overall objective is to find a result that leaves both the issuer and the investors happy. We help the issuer raise money and develop a good reputation in the capital markets in order to ensure and enhance future access, and we want to make sure the investors see enough upside to keep participating and playing in new issues.

This is the essence of the syndicate job. I gave this same summary almost every year to the group of interns rotating through fixed income. I'd take over the corner conference room during lunch on a quiet summer day, walk them through the entire syndicate process, and then spend some time doing Q&A.

One year, my boss is walking by and, upon seeing me jovially gesticulating to a roomful of twenty-one-year-olds, understandably decides to see what I'm up to. The door swings open; he looks at the kids, looks at me, and then looks over at the white board, shakes his head in dismay, and just walks out without saying a word.

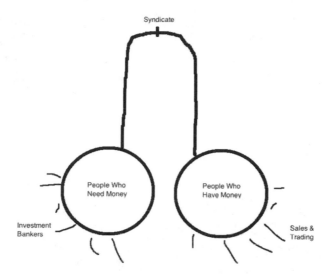

I had always found it far easier to actually draw a diagram of where and how the syndicate desk operates within the capital markets framework. The indirect path I have drawn between issuers (People Who Need Money) and investors (People Who Have Money) is designed to represent the fact that these entities are separated by a Chinese Wall and also to illustrate that the capital markets process is not always entirely efficient.

In practice, once it comes to actually doing deals, the syndicate process is much more fluid, particularly in Asia. There are no diagrams that can possibly represent that, or if there are, they would be written in disappearing ink.

The process starts with a company—the issuer—mandating (selecting) banks to serve as bookrunners for the purpose of helping them raise money. Let's say a company already has an established relationship with many Wall Street banks; a common practice would be for them to send out a request for proposal, or RFP. They want to hear each bank's recommendations on pricing, structure, timing, marketing, and fees. This is where I come in. I'll take a look at the credit; I'll look at the market comparables—where their outstanding bonds, and those of their peers, are trading. Then I will incorporate this knowledge into my overall sense of market conditions, investor appetite, and structural preference and come up with recommendations.

For a complicated credit or an important pitch, I might sound out the deal to a few investors on a no-names basis, talking them through the credit profile and theoretical deal parameters in general terms for the purposes of getting feedback to help me refine my view. I might say something like, "I'm looking at a possible new high-yield issue for a Chinese property developer with a mid-/high single-B credit rating. They're predominantly high-end residential in the Hangzhou Province." From there, we'd get into the nitty-gritty in terms of their property portfolio, leverage, and other specific financial and business metrics. In many cases, a good credit analyst or portfolio manager can easily figure out whom I'm talking about, especially if they are getting calls from other syndicate bankers also sounding out the market for the same deal.

It's not always easy to dance around the barrage of Twenty Questions from the investors, which can often culminate with "Dude, come on, don't waste my time. Just tell me who it is."

The truth is that if we really want to have the best quality feedback on a credit or possible deal structure, and therefore be more credible in the RFP pitch, we'll tell the investor the name of the soon-to-be issuer. What Chinese Wall?

"All right, man, I'll call you on your cell phone." A couple of minutes later, I'm back on the phone, this time from the safety of a conference room. We can't make these calls from our desks because all the dealerboard lines are recorded for compliance reasons. "Okay, between you and me, we're looking at a $500 million seven-year deal for ███████████. What kind of appetite do you have for China property in general, this credit, and at what kind of yield?"

This is simply how business is done. Is it legal? "Well, I'm not a lawyer" is always the running joke on the syndicate desks.

If we don't do it, we suffer. Our European competitors tend to be more aggressive when it comes to disregarding the rules. If we lose the mandate, the investment bankers who are directly responsible for the client relationship will argue it's because our competitors were armed with a better read of the market, placing the blame squarely on my shoulders, which won't be forgotten come bonus time.

I've gone to plenty of pitches and confidently pounded the table, saying, "Mandate us. We're in touch with specific investor appetite for your name and size." This is an attempt to coax the client into doing a deal and to demonstrate to them that we're better informed. Sometimes we just make it up; but other times, it actually comes on the heels of having sounded out the market.

Beyond helping us win business, sounding out possible deals with investors is also helpful in terms of our relationships with them. If we're working on a deal, or if there is an issuer considering coming to market, the investors would obviously love to know before this potentially market-sensitive information becomes public. I don't want to receive angry calls from a hedge fund saying, "Why didn't you tell me X Chinese property company is coming with a deal?" The implication is that he would have sold or shorted other Chinese property names on the expectation, depending on the market, that new supply will put pressure on existing bonds.

Hence, hedge funds love helping bankers sound out deals. They get early access to nonpublic information that they can trade on. They also like that it gives them some leverage come allocation time. *Hey, don't fucking forget, I helped you when you were pitching this deal. I better get the bonds I want.*

Those "I'll call you on your cell" messages on Bloomberg chat—the instant messaging service used by the vast majority of relevant market participants—are the greatest messages ever, because we know we are about to have an off-the-record conversation about something market sensitive. Or, if it's not deal related, then we know we're about to hear some outrageous X-rated or inappropriate story that we don't want on a recorded line or chat room.

Most trading floors prohibit cell phones on the floor, so the usual response to "I'll call you on your cell" is "Cool. Gimme five."

The other thing syndicate desks (at least the good ones) do in response to an RFP is quietly collude with one another. We'll collaborate with other banks on the nature and specificity of our individual recommendations in order to improve our chances of winning the deal. If a client sees an identical recommendation from Citi, JPMorgan, and Deutsche Bank, it's more likely that they'll pick those three together over an outlier recommendation that is now perceived to be riskier or less credible.

If I know that a specific bank is really close to a company in Singapore that is rumored to be looking at a deal, I'll call up their syndicate guy (from a cell phone) and say, "I'm mandated with two yet-to-be-determined banks on this Korean deal. If you get me on your deal in Singapore, I'll show you the pricing, structure, and fees that we showed in Korea so that you're giving them the same recommendation we did. And then I'll put your name forward."

One of my biggest non-sovereign trades, a US$2 billion multi-tranche deal for an Indian bank, was secured in this manner.

It can be a dangerous game because if I'm not 100% sure I'm on that deal, and that I can trust my competitor to play fair, they could take that information, undercut me on pricing and fees, and then go team up with someone else and steal the deal.

From the issuer's perspective, besides the pricing recommendation (i.e., how much is this going to cost me?), one of the biggest concerns for Asian borrowers is the question of underwriting fees. In the US, markets are so established and efficient that the treasurer of General Electric or IBM isn't going to waste time negotiating from 0.20% to 0.15% in fees ($2 to $1.5 million per $1 billion new issue), because it's irrelevant in the grander scheme of things. They know from experience that execution is more important than trying to shop around bookrunners on fees.

However in Asia, markets are still developing. Also, it's a cultural thing; it's almost like a game—issuers want to negotiate fees for the sake of negotiating fees. And banks play right along, undercutting one another as much as it takes. After all, getting in on a deal for less money is better than explaining to your boss why you missed the trade.

There was actually an off-the-record meeting held at a hotel in Hong Kong several years ago, attended by most of the senior Asian syndicate managers from the big Wall Street firms, to try to stem the tide of banks undercutting one another on underwriting fees. I know because I was there. We covered the full spectrum, from high-yield corporates to sovereign frequent issuers—namely Indonesia, Korea, and the Philippines, where underwriting fees had dropped to as low as 0.02%. Some guys flew in from Singapore just to attend the meeting, and then following a handshake agreement, we all went out drinking.

Just to quantify that, I could do a $100 million sole-bookrunner Indonesian palm oil high-yield deal that paid 2.0% in fees and make $2 million. Or I could do a $3 billion multi-bookrunner deal for the Republic of the Philippines that paid 0.02% in fees and, after splitting it with the joint books and paying expenses, I'd actually lose money. This was the nature of the business. Why would we consciously do deals that lose money? Sometimes, it's in the long-term interests of the firm's relationship with the client, and we know we can make money from them in other areas of the bank—although that doesn't help me come bonus time. For us, as a firm that defines ourselves as a bond house, we had to be in on those deals for the league table credit. Big banks take their league tables—the rankings of banks based on the number of deals they have led—very seriously. Being able to advertise to prospective is-suers that we are the number one bond underwriter in Asia helps us win more business, which is why we're happy to lose money on large benchmark deals for frequent borrowers to boost our league table position. Also, even if we lose money underwriting a deal, we can make money trading those bonds as a market maker in the secondary market. Being an active market maker also gives us better market information and traction with investors.

The secret syndicate meeting was long overdue. We needed to find a better way—there wasn't enough lucrative business to go around to sustain or subsidize doing deals for free, espe-cially once we started cutting high-yield fees down under 1%. During this meeting, all the bankers agreed to set fees at mini-mum levels, and we all promised to not be the ones to break the agreement. Of course, a truce like that was never going to last long; I'd rather explain to a competitor why I welshed on a secret illegal agreement than explain to my boss why I was stupid enough to think they weren't doing the same thing.

Once an RFP is finalized, the bankers are summoned by the issuer for a little dog and pony show, also known as a "bake-off." Syndicate guys usually don't have to attend the pitch; our job is to stay glued to our seats on the trading floor and keep our fingers on the pulse of the market.

One time, I received a frantic call from one of my coverage bankers: "Hey, I just heard that Deutsche Bank and Credit Suisse are bringing their syndicate guys to the pitch. Can you please get on a plane first thing tomorrow morning?"

I couldn't say no to that. If we lost the deal, I was the one getting thrown under the bus. So I caught the 8 A.M. to Jakarta and flew four hours for a forty-five-minute meeting, during which I might have spoken for five or ten minutes. As it turned out, the Deutsche Bank and Credit Suisse syndicate guys had in fact flown in, but that was just to go whoring and play golf the following day. For them, the meeting was an excuse to expense the trip.

I'd rather go to the dentist than attend most bake-offs. But it's always funny to see what ends up in the final version of the presentation, because the bankers usually assume that we won't be in the meetings. After all of my credit work, sounding out a handful of savvy investors, and even checking a couple of close hedge fund relationships on the specific credit, I make my recommendation: $200 million five-year note at 9.5%. I get to my slide—the most important one—and my page says $300 million seven-year deal at 8.75%. The bankers will say and do anything to win the deal, including drastically overpromising the client with respect to market access. Pitch after pitch, the response is always the same. "Bait and switch." "Let's just get them pregnant." "We'll moonwalk them back once we win the deal." So I just embrace it and accept the fact that come execution, it's going to be me doing the moonwalk.

"Getting them pregnant" is the easiest part. All we have to do is announce the deal and get them on a roadshow. Once a treasurer or CFO gets board approval to go out and raise hundreds of millions of dollars, they're not inclined to go home empty-handed, especially after a lengthy roadshow. So what if it's not the deal they signed up for—it's still better than looking totally incompetent. We're quick to remind them: "If you walk away from this deal, it's going to be much more expensive for you next time just to reengage the investors."

Once we're mandated and the deal is announced, my focus shifts from the issuer client to the investor clients. Along with our sales force, I now need to go out and build a big enough order book at the right price.

Occasionally, when a deal is announced, a second-rate hedge fund client will call up and say, *Dude, I spoke to you yesterday. Why didn't you fucking tell me this deal was coming? I'm long a shit ton of this paper.* The answer should be pretty simple, "That would be illegal." But it comes out more like, "Sorry, bro. Things were moving quickly. I'll make it up to you." The reality is that if he didn't know about it, he's probably not that important to us. After all, many of the other guys whom we had "sounded out" the deal to ahead of time have no such complaints.

The book-building process varies significantly from a single-day drive-by to a heavily marketed two-week roadshow. The simple idea is to work with the sales force to bring in orders and solicit price sensitivities and feedback from the investors. This "market color" is reflected by me to the issuer. It's then my job to convince the issuer to agree to a price that reflects where a market-clearing deal works. Once we get the issuer to sign off on the deal terms, we're ready to allocate bonds to investors, get the deal across the finish line, and then move on to the next one.

The allocation process is one of the most nuanced and contentious aspects of the execution process, and probably the most important. Our primary focus when it comes to allocating bonds is to do what's in the best interests of the deal—place the bonds in safe hands (i.e., serious long-term buy-and-hold accounts who are participating in the deal because they know and like the credit, not because they think it's a hot deal and they can "flip the bonds on the break," or sell them immediately after the deal prices). However, it's not always as straightforward as that. Part of what makes the allocation process such an art form is that we have total discretion to allocate bonds to whomever we choose and for whatever reason. Some of this is fairly benign and is in the best interests of the deal. Investors who met the company on the roadshow, or helped drive the pricing discussion, or supported the deal early on all expect to be rewarded for that.

Obviously, if we give every big-name investor all the bonds they want, there will be nothing left for most of the other investors—and they're our clients too. For example, a hedge fund might mean very little to my business, but they could be important to the equities or foreign exchange guys. So generally speaking, in most deals, we'll spread bonds around, even to accounts that we know are going to try to make a quick buck, otherwise known as spivs. If all the bonds disappear and get locked away, we don't make as much money trading them.

This isn't entirely self-serving. By leaving some quality accounts hungry for more, the expectation is that they will come back in the secondary market and scoop up any loose paper, which helps ensure that the deal performs well, just as you'd want an IPO to go up in value on the first day it's listed. This helps solidify the issuer's reputation in the market for doing good deals and keeps investors happy with us as bookrunners.

Side deals and favor trading are still a huge part of the allocation process. It's amazing the number of times I get invited out by a hedge fund in the days leading up to the pricing of a hot deal. Sure, a nice bottle of wine over lunch will probably get him a few extra million bonds the next day.

If an investor is considering being an anchor order (early and sizable) in an unrelated high-yield deal, or is doing his homework on a lucrative private placement I'm working on, then we will definitely hook him up on a few hot deals when it comes to allocations—using one deal to help make other deals easier.

However, much of our allocation pressure also comes from within. If prime brokerage is wooing some hedge fund and they want to impress them, they call us and say, "Take care of my guy on this deal, and then tell me before you release allocations." Their intention is to front-run the news by calling the hedge fund and taking credit for hooking them up with a generous allocation. Or if the equity or credit derivative desk owes a guy a favor, they might ask us to repay him via a generous allocation. On one deal, a more senior New York counterpart asked me to "take good care of" a new hedge fund because our senior management had invested their own money in the fund.

Considering that the vast majority of deals are done with at least two bookrunners, we also have to contend with the allocation pressures that our joint bookrunners have as well. All allocations have to be agreed on by all syndicates before a deal can be priced, which is why some allocation conference calls can last several hours, often delaying the pricing of the deal—and exposing the issuer to unneeded market risk.

The process is generally pretty smooth; the syndicates have a vested interest in ensuring the success of the deal, and we all have a similar view with respect to the quality of the investors— long-term buy / hold vs. short-term trading / flipping. But at the same time, we each have our own agenda to contend with. So when my bookrunning counterpart at JPMorgan asks me, "Why do you want to give that shitty hedge fund more bonds than we're giving this real money asset manager who partici- pated in the roadshow?," I can't simply say, "Because he bought me a 2008 Grange and a lap dance three nights ago."

The smoothest way that we have found to address our re- spective axes (priorities) is to formally assign each bank a num- ber of bullets that they can use on the allocation of each deal, no questions asked.

Once the allocation process is done, we're ready to price the deal, which all the joint-bookrunner syndicates do together on a ceremonious call with the client. Then we meet at a bar and drink.

Why would I marry? It's betting some chick half my net worth that I will love her forever.

I can always tell a banker within the first two minutes of meeting him in a bar . . . because he tells me.

China is our landlord and we know he's beating his wife but we're 2 months behind on rent so we let it slide.

It's hard not to judge someone when their favorite movie sucks.

Build 1,000 bridges and no one calls you a bridge builder. But suck one cock . . .

Networking

As I said my good-byes in the London office, one of the traders pulled me aside. Artie had not only been a colleague but also a close friend during my time in the UK. Our shared interests include golf, drinking, and posh British chicks (specifically Sloane Rangers).

We lived within blocks of each other in Chelsea and would spend several nights a week rotating between the Big Easy, the Admiral Codrington, and any number of regular spots on Walton Street, fending off the semipros and cougars who dominate that scene.

"Listen, when you get to Hong Kong, I want to set you up with a friend of mine," Artie said. "She comes from a prominent Hong Kong family, so she's rich. She's hot. And I think she went to Hotchkiss or one of those prep schools, so you might have a lot in common. More important, she's just a good, cool person to know. Trust me, she knows everyone and can definitely plug you in with the right people."

"Definitely. Hook it up," I said. "I'd love to meet her."

It's like when you run into an acquaintance on the street, and they say, "Hey, we need to get together soon," and you respond with "Sure. I'll give you a call." It's a lie for a lie. I'm not sure if he's just trying to be polite, but I know I had no real intention of ever connecting with her, not because she didn't sound great, but just because I'd grown so tired of these tedious American-abroad, name-game, find-some-common-ground unsolicited introductions that are almost always a huge waste of time. "Oh, you're from the South? You should look up my friend." Fuck you. "You went to boarding school? When you get to Paris, call my old roommate to show you around." No thanks. But then again, Artie is a good friend of mine, and he's never steered me wrong.

After one month on the ground in Hong Kong, I've completely forgotten about his offer. So far, the only people I have met socially, as expected, have been fellow expats and investment bankers. Most of my socializing has been with colleagues or clients. I've been working long hours and then going out and partying until two or three o'clock in the morning. I'll catch a few hours of sleep and then make it back into the office at 7:30 A.M., where the process will repeat itself.

After a few more weeks of killing myself with long hours and longer nights, some subconscious survival instinct kicked in to remind me about Artie's friend. I need a respite from my monotonous work-drink-sleep-repeat existence and would like to meet some more interesting people. Artie enthusiastically arranges a date.

When the day comes, I'm excited, not because I think I might get lucky, but because I'm legitimately looking forward to broadening my social circles. As per my daily routine, I hand over my responsibilities to the New York desk around 7 P.M. and head out. I stop at the ATM machine in the lobby where Citibank Tower, ICBC Tower, Bank of China Tower, and Cheung Kong Center all converge. Walking out at this time of day is like running a gauntlet of temptation. It's the witching hour for wayward bankers, and everyone seems to have a devious plan for the night. Unlike in London or New York, bankers in Asia are friendly with many of their competitors, and socialize together.

I run into a friend and colleague, Ben, who suggests going out for a few drinks. He moved to Hong Kong not long before me, and as a fellow London transplant, he is also friendly with Artie. So, I counter by inviting him along to my drinks date. It's a fairly good hedge. If the girl is hot and into me, I can tell Ben to fuck off and I know he will respect that. And if I have no bid, then we can ditch her and go out drinking together.

"What!? You're meeting Artie's friend Lillian? Tonight? You motherfucker. He's been trying to set me up with her for months. Fuck yeah, I'm coming." So my hedge might have just turned into a bit of a sword fight, but oh well.

We have thirty minutes to kill before I'm supposed to meet Lillian at the Captain's Bar, which conveniently happens to be in the lobby of the Mandarin Oriental, where I'm still living. We head upstairs to my room and pour a couple of Johnnie Walkers. I need to change anyway since I am still acclimating to the Hong Kong pollution and tropical humidity.

By the time I emerge from a quick shower, Ben has made himself at home and already has a plateful of cocaine laid out and ready to go. "Hey, man, you want?" Well, isn't that considerate of him.

Forty-five minutes later, we're still blowing through lines. That's when it occurs to me, as I am sitting in my hotel room half dressed with another dude, ripping lines of cocaine, that a hot, young, rich girl is downstairs sitting by herself waiting for me.

I am now going to show up late for a date, tipsy and high, and bring with me another guy as the third wheel, one who himself intends to turn me into the third wheel. This night is off to a great start.

We have one bag of cocaine left, which should be plenty for a Tuesday night. The only problem is that, having torn the first bag, we have only one functional bag left, thus no ability to split up our supply. I lay out the ground rules: "Okay, here's the deal. I'll keep the bag, and then when you want it, just signal me. And then you keep the bag until I signal you. The only rule is that you can't do more than two lines until the other person has a turn. Agreed?"

I already know this is going to be a disaster. The bathroom at the Captain's Bar is probably one of the worst places ever to do drugs. The bar is ground zero for traveling business executives and captains of industry, and is otherwise packed, almost exclusively with banking colleagues and competitors. There's only one stall and one urinal, and a constant parade of drunken pinkie-ring-wearing toffs stumbling in and out.

Of course, Lillian is already there. Perfect. The place is packed and she has a table that fits the three of us. She is just as Artie has described—smoking hot, exuding Asian glamour and Hong Kong sex appeal, i.e., everything about her looks expensive.

She's not fazed at all by the sight of two of us. It's as if she ordered one pizza and the delivery guy accidentally brought two.

Things start off with the usual meet-my-friend icebreakers, from "How do you know Artie?" to "Where'd you go to school?" Two things are becoming very clear rather quickly: that she's a really nice, cool girl who likes to party, and that both of us want her.

Ten minutes in and we're on our second round; the only thing holding us back is the pace at which the drinks can be brought to us. Ben makes eye contact with me and clears his throat. It doesn't register. Five seconds later, he does it again, this time clearing his throat twice and nodding his head. I get it now. So I take the bag from my pocket, slip it into my napkin, and pass it to him underneath the table.

"Excuse me," he says, and gets up and heads to the bathroom. This is great; now I have her all to myself. I can't help but notice that right after Ben gets into the bathroom, another guy goes in there too. Good: it's going to take him a while to find a safe execution window.

The more we drink, the less subtle our coke signaling becomes. We started with the double-throat-clear and a nod. Pretty soon, I have added a wink, and not long after that, Ben punctuates it with a table slap.

After Ben returns from yet another lengthy disappearance, Lillian's slightly bemused. "Are you okay?"

I jump in. "Nah, he's fine. He had lunch at that Indian place in Sol Io, and it hasn't really agreed with him." Boom. That one's a bit below the belt, but I can't resist. Now, there is no way she's thinking about fucking the guy with swamp ass.

Meanwhile the drinks keep flowing. And maybe it's because I'm drunk, but I'm thinking Lillian is getting into me.

Pretty soon, it's my turn to recharge again. This time, I opt for a single-throat-clear, double-wink, under-the-table-leg-kick. The only problem is that I accidentally kick the table stand with such force that Lillian's martini glass crashes to the ground. I guess I am getting pretty wasted.

"Fuck. I'm so sorry."

At this point, she's a little suspicious or at least very confused. It's a good thing she's having a great time and knocking back cocktails along with us, albeit at a slower pace. Our waiter rushes over, apologizes profusely, and proceeds to sweep up the broken glass under Lillian's feet, creating the perfect diversion for Ben to make the handoff to me once again. The bag is getting pretty light, so I know I want to make the most of this trip.

"I'm sorry. Please excuse me. I will be right back."

Drunk as she is, Lillian is onto us. "Did you have lunch at that Indian place too?"

"No. No. It's nine P.M. so I just have to step out into the lobby real quick and dial in to this weekly conference call with New York. I'll literally say a few words so they know I'm on, and then I'll be right back."

With that, I shoot Ben a look that simply says, "Game. Set. Match. Motherfucker."

I move out into the part of the lobby that is still visible from Lillian's vantage point, pretend to dial on my BlackBerry, and then pace slowly toward the stairs. Once I am confident that she can't see me, I jog up the stairs and race to the mezzanine-level bathroom.

Holy shit. I am in heaven. This is where having the home field advantage comes in handy. It's a ghost town, and I've got five stalls to choose from. Dimmed lights, a sea of black marble, and oak stall dividers that go all the way down to the floor, creating a womb of comfort and privacy. I don't want to just do coke here, I want to live here, that is, if I wasn't already living upstairs. That's when I see my double rainbow, the horizontal marble surface above the commode, giving me a perfect seat and a table. Incidentally, as a WASP, I am also comforted by the fact that the toilet paper end is folded into a neat triangle, a gentle reminder that the stall had been sanitized subsequent to its previous use.

Relative to previous trips, I have ample time to carve out my allotted two lines, making them extra healthy to celebrate the splendor of my surroundings.

I stroll back to the table and, seeing that Lillian is busy on her phone, quickly hand off what is left in the bag across to Ben. Now it's time for me to focus on her. "Sorry about that. Should we get another round of drinks?" She shoots me one of those "hell yeah" looks, and my heart melts a little bit. I think back to the Asian kids at boarding school, segregating themselves in the dining hall and spending all of their time in the library. Sitting among the blond girls and the lacrosse players, we thought we were the cool ones. We didn't have a clue. Back in Hong Kong, those "nerds" are actually the kids with the green Lamborghinis and the nightclubs and the racehorses.

In between all of these shenanigans, the three of us are having a really great time, a natural rapport that you wouldn't have expected considering the way the evening started. She's making plans to take us to the Jockey Club and on a junk trip, to this private kitchen and to some local dim sum house. Things are really looking up in terms of the quality of my Hong Kong experience.

It doesn't take long for Ben to give me the signal, this time starting off a bit more subdued—only a double-throat-clear and a nod. It's apparent that he's pretty drunk and has forgotten that I've already handed the bag back to him. Trying to help him out, I cough in response, while pointing to his pocket with the hand that I use to cover up my cough. Slightly more frustrated, he goes again—a double-throat-clear, a nod, and a wink. So I respond back again, this time with a throat-clear, and then I thrust my head forward as if to point in the direction of his pocket with my chin. I do my best to get through to him, but he's clearly getting increasingly aggravated and confused.

He remains undeterred. Losing any sense of subtlety what-soever, he goes all-in with a double-throat-clear, followed by two nods with simultaneous winking. Just to make sure that I see him, he takes his index finger and points directly at his eye with each wink in exaggerated slow motion. He's hammered.

"What the fuck are you doing?" Lillian snaps, implicating both of us but glaring only at him. "Are you guys doing drugs? Because I like to have fun, but I am not cool with anyone who feels the need to use drugs."

"What? No. Of course not. We don't do that," I jump in, adding some confused-looking body language. "Let's get some more drinks."

This is where things get a bit hazy for me. I experience a complete and total blackout. The next thing I know, I'm in a bed. Next to me is a girl. It takes me a few more seconds to process; it's Lillian. I look around; it's not the Mandarin. Why the fuck didn't I just go upstairs to my room? That's the entire point of drinking in my hotel bar. Apparently, despite every-thing and in spite of myself, I have somehow ended up back at Lillian's apartment and in her bed.

Amazingly, I have also come out of a blackout just as things are starting to get hot and heavy; I didn't miss a thing. The plan has worked out after all. I sit up and look around, just to make sure I haven't emerged into the middle of some freaky shit. Thankfully, Ben's nowhere to be found.

Things are just about to happen, when I realize that between the quantities of alcohol and the cocaine, there is zero chance of me being able to perform right now. To buy some time, I employ my go-to move in this scenario and head down south. This gives me a chance to make sure she's satisfied, while also freeing me up to try to jump-start my own engine.

A solid twenty minutes pass, and my ignition isn't even turning over. Fuck. I pull myself up, drenched in sweat from the suffocating bowels of an obviously expensive duvet. "Sorry. I'll be right back," I say as I rush toward the bathroom. I'm not typically self-conscious but it's always a little weird walking around a girl's bedroom totally nude on a first date.

I lock myself in her bathroom, turn on the lights, and just stare at myself in the mirror. I imagine this is how Larry Bird or Rickey Henderson used to get himself psyched up before a big game.

I run the faucet so that she can't hear me, and then I start masturbating feverishly, with the only objective of marching back out there like a champion. That's when I look down and see my crumpled jeans on the floor at my feet. Staring back at me, peeking out of the front pocket, is a small white baggie. Of course, I have no idea how it ended up back with me, but miracles do happen. Not that this will in any way help my cause in this situation, but in my inebriated state, I decide that the right thing to do is to rip as big a line as that small bag will afford me.

"Hey, are you okay?" She's so sweet.

"Yeah, just washing my face. I'll be right out."

Apparently, Lillian also has two dogs—little fucking Pomeranians—and they've just emerged from who-knows-where and are now scratching and sniffing around in front of the bathroom door. But, at this point, I'm not going to let anything stop me.

I dump the contents of the bag onto the sink's edge. There's surprisingly more in there than I had thought. Using the bottom flat edge of her face wash, I shape the small pile into what loosely resembles a line and then kill it.

After that, I get back to the mission at hand—getting myself hard. The dogs clearly sense something strange happening and start yapping in sporadic little pips. That's not helping my cause. They continue, speaking to me in Pomeranian: *Margaret Thatcher. Margaret Thatcher. Baseball. Kevin Spacey.* Cockblocking asshole mutts.

I tear open the empty bag, turn it inside out, and lick its remnants. Surely, that'll give me the boost I need. Once again, my logic is totally backward.

"You're not doing drugs, are you?"

Here I am, locked in a stranger's bathroom, staring at myself in the mirror, sweat pouring down my face, white powder all over my nose, and my limp cock in my hand.

I've been in Asia for all of eight weeks.

When I hear, "Got a minute?" I know I'm about to lose a half hour of my life that I can never get back.

My personality is 30% the last movie I watched.

I never give money to homeless people. I can't reward failure in good conscience.

For people who believe everything happens for a reason, that reason is that they're idiots who make shitty decisions.

If my wife offers me a blow job, I know it's time to check my Amex statement.

Carpet or Cock

Living in the Mandarin Oriental is great while I get accli-
mated, but after a few months, I'm ready to move into my
own apartment, which according to my company's housing
allowance turns out to be a three-bedroom on the forty-sixth
floor of a brand-new luxury Mid-Levels tower. Bear in mind
that the average-sized apartment for a family of four in Hong
Kong is approximately 550 square feet, and that I'm coming
in at over three times that size, as a single guy who will spend
most of his time in the office or on an airplane. That, added
to the legacy of decades of colonial rule, may help explain
why there is some resentment toward expats in Hong Kong,
particularly in the office.

My first order of business, after taking down half the Minotti
store, is to find a suitable maid. There is no shortage of experts
to guide me in this process. During my many "Welcome to
Asia" dinners, this becomes a frequent topic of conversation.
What's the deal with Macau? I hear Thailand is full of hoi
polloi? Can you recommend a good tailor? How do I find a
reliable and trustworthy maid?

During one such dinner, I am sitting next to ▬▬▬▬
▬▬▬▬▬, the head of fixed income for Japan, who is visiting

Hong Kong for the week. He doesn't even live here, and he's an expert on the subject. "Here's what you want to do—go to one of those agencies and they'll give you a phone book full of headshots to choose from. Then pick a young, hot Filipina girl."

Apparently this advice comes tested. A friend of his has a maid who, having failed as an aspiring model, chose the next best line of work for a person in that situation: working as a live-in helper rather than have her visa revoked and be sent back to the Philippines. Among many other things, leading up to and including sexual favors, this guy (in all fairness, he's a broker, not a banker) likes to make her dress up in ridiculously skimpy outfits for his weekly poker nights.

"This way, if you strike out at the bars and come home wasted and alone, all is not lost. Trust me, she knows the drill."

The guy sitting across from us chimes in. "Yessss! But the trick is to make sure that she's not too hot; you don't want her thinking she actually has a chance with you and then getting jealous when you bring other girls home."

The next night, I'm having yet another dinner, but this time with more of the working-level capital markets origination bankers. These guys are considerably more risk averse; they don't have the stomach for sales and trading and lack the smarts for M&A. Just to be provocative, I throw the advice out to the table. "I think I'm going to get a hot maid; she'll know the drill."

"That's a terrible fucking idea," Rob Chen jumps in. "I'm married so I can't say that I've ever tried it. However, we did make the mistake of hiring a young maid. She wasn't even hot; she just wasn't terribly ugly. One afternoon, when my wife and kids are out of town, I have to run home unexpectedly to grab my passport. I walk into my apartment only to find my maid, down on her knees, giving some random guy a blow job—on my daughter's bed. There he is, just sitting there, with his sweaty ass soiling my daughter's Little Mermaid comforter, staring back at me. I wish I could say he looked shocked, as if this was some crazy, fucked-up situation, but he just stared back totally unfazed, like it was just another day in Hong Kong. Maybe he thought I was next in line."

It turns out his maid had been turning tricks in the apartment with the steady stream of construction workers in the building for the various renovation projects.

"Ugly and old is the only way to go," he concludes.

I'm sure as hell grateful I had this conversation; my mind is made up. Fortunately for me, Dennis Lipton offers to let me have his maid, Fé, once he completes his move back to the US. She's old and she's hideous—perfect. The best part is that, having worked under the watchful and demanding eye of Lipton's wife, she's very well trained.

Maids in Hong Kong generally work fourteen hours a day, six days a week, fifty weeks a year. Their minimum wage is set at US$500 per month by the Hong Kong government, which coincidentally, also tends to be their maximum wage. For the most part, they live in storage rooms (called maid's quarters) connected to the kitchen, rooms that are often scarcely larger than a closet. For many of them, their quarters are so small that in order to lie flat, they fold out a cot and sleep in the doorway straddling the kitchen and their room. The designated space for the toilet, sink, and shower is often overlapping, such that the shower nozzle hangs down directly over the sink and toilet.

They have one day off a week—Sundays. With nowhere to go, and no means to do much of anything, they gather in groups and sit on the sides of the streets, the walkways between buildings, and in the other designated public areas.

They construct cardboard box forts and spend the day (irrespective of the weather) playing cards, chatting, giving each other pedicures, and enjoying a homemade street-side buffet. For the most part, the maids are dedicated, hardworking, and devoutly Catholic. They save as much as they can to send back to their worse-off extended family members in the Philippines.

The Hong Kong government is so discriminatory against domestic helpers as a class of people that, as a means of keeping them out of the public parks, they've made it illegal to consume food in parks—but only on Sundays. Also, many of the businesses and malls will close their bathrooms for "maintenance"—again, only on Sundays.

Nonetheless, my new maid is ecstatic to have me as her sponsor. Not only do my requirements pale in comparison to those of her previous employer, I allow her to earn money on the side, which perversely is also illegal under Hong Kong law. Working for me and also for a few friends of mine, she's going from killing herself for a family of five, earning US$500 a month, to making more than US$1,500 working for a few laid-back, single expats, who all work long hours, travel frequently, and aren't particularly demanding. Given my busy work schedule and social habits, I don't even require much in terms of cooking.

Having said that, I still have needs. I need fresh orchids for the living room and cut flowers on the bedroom nightstands. My T-shirts, boxers, and socks must be crisply ironed. The pillowcases and sheets must also be ironed, and the duvet must have a perfectly perpendicular checkerboard pattern of subtle creases. Initially, as a legacy of hotel living, I request clean towels and fresh sheets daily, but in order to minimize the wear and tear on my expensive linens, I cut that back to three times a week. It has nothing to do with the environment; it's just that good sheets are hard to find.

I don't need an alarm clock anymore; I've got the fresh juice wake-up call. Monday, Wednesday, and Friday is a ginger-carrot-pear detox. Tuesday and Thursday is orange or grapefruit juice: "I don't care; surprise me." I'll follow that up with a to-go coffee and toasted bagel, perfectly timed and still warm for my short commute into the office.

As bad as it might be to work for a crazy expat, nothing is worse to a Filipina than working for a Chinese or Indian family. By comparison, they tend to be cruel and relentless, forcing helpers to work longer hours and frequently on Sundays. They have been known to install locks on the outside of maid's quarters so that they can lock them in their tiny rooms. They dock their wages arbitrarily to the point that employment borders on enslavement. In fact, there are often cases of retaliation or retribution, during which a foreign domestic helper will murder her Chinese or Indian employer, or vice versa.

One of the more senior guys on the capital markets side, Wisal Lari, actually sent his maid to live with his mother in Pakistan for eight weeks so that she could learn all of his favorite childhood recipes. While I don't have a huge amount of respect for him generally, I have to admit the food at his house is amazing.

Another time, I am at a dinner party at the apartment of an Indian colleague of mine, the head of high-yield capital markets. On the table, they have this small remote control. It's amazing; any time it is pressed, the maids (they have two) will come running out of the kitchen to service us.

"Damn, where can I get me one of these?" I sarcastically ask my colleague's wife.

"I couldn't find it here, so we had ours sent from home. In Mumbai, you can't live without it because the Indians are so lazy and unreliable. The most annoying thing here is that the walls are so thick, I can't get reception upstairs. So, if I want something, and I am in bed, I physically have to get up and walk halfway down the stairs in order to alert one of the helpers."

"Who knew that the reinforced walls that protect us in typhoon season would be such a pain in the ass? Why don't you just call or text down your breakfast order?" It'd be impossible for me to be any more sardonic. But she doesn't get it all.

"Well then, what's the point of having this one button if it doesn't even work?"

By comparison, I am saintly, but far from a saint. For Christmas, on top of a generous cash bonus, I get Fé a really nice shine box and shoeshine kit. For Easter, in addition to a few extra days of vacation, I surprise her with an extension device that allows her to clean my exterior windows without putting her life at risk. (Okay, the shine box and extension device weren't actually part of her present, but I told my friends they were and they thought it was both hilarious and practical). It's no joke; there are multiple fatalities in Hong Kong every year from helpers leaning too far out, or even climbing onto the ledge of their apartments, attempting to clean the windows.

Despite our many foibles, the Filipina helper community loves working for the *gweilos*. And by foibles, I mean behavior that is in complete disregard for all societal norms and basic human decency. My Fé has to deal with the carnage that comes with me coming home blackout wasted several nights a week. Each morning, she has the privilege of digging through last night's suit pockets, pulling out receipts and wads of discarded cash, the totals of which would feed her village for months. She knows that I have no clue what's in there, but it's just not worth the risk for her to steal from me, even if she were so inclined. One mistake, or even the suspicion of one, and I, as her work visa sponsor, could have her deported almost immediately—no questions asked. Her life, or, at the very least, her livelihood, is completely in my hands.

Occasionally, after a particularly outrageous misadventure, I will text her from the safety of my office and ask her to kick a girl out of my bedroom. That's bad, but probably not as bad as the time I had an old boarding school friend visiting from Tokyo, and she walked in on him getting intimate with a transsexual prostitute. At least I enjoyed hearing her tell me about it.

One day, Fé comes to me in a state of distress. "Hello, sir. I cannot work for Mr. Randall any longer. Is that okay?" She wants to stop working part-time for one of my friends who lives just a few blocks away from me. She'd rather earn substantially less money than have to deal with another version of me and the eccentricities that go along with being a single white expatriate banker in Asia—a job assignment most maids would kill for.

"What's the problem, Fé?"

"Well, sir. Mr. Randall yell at me because I make mistake. He say I throw away his drugs too many times. I try to do my job, sir."

I just start laughing and immediately call him up. "So apparently you went apeshit on Fé and now she wants to quit cleaning your place. What the fuck happened?"

He's still seething. "That dumb bitch. I left a bunch of coke out on a plate last night. It wasn't just a little bit. I was Jack fucking Nicholson in *The Departed*. The next day, when I get home, it's all gone. And when I ask her about it, she just says that she cleaned everything up. What the fuck am I supposed to do? Should I garnish her wages for the cocaine? She'll have to work like nine months to pay that off."

I gradually manage to calm him down; he forgives her, and she agrees to not quit. But from that point on, she is exceptionally diligent—with all of us. Any time she comes across a little white baggie in one of our pockets, she carefully places it on the nightstand. If there's a plateful of coke laid out on the coffee table, she carefully cleans around it, even making sure to leave the residue that has spilled onto the table—just in case we get desperate. At one point, I look in a random drawer in my kitchen and find an entire collection of tightly rolled HK$20 banknotes.

Deep down, I know that Fé loves me. She even leaves a note one Sunday telling me that she said a prayer for me at Mass that day. It's comforting to know that Fé doesn't want to spend eternity without me.

This aside, Fé's life is amazing in contrast to that of her peers, and she knows it. One day in the office, I get a text from her: "Hello sir. May you please help me. My daughter in Manila has a school exam and needs books. Please sir, can you borrow me HK$3,000 of my salary. Thank you, sir. God bless."

I relay the message to a Chinese colleague sitting next to me and ask for some advice. "Fuck her, dude. They know they can just take advantage of you white people. It's a fucking scam."

"It's just an advance on her salary. What's the big deal?"

"Don't fucking do it. It's the principle. If you give her the money, then she knows you're a sucker. It's all over after that."

I seek a second opinion. I stand up and shout across two rows of the trading floor, to one of our credit traders. He's an ABC (American-Born Chinese), so I'm hoping for a more balanced opinion. "Hey, Andy, my maid just texted me. She wants to borrow money; she says it's for her daughter's schoolbooks back in the Philippines. What should I do?"

"Fuck that. She doesn't need any schoolbooks. She knows the only thing her daughter needs to learn is how to suck carpet or cock." And then with that, everyone in the immediate vicinity just starts laughing, and a few people jump on in agreement: "Yeah, are you fucking stupid?" or "Fuck that."

I'm not hugely surprised. I had previously been chastised in the office for innocuously mentioning that I allow my maid to take a taxi any time she's going grocery shopping for me. Some of my colleagues got seriously annoyed. "Dude, make her take the bus. You're setting a bad precedent. She's just going to tell her maid friends and then they're all going to want to do it."

Fortunately, not everyone in the office shares the same dismissive attitude toward the Filipina helpers. After all, they're only human. We can't lose sight of the fact that the life of a Filipina maid must be a monotonous, solitary, and soul-destroying existence. It should elicit some sympathy—or in Ken Davies's case, sympathy and opportunity.

Ken is one of our back-office guys; he transferred to Hong Kong from the UK, specifically to satiate his yellow fever. Every Sunday, Ken will religiously patronize the bars frequented by the lonely Filipina maids looking for company on their day off—it's not like all of them go to church and sit on cardboard boxes. Sometimes, he'll have two or three "dates" on a given day. Ken's dedication runs so deep that, unlike most expats, he chooses to live in the Wan Chai red light district just so that he can be closer to the action.

He even attended a colleague's traditional Chinese wedding with a maid as his date. Watching our boss, the head of fixed income, and in particular his wife, attempt to make polite conversation with this woman, who had clearly borrowed an "evening dress" from one of her prostitute friends, had all of us rolling for days.

While he says he prefers the Vietnamese girls because "they really know how to hold a position," Sundays and public holidays are all about lonely Filipinas. One day, as he proudly tells it, he meets and spends the afternoon drinking with a nice young Filipina girl in Wan Chai. Many cocktails later, she boldly invites him back to her employer's apartment because he and his family are out of town.

She takes him to a palatial place up on Old Peak Road, where he spends the night. Of course, they're not going to confine themselves to the maid's quarters; they make full use of her employer's apartment.

The next morning, Ken is in the kitchen helping himself to some juice, when he decides to check the place out in the light of day. Walking through the living room, he admires the tasteful contemporary Asian decor and impressive collection of artwork. He then moves across to a sideboard, showcasing an array of framed family portraits and travel photos. And that's when he sees a very familiar face in almost every single picture. It's Charles Widdorf, our regional head of equity capital markets.

Our piece-of-shit back-office geezer just fucked Charlie's maid in the bed Charlie shares with his wife.

Some chick asked me what I would do with 10 million bucks. I told her I'd wonder where the rest of my money went.

"Work hard, play hard" is the mantra of a drunk who doesn't work that hard.

Checking your phone after someone else checks theirs is the yawn of our generation.

As a society, we're actually smarter than ever. It's just that technology has given a voice to the unsophisticated masses.

Not only did I forget her name in the morning, I forgot what I told her my name was too.

The Roadshow

Selling a new high-yield bond (also called a junk bond) for a company usually involves conducting a full investor roadshow. It is an integral part of the deal marketing process and can be of pivotal importance in terms of lowering a company's cost of borrowing. London-Paris-Frankfurt-Milan-Madrid is a typical European circuit, often traveling by private plane, always dining at the best restaurants and staying at the finest hotels. This might sound exciting and glamorous, but I can assure you, it's anything but.

In a nutshell, a roadshow involves taking borrowers—the bond issuers—to meet and sell their story to potential investors, who range from hedge funds and asset managers to insurance companies and pension funds. The issuers and their bankers go through a scripted PowerPoint presentation; address any structural, disclosure, or financial issues in the offering prospectus; and finish with a Q&A.

Each day is a series of back-to-back meetings and group investor lunches, flanked by market update and strategy conference calls and punctuated with mad dashes to the airport. Roadshows are arduous, grueling, and often stressful.

The worst job, by far, on any roadshow is that of the analyst. Analysts are the pledges of the financial world. It's where
everyone has to take his or her three years of licks after coming out of the training program. It's masochism born out of
stupidity. What at first seems like the big time soon turns into
sixteen-hour days, seven days a week, most of it mindless crap
like churning out pitch books and any other shit-work the associates don't want to do.

On a roadshow, the responsibilities of the analysts are to
carry the presentation materials and to oversee the logistics,
such as hotels, flights, cars, and dinners. All of this has to be
done without fucking up—period. The job sucks, but analysts
want to do it; it's a coveted badge of validation. Just as the slow-
est and dumbest analysts rarely get asked to do coffee runs,
and the boring-as-shit ones never get invited out for drinks,
I'll pick the most competent analyst to go on a roadshow. And
if I'm going too, they better know how to have a good time.
Nothing is more painful than being stuck in an airport lounge
with a teetotaler from the Indian Institutes of Technology.

At this point in my career, I'm senior enough that I don't
have to worry about any of the analyst bullshit on this roadshow. I'm here to represent our firm's relationships with the
investors and to help sell the deal. More important, I'm here
to demonstrate to the issuer just how much we value our
developing relationship with them. For frequent borrowers
or less important clients, I usually delegate the roadshow leg-
work to a capable associate so that I can focus on executing
other deals or winning new business. However, this particular
deal is for a company that will pay Wall Street banks approximately $30–$40 million in fees this year alone, across capital
markets and M&A advisory. While the fees on a bond deal
might not be spectacular, being a bookrunner on these deals

creates incremental trading revenue as a corollary. And since we are just starting to establish ourselves as one of their key counterparties, I'm there to shine. After all, my next bonus and promotion depend on it.

It's my job to shine; ergo, it's also my job to proactively throw my competitors under the bus at every possible opportunity, regardless of the fact that we're technically partners on this deal. So I'm the one taking personal credit for setting up the most important meetings, and then, when we get a big order, I'm the first one to deliver the good news. Conversely, this also means that I'm a matador when it comes to strategically sidestepping the task of delivering any bad news. On a deal that involves multiple bookrunners, banks rotate leading client update calls. So, if there's a chance that it will be my turn to deliver a recommendation that the client isn't going to like, I will disrupt the alphabetical rotation by inserting a last-minute "market update and investor feedback" call into the schedule. Not only do I now get to avoid delivering the bad news, I can purposefully paint a rosier picture on my call, just so that the next bank's job is even more challenging. It's all one big game; I didn't make the rules. "I'll let you know how your fucking lunch tastes" is my typical not-so-subtle reminder to my counterparts at the onset of any deal.

It's a war waged on all fronts, irrespective of what's in the best interests of the client or the deal. When I was an analyst, if another bank was responsible for roadshow logistics and I wasn't traveling with the team on the road, I would often give their analyst intentionally incorrect information—the wrong floor or the wrong tower for an investor meeting, anything to make them look bad. I don't care if it causes the entire roadshow team to show up ten minutes late; that's Deutsche Bank's or JPMorgan's problem. Although the banks may be working together on this deal, we're always competing for the next one.

So far, this particular roadshow has been a breeze. Investors love the deal. The client is happy, and the bankers are all playing nice. Heading into the home stretch, the day starts off just like the others. My BlackBerry alarm clock goes off at 6:45 A.M. The auxiliary wake-up call comes at 6:50 A.M., and the "waffle wake-up call" arrives at 7 A.M. sharp. A "waffle wake-up call," a move that I am credited for having started, is more or less exactly what it sounds like. Upon first checking into a hotel, I prearrange breakfast room service with strict instructions for the butler (their term, not mine) to come in and make sure that I am awake and/or still alive. You can't risk waiting to arrange this until right before you go to sleep in the likely event that you won't have any recollection of getting back to the hotel at night.

A 6:45 A.M. wake-up isn't particularly early by my standards, but it is after the typical night out on a roadshow—wining and dining the client over dinner and enough drinks to recover from an exhausting and tedious day of nonstop meetings. Banks generally pay for the roadshow expenses out of deal fees, which are typically in the region of 2% for a decent high-yield deal. So the client wants and expects to have a good time, especially if the deal is going well. In many cases, it's the most exciting thing these fuckers will do all year, so they want to make the most of it.

Corporate executives are just not cut from the same cloth as investment bankers, so the client festivities usually wrap up by midnight. From there I'll get into the elevator with the clients, talk about what a pivotal day we have coming up, drop them off on their floor, and then double back downstairs. (Never stay on the same floor as a client; a shared stroll to the elevator at 7 A.M.

with a UK finance director and two prostitutes taught me that lesson, a situation that was made even more awkward by the fact that the hookers were his.) By the time I manage to shed the deadweight, I have arrangements to meet anyone I can—friends, colleagues, competitors, or even other clients for more drinks. Having played the part of babysitter all day, this is my chance to blow off some steam. My mission is to push myself to the limit of what I can handle and still be able to function the following day, a formula that I don't always get quite right. Deviant proclivities tend to set the pace; however, I generally try to work my way back to the hotel for a civilized nightcap before 3 A.M., when we can sit back in the lobby bar and watch the whores on parade as they escort the drunken businessmen back up to their rooms. I don't think there is anything in this world quite as brazenly entrepreneurial as a prostitute soliciting me in the corridor of a hotel, just as she's leaving some guy's room and I'm staggering toward mine. I know a few guys who have made that trade, but the "hot pocket" isn't my thing.

To kick off a roadshow day, the client breakfast ordinarily starts downstairs at 7:30 A.M. Having already scarfed down two coffees and some waffles in my room, this is when I'll deliberately order a jasmine tea and a fruit plate just to make a point to the client that I'm a serious and disciplined professional. I usually accompany that with a quick line about how shitty the hotel gym is. "The treadmill shakes too much at high speeds" is a fan favorite. The client is almost always impressed.

Our first investor meeting, and my third coffee of the day, starts at 9 A.M. Four hours, three meetings, one shitty investor group lunch, and an unknown number of coffees later, we're just halfway through the day. Come 6 P.M., it's finally time to head to the airport. I'm fucking exhausted, and I feel like shit. It is the end of yet another tedious day of the roadshow.

Thankfully, all that stands between me and the warm embrace of an evening in Madrid is a two-hour flight.

For this roadshow, given the schedule of meetings and travel logistics, it makes sense to travel by private plane. On a commercial flight, with some basic preparation, you can make sure you aren't seated anywhere near a more senior colleague or a client. Instead of working or reading the latest issue of *Institutional Investor* or *International Financing Review*, you can watch a movie, get some sleep, and, most important, have a few drinks. The best part of any airport lounge or first-class cabin is that no matter what time of day it is, it's generally socially acceptable to drink. Sadly, our travel arrangements today afford me no such opportunities for a much-needed elixir.

I'm a really nervous flyer to begin with, and I am immediately reminded of the endless number of statistics that say flying private is substantially more dangerous than flying commercial, not to mention all the anecdotal evidence running through my mind, thanks to the Discovery Channel. As exhausted as I am, I don't think too much about it and quickly try to settle into my seat for the easy jaunt to Spain.

Just over halfway through the flight, all the coffee in my stomach feels like it's percolating its way into my lower intestine. It's nothing out of the ordinary, and my internal body clock comforts me with the knowledge that my next BM should be right around ten minutes after hotel check-in. After all, I haven't dropped heat on a plane in about ten years, and there's no reason to think that streak will end on a relatively short trip on a private jet.

I hunker down and focus on other things, like playing *Snake* on my *Matrix* edition Nokia. Twenty minutes pass, but feel like an hour. We then start to experience, even by my standards as a seasoned traveler, some pretty violent turbulence. With each bounce, I have to fight my body, trying not to shit my pants. *Thirty minutes to landing, maybe forty-five,* I try to tell myself, every jostle a gamble I can't afford to lose.

On a plane like this, the flight attendant isn't really as much an attendant as she is someone who keeps the pilots company. Trying not to draw attention to myself, I signal to her and she heads toward me. I start to think about insurance; am I wearing boxers or boxer-briefs? I've got no fucking clue; I was still drunk when I got dressed this morning.

"Excuse me, where is the bathroom, because I don't see a door?" I ask while still devoting considerable energy to fighting off what feels like someone shook a seltzer bottle and shoved it up my ass.

She looks at me, bemused, and says, "Well, we don't really have one per se." At this point, she reads my mind, and preemptively continues. "Well, technically, we have one, but it's really just for emergencies. Don't worry, we're landing shortly anyway."

"I'm pretty sure this qualifies as an emergency," I manage to mutter through my grimace. The turbulence outside is matched only by the cyclone that is ravaging my bowels.

I can see the fear in her eyes as she nervously points to the back of the plane and says, "There. The toilet is there." For a brief instant, relief passes over my face. "If you pull away the leather cushion from that seat, it's under there. There's a small privacy screen that pulls up around it, but that's it."

At this point, I am committed. She just lit the dynamite and the mineshaft is set to blow. I turn to look where she is pointing and it makes me want to cry. I do cry, but my face is so tightly clenched that it makes no difference. The "toilet" seat she is referring to is the seat occupied by the CFO, i.e., our fucking client. Our fucking *female* fucking client.

Up to this point, nobody has observed my struggle or paid much attention to my discreet exchange with the flight attendant. "I'm so sorry. I'm so sorry." That's all I can say as I limp toward the back like a drunk Quasimodo impersonating a penguin and begin my explanation. Of course, as soon as my competitors see me talking to the CFO, they all perk up to find out what the hell I'm doing.

Given my fun-loving attitude thus far on the roadshow, almost everybody thinks that I'm joking. She knows right away that this is no joke and jumps up, moving quickly to where I had been sitting, which must have felt like slipping bare feet into still-warm bowling shoes, or the previously mentioned "hot pocket."

I now have to remove her seat top—no easy task when I can barely stand upright—the small cabin continues to bounce around, and I am valiantly fighting a gastrointestinal Mount Vesuvius. I manage to peel back the leather seat top to find a rather luxurious-looking commode, with a nice cherry or walnut frame. It has obviously never been used, ever. Why this moment of clarity comes to me, I do not know. Perhaps it is the realization that I am going to take this toilet's virginity with a fury and savagery that is an abomination to its delicate craftsmanship and quality. I imagine some poor Italian carpenter weeping over the viciously soiled remains of his once beautiful creation. The lament lasts only a second as I am quickly brought back to reality, concentrating on the tiny muscle that stands between me and molten hot lava.

I reach down and pull up the privacy screen with only seconds to spare before I erupt. It's an Alka-Seltzer bomb, nothing but air and liquid spraying out in all directions—a Jackson

Pollock masterpiece. The pressure is now reversed. I feel like I'm going to have a stroke; I push so hard to end the relief, the tormented sublime relief.

"I'm so sorry. I'm so sorry." My apologies do nothing to drown out the heinous noises reverberating throughout the small cabin. If that's not bad enough, I have one more major problem. The privacy screen stops right around shoulder level. So I am sitting there, a sweaty disembodied head, in the back of the plane, on a bucking bronco of a commode, all while looking my colleagues, competitors, and clients directly in the eyes. "Pay no attention to that man behind the curtain" briefly comes to mind.

I'm so close I could reach out with my left hand and rest it on the shoulder of the person adjacent to me. It's virtually impossible for him, or any of the others—and by "others" I mean high profile banking competitors and clients—to avert their eyes. They squirm and try not to look, pretending as if nothing out of the ordinary is happening—that they are not sharing a stall with some guy crapping his intestines out, vociferously releasing smelly, sweaty shame at one hundred feet per second. "I'm so sorry. I'm so sorry."

People who drive the speed limit are either huge pussies or have a car full of drugs.

Each comma in your bank account adds an inch to your dick.

If she thinks fellatio is a Shakespearean protagonist, I don't know if I should cut my losses or go all-in.

Insider trading is like pissing in the pool. It sounds dirty, but really isn't that big a deal.

I'd marry for money. And I already have money.

The
Wild Wild East

The first time I flew down to Jakarta, I waited one hour in immigration and then another three hours in traffic without BlackBerry reception, only to arrive at the Ministry of Finance to discuss their proposed $3 billion sovereign benchmark deal twenty minutes after our pitch ended.

No wonder they need the money: Jakarta is a shithole.

To avoid making the trip a complete waste, the local banking team invited me out for dinner. We started with drinks at my hotel, the Hotel Mulia. As the only locally owned five-star hotel in Jakarta, the Mulia is considered less of a terrorist target than Western hotels like the Grand Hyatt or Four Seasons.

My local team was quite proud of having arranged to take me to one of Jakarta's hottest and most exclusive spots for dinner. When we arrived, my first thought was that it looked like a prison—a walled compound draped with razor wire. We were greeted by several security guards, a German shepherd, and one of those guys with a primitive mirror-on-a-stick bomb detector, the mascot of the third world.

Another guard opened the imposing gate and waved us through. As we drove inside, I was amazed—lush green gardens, tropical flowers, perfectly manicured landscaping, and elegant fountains. There was probably a koi pond too, but I was too distracted by the row of exotic cars lined up in front of the entrance: Ferrari, Ferrari, Porsche, Lamborghini, Mercedes, Ferrari, and Ferrari.

The inside of the restaurant was equally striking, a minimalist Asian decor overflowing with beautiful people—models, socialites, and titans of industry, or certainly their offspring.

While we were making our way to the bar, a stunning girl smiled and said hello to me. Not that I think I'm ugly, but that kind of thing doesn't usually just happen to me. I had to check with my local capital markets head and host for the night. "That's a pro, right?"

"A hooker? Nah, man, people are just really friendly here." He was more amused than offended.

He wasn't joking. What I encountered over the many drinks that followed were some of the kindest and most outgoing people I have ever met. It was explained to me that just by virtue of being at this club, we were accepted as members of the local elite. Everybody was friends with everybody.

I went ahead and stayed an extra night: Jakarta is fucking awesome.

Now, a year or so later, I'm flying back to work on a high-yield deal for the Mulia Group, an Indonesian property company. They own one of Jakarta's premier shopping malls, condo towers, and, of course, the before-mentioned hotel.

Just a few days before, I spent four tedious hours on the phone with senior officials at the Korean Development Bank, arguing over a 0.005% difference in their funding cost. Now, here I am working on a deal for an Indonesian tycoon named

Djoko Tjandra, the CEO and largest shareholder of Mulia. He's an outrageous character, chain-smoking his way through meetings and never without his Biggie Smalls Versace sunglasses, even indoors.

It's our job to find investors willing to lend this Bond villain $150 million.

This is why I love working in Asia. You never know what to expect; anything goes. I've always embraced that aspect of my job. From the day I landed in Hong Kong, I have been constantly shifting my expectations and realigning my moral compass in every aspect of my life.

Even innocuous events like my first closing dinner in Hong Kong were totally different from those that I have attended in New York or London. Closing dinners are a global banking tradition, where the bookrunners and clients celebrate the success of a deal in the private room of some fancy restaurant, getting drunk and handing out tombstones (Lucite deal trophies). Toward the end of dinner, a senior banker quietly made it known that the Chinese CEO wanted the party to continue at a karaoke bar. To avoid creating an embarrassing scene for the client, the female bankers were discreetly asked to excuse themselves from dinner. The young analyst next to me got a BlackBerry message from her boss: "Hey, maybe you should go home now."

I was used to explicit sexism from my time in London; after all, my first boss insisted on only interviewing prospective female candidates, which he called the "Office Beautification Project." But Asia takes this to a whole new level. My boss in Hong Kong once asked me to interview a research candidate and then gleefully suggested that we should hire her because "you know, we should probably tick that box"—implying that with her butch haircut, pantsuit, and masculine demeanor, she was, in his mind, quite obviously a lesbian. "She's good for the brochures."

Everything in Asia is amplified, fueled in part by the benefits of being an expat, with the extra compensation packages, the housing allowances, and more senior reporting lines. And because of the lingering effects of colonialism, foreigners are often treated better than the locals. Many of my Chinese friends will speak English when they make dinner reservations or if they walk into an upscale department store, because even acting like an ABC will get them better treatment. If I'm hosting a dinner in my Mid-Levels apartment, the *gweilos* are allowed right up, no questions asked, whereas the locals are stopped by security at the gate and then again by the Chinese doorman in the lobby, who will call up to confirm the visitor.

When we had a company off-site in Thailand, the local employees flew Dragonair economy class, while the expats flew Cathay Pacific business class. Although the rules were subsequently changed, there's a resentment that remains today. "How come I don't get a housing allowance?" or "Why'd they send you from London to be our boss instead of promoting one of us?"

In short, there are no rules and we are all part of an entitled class that is overpaid and protected. This identity cuts across the usual banking boundaries found in the United States and Europe, where bankers tend to do their jobs and go home.

After work one evening, I'm having dinner with a group of colleagues, all of whom are Americans, at an open-air restaurant in SoHo. For no particular reason, one of our traders suggests a contest to see who can walk into the Chinese restaurant across the street and yell "Suck on my balls" the loudest. After the third guy walks in and yells, it's my turn. By this point, I know they are going to be suspicious of any white guy walking in alone. So I patiently go through the motions of getting a table, sitting down, and ordering a beer and appetizer.

Once I have alleviated all suspicion, I jump up on top of my chair and yell at the top of my lungs—"Suck on my balls"— unequivocally winning the contest. I jump down and hightail it out of there, taking my beer with me of course.

It's not that bankers in New York or London are any less deviant, they just can't get away with what we can. That's why they are always trying to drum up any excuse to attend one of our conferences, or to convince their clients to "develop relationships with the Asia investor base" with a weeklong roadshow, where the most important meetings are with tailors, watch retailers, and karaoke companions. To echo the sentiments of a visiting managing director from New York: "Damn, it doesn't take long in Asia before I've seen all your cocks."

In fact, my trader friend Andy's unexpected promotion was primarily based on his ability to entertain visiting senior management, taking them on helicopter "missions" to Darlings or the Rio in Macau.

We even had a visiting colleague from New York get drunk and hook up with one of our interns (an offense that can get you fired in New York). He was so drunk that he couldn't remember which girl it had been—as he said it, "They all look the same." So the next morning in the office, he somewhat jokingly walked around the trading floor trying to identify her by the top of her head, much to the amusement of the rest of us.

I arrived in Hong Kong in the fall of 2004, but didn't fully understand the magnitude and pervasiveness of this entitled and deviant mentality within broader banking culture until the inaugural Asian debt syndicate Christmas dinner at the end of that year.

That night, we take up a single long dining table in the middle of the Mandarin Grill. Representatives from every meaningful bank are in attendance—Morgan Stanley, Deutsche Bank, JPMorgan, Goldman Sachs, Lehman Brothers, ABN, Credit Suisse, HSBC, Citigroup, Barclays, Nomura, UBS, and Merrill Lynch. The only relevant bank that isn't there is Bank of America, and as I am quickly informed, their syndicate head wasn't invited, not just because she is a woman, but primarily because she is a "minger" and a "snoozer."

We start with four bottles of tequila spread out across the table and a simple rule: if you check your BlackBerry or answer your phone, you have to do a shot. This sets the pace for the evening. "Sorry, this is New York calling; I need to take this" is met by a chorus of "Do a shot, bitch."

Even some old boarding school tricks get resurrected. ████████ █████████, a senior banker at Nomura, walks over to my end of the table, stands between me and the ABN banker next to me, and says, "Hey mate, did you guys get bread rolls down at this end?"

Without thinking, I peel back the napkin, only to discover (at eye level) his freckled ginger cock and balls resting comfortably on top of the rolls. I leap out of my chair, sending it crashing to the floor and filling the dining room with the sound of the laughter and high fives.

"Wait, wait. Where's Peter? Did he miss it?" someone shouts. My colleague Peter, who is in the bathroom, had missed the dick-in-a-bread-basket gag.

Upon his return, he is courteously offered a roll from the soiled basket, which he immediately devours. That's his punishment for being suspected of pretending to go to the bathroom just so that he could use his phone without having to do a shot. Also, no one likes or respects him. As he reaches for his second roll, we're rolling on the floor laughing.

"What's so funny?"

Since no one else is going to eat the bread, there isn't much we can do with it except hurl it back and forth from one end of the table to the other. As we see it, hitting someone in the face is tantamount to slapping him with a cock.

We haven't even ordered food yet, and people all around us, having been overwhelmed by ricocheting bread rolls and every imaginable combination of profanity, are requesting to be relocated to tables in far corners of the restaurant. Tonight, "Siberia" is the best seat in the house.

One complete stranger makes the mistake of pleading with us to keep it down. Not only is he heckled as he scurries away from the table, but he is subsequently followed into the bathroom by two managing directors, pushed into a stall, and reminded to mind his own FUCKING business.

The final tab—including the tequila, miscellaneous beers and cocktails, and at least two dozen bottles of wine—is split by the three most senior guys (who would have the least difficulty expensing it). Still new to Asia, I'm not quite in the inner circle yet and am therefore NFI (Not Fucking Invited) to the post-dinner activities, which include an ample supply of narcotics and love monkeys (prostitutes) galore.

The festivities don't end there. The last person into their respective office the next day, as measured by their Bloomberg login status, has to pay for the liquid lunch that follows, where we spend three hours nursing our hangovers and reliving the events of the previous evening.

Subsequent syndicate dinners are moved to private rooms, and for good reason. As the tradition continues, so do the antics—bowling with wineglasses and ashtrays, fistfights, BlackBerrys mysteriously ending up in wine buckets, suit jackets finding their way into urinals, communal stashes of cocaine, and at least one trip to the hospital.

This deviant mentality isn't simply a by-product of living up to the "work hard, play hard" cliché; it is firmly engrained in how bankers act and how business is conducted. The people are the same. The mentality is the same. Asia just happens to be the place where we can show our true colors without accountability or consequence.

Against this backdrop, and with the help of a bull market, the deals continue to flow. We did a roadshow for a government-related Korean entity and frequent bond issuer. The finance director cared more about the hotels and dinner plans than he did about the lineup of investor meetings. He famously strolled through the duty-free store in the Heathrow concourse, pointing out luxury items that caught his eye: a classic blue Ferragamo print tie and a Montblanc fountain pen. By the time the roadshow team landed in New York and checked into the Palace Hotel, he had two ties and two pens waiting for him in his room. Both relationship managers at ▮▮▮▮▮▮ and ▮▮▮▮▮▮▮▮ had sent their junior bankers scrambling back to make the purchase—whatever it takes to increase your chances of being on the next deal.

A Ferragamo tie is a small price to pay. We once lost a high-yield mandate to ▮▮▮▮▮▮▮ because their head of debt capital markets sent an analyst to Jakarta to personally deliver a sought-after Hermès Birkin bag as a gift for the CEO's wife.

On one very memorable deal, we're trying to price a $1 billion five-year bond for ▮▮▮▮▮▮▮▮▮, one of the government-related Korean banks. They are by Asian standards regarded as a frequent borrower and are crucially important to the franchises of any top-tier bank in their region. These deals don't pay much in fees, but they help put you on top of the league tables. Moreover, the team that runs ██████████'s borrowing program also advises the Republic of Korea on their capital markets activity. For all syndicate managers, winning the trust and faith of the ████████ team can mean the difference between having an average year and a great year.

Given their frequent borrower status, they are also well known to the global investor base. They could theoretically announce a transaction in the morning and price it that night, significantly reducing their market risk, like a big move in rates, equities, or investor sentiment, and headline risk, like North Korea deciding to test-fire a new rocket. Either scenario represents an event that could derail their ability to borrow money attractively from the international capital markets.

However, a one-day execution process isn't much fun for a bunch of Korean bureaucrats. So, of course, we all tell them what we think they want to hear if it will help us win the mandates—a global roadshow is in order.

One bank gets into the deal by adding Paris to the recommended roadshow schedule—ostensibly for sightseeing and shopping, because there's not a single investor in France (besides Dexia, but they don't need a meeting) that buys their bonds. Another bank impresses the client by pitching a roadshow schedule that straddles a weekend, so they can spend two days golfing in New York.

Midway through the roadshow, it comes time to release initial price guidance to investors, letting them know where we think this new $1 billion five-year bond is likely going to price. This isn't rocket science—we have investor feedback, trading levels of existing comparable bonds, and a sense of investor sentiment and overall market backdrop, all of which gives us a fairly precise idea of where a new deal should price.

We recommend Libor +20 basis points area. "Basis points," or "bp," represent one hundredth of a percent, in reference to the yield, or cost of borrowing. "Area" is a term that simply means "plus or minus"; sometimes it is quantified and sometimes it is left intentionally undefined. This gives us scope to price tighter than +20 bp if the market backdrop is constructive, or slightly wider than +20 bp if the market is adverse, therefore allowing the company optimal flexibility.

Price guidance is also an important tool for us in generating deal momentum so that we can still entertain reflections of interest at wider levels than our intended final outcome. Our strategy is simple: generate strong interest at that guidance, and then aim for a final outcome in the context of L+18 bp. All the investors who were initially reluctant at anything inside of L+20 bp will usually end up staying in the deal.

That's all the company hears. They don't want to even consider a scenario whereby the end result could be anything less than stellar.

Director Park speaks up on behalf of ████████. "We don't agree with that +20 area recommendation. If you are so confident that +20 area gets us to +18 as a final outcome, then let's just go with +18–20 now." In their minds, this removes the possibility of pricing wider than +20.

The syndicates hold the line and refuse to accept the counterproposal. Our response is simple: "Starting at +20 area has a better chance of getting to +18 as a final result. If you squeeze too early and go out +18–20 then it will scare away the momentum players and push large accounts into putting limit orders in at the wider end of that range."

We've been on the phone for more than two hours now—thirty bankers and five stubborn Korean clients—and it's really starting to jeopardize the viability of the execution timeline.

It's imperative to convey a number that the market receives favorably as soon as possible into the Asia morning, so that orders can be confirmed and momentum can be reflected into the European investors in the afternoon. It's already after 10 A.M., and the radio silence is letting investors know that we're having issues; they're smart enough to know that it's usually the result of a disagreement on pricing.

After much back and forth, Director Park breaks the deadlock. "Fine. I will reluctantly accept your recommendation of Libor +20 bp area, but only if you agree to backstop the deal at that level." Thus, he wants to lock himself in at Libor +20 bp, keep any upside, and give all the downside to us.

Having expected this kind of scenario, we're quick to respond.

"Barclays agrees."

"Citigroup agrees," I chime in, caveating our commitment with some language to protect ourselves in a worst-case scenario, like a North Korean invasion or another 9/11. Otherwise, I'd have to reach out to New York for approval.

"Deutsche Bank agrees."

After a long pause, "Um, this is UBS. Can you all please hold on for just one moment?" It's Sam, the junior syndicate banker at UBS. He's not in a position to sign off on underwriting the entire deal without the approval of his boss, the managing director and head of syndicate at UBS, Johan Hanson.

"Okay. Hurry up." Director Park is agitated.

Of course, we all seize on this opportunity to throw UBS under the bus, trying to make sure they get excluded from the next ███████ or Korea sovereign deal.

"Sam. Hurry up," Deutsche Bank pipes in. "We're losing valuable time. We're dead if we don't give Asia enough time to confirm their orders before Europe gets in." It sounds silly, but it's important when dealing with clients whose first language is not English to speak in memorable bullets, using easy-to-comprehend (and scary) words like "dead."

Everyone on the line sits in silence as UBS tries to get approval internally. All of a sudden, we hear ringing, followed by a voice. "Thank you for calling the Mandarin Oriental, how may I direct your call?" Then we hear Sam again. "Room 1312. Johan Hanson, please." It's now clear that instead of calling his boss on a different line, he has inadvertently patched the call directly into the conference line.

We hear ringing again. And ringing. And ringing.

Finally, a voice answers. It's Johan. "Heeelllllo?" He sounds like he's on his deathbed. More important, he has absolutely no idea there are thirty bankers and five high-level clients from █████████ listening on the call.

"Johan. Johan."

"Sam? What the fuck do you want?"

"You didn't answer your cell and I need your help on ██████████."

"Dude . . ."

"Johan?" Director Park interjects.

"Director Park?" It's obvious that Johan has just woken up and is thoroughly confused.

I jump in. "Good morning, Johan. Yes, that is Director Park. In fact you've got the entire ██████████ deal team on as well."

"Time-out. Sam, did you just fucking patch me into a conference call?"

Sam doesn't say a word. Johan pauses to clear his throat and jump-start his vocal cords. "Good morning, Director Park. Is this an important call?"

"Yes. Yes. We need to agree on price guidance urgently."

"Okay. Hang on. Let me kick this girl out of my room."

We wait patiently for about thirty seconds, listening to a barely audible conversation between what sounds like Johan and a prostitute. My line is muted, but some of the Korean bankers on the line can't help but snicker.

"Okay, now I am ready. What's up, guys?"

We succinctly explain to Johan that the joint syndicate team had recommended Libor +20 bp area price guidance with the hope of getting to +18 as a final result. ██████ wasn't happy with this recommendation and is only willing to accept it if each bank agrees to underwrite the deal at +20 in the unforeseen event that we price at a wider level than that.

"Yeah, fine. Whatever. We'll backstop the deal at that level you just said." And just like that, Johan now owns $250 million ██████ five-year bonds at Libor +20 bp.

"Director Park, now I have a question for you."

"Yes, Johan?"

"Can I go back to bed now?"

"Yes. Yes you can." The line erupts in laughter.

The client loved it. For all subsequent calls that required a syndicate decision, Director Park would say, "Wait, we can't begin without Johan." They loved his honesty and lack of pretense.

After my trip to Jakarta, the banking team spends the next two months working through the due diligence and documentation process for the Mulia deal.

Once we start the roadshow, I know that I'm going to have my hands full. We have a few serious hurdles with trying to help them raise the $150 million.

International investors have had a contentious relationship with Indonesia ever since the default of Asia Pulp and Paper in

2001, which caused a collapse of asset prices in Indonesia and across Southeast Asia. It was a painful and expensive shock to the bondholders given the reputation of APP's management-owners, the well-connected Widjaja family, and the deal's bond underwriters, Credit Suisse, Goldman Sachs, JPMorgan, and Merrill Lynch.

As a result, many emerging market investors still refuse to participate in any Indonesian corporate bond deals. This disdain goes beyond APP; the Indonesian courts are notoriously corrupt and have a long history of disregarding international law.

For our Mulia deal, there really isn't much recourse for investors in the event that the company decides to stop making interest payments. In this case, we have securitized the bond by ring-fencing some of the hard assets into a newly created offshore entity. Theoretically, in the event of a default, the investors would own the Hotel Mulia, the condo towers, and the shopping mall, but good luck getting a court in Jakarta to enforce that.

Then there's the small issue of the CEO's nefarious reputation as a "crook" or "Suharto crony." We try to address this by pointing out that we, as a firm, have conducted thorough due diligence and have received internal approval from our New York–based commitment committee to proceed with the deal—so investors are buying into our reputation as well. "Hey, we wouldn't be doing this deal if it wasn't legit."

Another issue we have is over the stated use of proceeds. The company wants to borrow $150 million from investors for the purpose of repaying loans. The fundamental problem is that these loans are from a handful of their principal shareholders (i.e., themselves), all through dodgy British Virgin Islands shell companies with suspicious names that would make the

Enron lawyers who dreamed up the infamous JEDI, Chewco, and Raptor SPVs blush. Unfortunately for us, we actually have to detail each of these shell companies in the offering circular. It's a good thing many investors never bother to read the bond documents anyway; in a bull market for credit, all they care about is yield and if the order book is oversubscribed.

This is going to be a very challenging deal, but there's a price for everything. However, that leads to yet another fundamental problem. Looking at the cash flow of the company, there is no way they can support a coupon payment of anything above 12%. Anything above that and default becomes self-fulfilling. And Djoko Tjandra sure as hell isn't going to give away any equity to add a "kicker" to boost the yield.

I'd rate this deal somewhere between challenging and impossible. But no one internally wants to be the person to say no to doing it. The banking team in Jakarta is just so happy to be doing a deal that pays real high-yield fees (2%), compared with what we might make on an Indonesian sovereign deal (0.05%). And Babar, our head of high yield, is happy to slash and burn his way through as many deals as possible, hoping that if a handful of them get done every year, he's a hero—a well-paid hero.

After the first day of investor meetings in Singapore, the Mulia team flies up to Hong Kong. Feedback from the meetings is not great; apparently, they are terrible at presenting and are ill equipped to answer investors' questions. That's when Babar tries to pawn the Hong Kong portion of the roadshow over to me. "Hey, man, I've got another deal kicking off. Can you step in and take them to the one-on-one meetings?" Once again, this is not a good sign.

Ahead of our first investor presentation, I meet the team for breakfast to give them a market update and an overview of the meeting schedule that is ahead of us. A presenting delegate of the Mulia team shows up wearing a garish Chanel suit, accentuated by gold Chanel-logo buttons. To complement the suit, she has an all-diamond Cartier watch, diamond bracelet, and jeweled rings on at least four of her fingers. It's going to be a shitty day.

She is asking investors to effectively lend her $150 million so that she can turn around and repay loans she and her cohorts have allegedly made to the company. At the first meeting, she gesticulates wildly as she leads a portfolio manager through our meticulous PowerPoint presentation. I'm not sure they hear a word she says; they're hypnotized by all the bling adorning her hands and wrists.

Now I know for sure, this deal is never going to work. But I still don't want to be the one who gets blamed for killing it. At the end of the second day of meetings, I try to gradually reset their expectations. "Look, we're facing a fairly challenging market backdrop, so there's no point getting on a plane tonight and going to London until we have more feedback and hopefully some indications of interest from the Asian investors you met with." In reality, I know they'd get laughed out of the room in London.

To alleviate the situation, I offer to take the team out to dinner.

We have a delightful dinner sitting on the terrace at Dragon-i. From my experience, the rich and unscrupulous tend to make for entertaining company. And we're in the perfect venue: an infamous restaurant, owned by the son of a reputed gangster, that turns into one of Hong Kong's hottest clubs as the evening progresses.

Toward the end of dinner, we've all shifted our focus from eating to drinking. I need them to get loose before I ease back into the discussion of the increasingly low probability of a successful deal. Just as I start talking about the deal, the wait-ress comes over and drops off the bill in front of me, and then just stands there next to me. My guests look confused. I pull out my corporate card and tell them it's not a big deal, that our table is probably reserved for later, and that we can go drink somewhere else, but they don't want to leave.

It's obvious that they're not used to being told they can't do something. To them, it's a reflection of status. Who could be more important? One of them starts berating the waitress, who is just staring at me helplessly. I didn't want it to come down to this, but I am forced to step in. "Guys, guys. Technically, it's my fault. I'm actually not supposed to be here after eleven P.M."

A few months before, I had received a lifetime ban from Dragon-i. Normally I wouldn't care about getting banned from a bar or restaurant, but it's hard to function personally (as an expat) and professionally (as a banker) in Hong Kong and not be allowed to go to Dragon-i. I went back and negotiated a truce with the general manager, whereby we agreed to a one-month ban, followed by a six-month probation period, where I would be allowed in but not permitted to stay past 11 P.M. Considering that I had been a loyal customer for years, they were willing to show some leniency. Hong Kong is a city of pragmatic capitalists above all else.

This potentially embarrassing situation is a big hit with the client. They just want to know the backstory.

I had been at Dragon-i with a group of my friends. At some point between 1 A.M. and blackout, I looked across from our table and saw most of the Manchester United soccer team danc-ing and standing around a table. I am a Chelsea fan, but I recog-nized the players from playing FIFA on PlayStation.

They had been doing an off-season tour of Asia and were in town to play an exhibition match earlier that day. I was at the game; the match was a joke—an insult. None of the big stars played more than twenty minutes. They warmed up in one uniform, started the match in another, and changed again at halftime. The entire trip was just about selling merchandise.

That's when we saw Wayne Rooney aggressively hitting on this relatively attractive blond chick. He's in a high-profile relationship, but I wasn't surprised. The British press had already exposed his alleged activities with a forty-eight-year-old prostitute and grandmother of two, later nicknamed the Auld Slapper.

I was pretty wasted by this point. What followed next was the Hong Kong equivalent of "Hold my beer and watch this."

I walked up behind Wayne Rooney. Because of the music, he was leaning right in this girl's face, oblivious to me standing behind him. Once I made eye contact with her, I start gently caressing Wayne's back, pretending to hit on him while he was hitting on her.

He snapped around and was obviously confused when he realized that it was me stroking his back. I held my hand up toward his face to initiate a high five and said, "Hey, you come here often?"

He pushed me back and yelled, "Fook off."

I glanced back over at my table of friends; they were dying. Within five seconds of our encounter, Wayne had forgotten all about me and returned his focus to the blond chick. So once again, I started caressing him, working my way down to the small of his back.

"Fook off." This time, he shoved me back with both hands.

I held my hand up toward his face and said, "High five?" He slapped it away, and I quickly retreated back to the safety of my table and the comfort of my drink.

Roughly ten minutes later, I saw that Wayne Rooney now had his arm around this same girl and was so close that he appeared to be kissing her neck or whispering in her ear. I felt this sudden compulsion, almost a moral obligation, to do something.

This time, I raced back over, leaned up next to him, placed my cheek on Wayne's shoulder, pushed my face up against the side of his neck, and gave a slow drawn-out exhale, while at the same time caressing the small of his back.

BANG. POW. BOOM. Punches were thrown; pushing, shoving, and shirt pulling ensued. Ryan Giggs and Paul Scholes jumped in to restrain Wayne Rooney, and my friend, a former college football player, jumped in to restrain Rio Ferdinand from trying to take my head off.

From there all I really remember is screaming, "Fuck off, ginger cunt," to Paul Scholes as two bouncers picked me up and carried me out. It's only when I showed up the next night that I was informed of my "lifetime ban."

The Mulia guys love the Wayne Rooney story. "Next time you come to Jakarta, we will take you out." I'm not sure I would have had the same response from some of my previous clients like Unilever, General Electric, or Rolls-Royce.

The following day, since they didn't fly to London, I finagle a few more meetings for them with hedge funds in Hong Kong—favors that I will have to later repay with allocations on hot deals. Somehow, we manage to drum up about $70 million of interest, ranging from 11% to 12%. But it's still not enough to justify continuing the roadshow in London. It was always going to be a tough credit to sell to European investors anyhow, and they won't be buoyed by the tepid demand out of Asia. Without heading to London with an oversubscribed order book, there's no hope for getting a deal done.

The time has finally come to pull the plug, send them back to Jakarta, and focus my time on deals that have a higher probability of success. As I am explaining this reality to them, they interrupt me. "You have $70 million that's good at 12%, right? What if you were to receive another $60 or $70 million in orders from ▆▆▆ Private Bank today? Then wouldn't we have enough interest to go to London and put this deal together, even if it ends up being a bit smaller than $150 million?"

The coverage banker loves this idea. All he sees are the 2% fees paid to us. Unfortunately for him, I also have to represent my other clients—the investors who would own this paper.

I respectfully play along. "Well, okay. But we haven't seen much private bank demand for this deal, so I don't see how we can expect to get $60 million from retail investors."

"Let us handle that."

Two hours later, our private bank salesperson gets a call from ▆▆▆ Private Bank placing an order for $40 million. Shortly after that, she gets a call from ▆▆▆ Private Bank with an order for $20 million.

At this point, it's perfectly clear what is going on. They're content investing their own money in their own deal knowing that the proceeds, minus 2% in fees, are flowing directly back to them anyway. This way, at least they'll still get the $70 million from the other investors.

I call my boss in New York, and he lays it out for me with remarkable clarity. "If everything you know about this deal were to appear on the front page of the *Wall Street Journal* tomorrow, what would happen?"

That was all I needed to hear. The next morning, we canceled the transaction, and I never heard from or saw the Mulia guys ever again. It didn't matter to us; we moved on to a jumbo project finance deal the following week.

Mulia's largest shareholder and CEO, Djoko Tjandra, was later sentenced by Indonesia's supreme court to two years in jail for embezzling millions in bailout funds from the now-defunct Bank of Bali. He fled the country and, at last count, is currently living large in Papua New Guinea.

If someone has a tattoo saying, "Only God Can Judge Me," I'm gonna prove them wrong.

I'd rather be me now than have been the quarterback in high school.

When it doesn't matter how much the drinks cost, it's always happy hour.

I start every cell conversation with "my phone's about to die" so they don't waste my time.

Who trusts a justice system where all the smart people get out of jury duty?

The
Lunch Break

On my first day working in Hong Kong, a few of my new colleagues take me to lunch at a decent Chinese place in IFC Mall. It's packed. An hour later, we're still eating leisurely, and the place is still packed.

"Hey, guys, thanks for taking time off the desk to bring me out to lunch." I'm assuming that this laid-back jaunt is an exception to normal office protocol. In New York and London, lunch on the trading floor typically involves running downstairs to the canteen and grabbing a sandwich to bring back and eat at your desk. Occasionally, during the summer lull or the holiday season, we will enjoy a long lunch. But those sacred occasions are few and far between.

In Asia, it's not only acceptable to take two hours for lunch every single day, it's part of the culture. The stock market officially closes. In fact, when the HKEx tried to implement measures to shorten the lunch break, there were protests.

In the fixed-income world, activity doesn't officially stop, but markets hibernate from noon until the London open. It's not so much a function of taking a break as it is waiting to get a sense of how European sentiment will influence market direction. This means the typical lunch break is informally either two or three hours, depending on daylight saving time. (The clocks never change in Asia.)

I have a feeling that this is going to get me in trouble.

A few days later, I am once again invited to join some new colleagues over lunch—this time for a trip to the spa. At first, I think they have organized this outing for my benefit, as part of my ongoing cultural acclimation; however, it soon becomes very clear that they do this all the time. I'm apprehensive, thinking it's going to be some grimy rub-and-tug joint. Andy, the ringleader and a rising star credit trader, reassures me: "Nah, man, don't worry about it. This is like a five-star resort. Besides, why you gotta be racist like that?" He's an ABC from California, or as he says, "I ain't Chinese. I'm from Cali, nigga." He was the kid in high school who was simply "cool" and not "pretty cool for an Asian kid."

The place is amazing. We change into plush bathrobes and follow the beautiful hostess into a giant Romanesque chamber, complete with marble columns and waterfalls.. We all get naked (if Asian dudes learned to manscape, it would look bigger) and hop in the hot tub. This completely redefines the notion of the "executive workout." We bounce our way from hot tub to ice-cold plunge pool to Jacuzzi (the size of a swimming pool) and back to the hot tub. From there, we hit the steam room, the sauna, and finally back to the Jacuzzi for a rinse, all at a rapid-fire pace.

"What's the rush?" I'm confused as to why we're condensing all of this amazingness into a twenty-minute hopscotch.

"This is just the warm-up; we can't waste too much time in here. And you'll have plenty of time to hang out here after your massage."

The hostess appears with new robes and slippers and directs us upstairs to a lounge area, which is filled with reclining chairs and lined with TVs broadcasting CNBC, Bloomberg, and several local Cantonese channels. Most of the seats are occupied by older Chinese men in robes, reading newspapers, eating noodles, chain-smoking, or sleeping. There's not another white guy in sight. The occasional sound of throat-clearing is a rather unpleasant reminder that this isn't quite the Elysium that the first room is.

We are immediately met by middle-aged women carrying stools, one for each of us. They hand us what looks like a menu, all written in Chinese, and then begin massaging our feet. Andy grabs my menu. "Don't worry about it, homie, I got you."

Five minutes later, four girls in bikinis lead each of us away in different directions. Andy preempts my obvious confusion. "I ordered you a sixty-minute massage. When you're finished, meet us back in the hot tub."

My girl takes me into a private room that resembles spa facilities you might see in at a Ritz-Carlton, but not quite at a Four Seasons. She skips the part where she's supposed to ask me if I prefer lavender or jasmine oil and jumps right into the massage. For such a nice place, I'm surprised that she's not more methodical. After rubbing my shoulders halfheartedly for no more than five minutes, she says, "Okay, you turn over now."

I roll over onto my back, and she immediately grabs my flaccid cock. Her bikini top is gone. "Whoa, whoa, whoa. Massage only," I say, somewhat reluctantly pushing her hand away.

After five minutes more of the world's worst shoulder rubbing, she says, "Okay, you turn over now." Again, I oblige. Surprisingly, she starts massaging my chest. Two minutes later, she grabs my semi-erect cock. Once again, I remove her hand, this time a bit more slowly. I roll back onto my stomach and say, "Massage. M̀hgòi." That's Cantonese for both "please" and "thank you."

This process repeats itself several more times, until one of us just gives up.

In terms of technical ability and effort, it's the worst massage I've ever had, but when considered in totality—not so bad. Exactly one hour later (I wasn't going to leave my Constantine in some triad locker room), I grab my robe and head back down to the hot tub, where my three colleagues are waiting for me.

"Where the fuck have you been? We've been waiting for you for over twenty minutes." They're more confused than pissed.

I'm equally confused. "What are you talking about? I thought we all got hour-long massages."

"Why would you get a massage from a whore?" They think it's hilarious.

Over time, I would discover a more comfortable, Western-friendly alternative to Andy's "jizz and jet" lunchtime tradition—in the form of a legitimate foot reflexology session. For many of us, it would become a regular habit of meeting for lunch and following it up with an hour-long foot massage. I'd also go by myself if I needed to sleep off a particularly nasty hangover.

As I quickly learn, the Asian lunch break is sacred. For the sake of my health and soul, I find some balance, gradually developing a routine of going to the gym three days a week and allowing two days for client lunches (usually just day drinking), internal or syndicate lunches (day drinking), massages or foot reflexology (a nap), or trips home (even more fun). If I am traveling (plane drinking) or mid-execution on a tough deal (stuck on the desk), I'll take it out of my gym time—thus preserving the two days of midday debauchery.

Thankfully, most of the local Cantonese clients get annoyed at the prospect of lunch meetings; it infringes on their free time. So my lunches are usually with hedge fund buddies and other *gweilos* (colleagues and competitors). At one of my first lunches in Asia, I tag along with Dennis Lipton. He wants to introduce me to all of his clients as "the guy who decides how many bonds they get on new issues." It's a smart move—now they'll call me if they don't like their allocations. We start at 11:45 A.M. with Bloody Marys and then switch to wine with lunch. They are appalled when I excuse myself at 2 P.M. to head back to the office. At 5 P.M., Lipton has his client, a prominent credit hedge fund manager, drunkenly call into our desk, yelling, "You fucking pussy," and vowing to keep calling every five minutes until I promise to meet them back out. I return just after six o'clock, and they haven't moved, other than making the necessary switch to vodka Red Bulls.

Another lunchtime ritual—more an obligation—is the road-show luncheon. We do so many deals that when markets are stable, it's virtually a weekly duty. Roadshow luncheons sound amazing—three-course meals in a private room at the Four Seasons, Ritz-Carlton, China Club, or Shangri-La. But as soon as that novelty wears off, they are dreadfully boring, needlessly high-caloric affairs.

Since we cannot avoid them, we learn to optimize the time. The syndicate bankers generally show up at the reception early so that we can shake hands with our issuer clients and give them any updates on the deal, along with a quick review of any market developments. Then we work the room, meeting and greeting our investor clients, thanking them for coming and for their interest in the deal. Wine is sometimes offered; I always make a point of being memorably disciplined: "Would it be too much trouble to ask for a grapefruit juice? But only if it's fresh-squeezed."

Once lunch starts, so does the PowerPoint presentation—one that I have seen and heard at least a dozen times. I wait five minutes, then pretend that my BlackBerry is vibrating, hold my hand over my mouth as I fake answer it, and whisper, "Hey, I'm in a meeting. Can I call you back?" I'll wait five seconds and say, "Okay, okay, hang on. Let me go outside."

I excuse myself politely, tiptoe out the door, abandon any pretense of being on the phone, and head directly to the hotel bar or one of its restaurants. It takes about twenty minutes for the scheduled group of bankers (mostly syndicate guys) to stagger their exits from the presentation and reconvene. If the weather's nice, we'll meet by the pool; there are some very attractive tourists who flow through Hong Kong.

Surprisingly, this is how many deals get hashed out and successfully completed; meeting face-to-face over a few drinks cuts through the gamesmanship, backstabbing, and other bookrunner antics. We'll spend twenty minutes talking deal strategy and then the rest of the time just hanging out and drinking. We generally take turns picking up the mostly liquid tab, not that it matters. All of us are expensing it, or using a deal code to charge it back to the issuer currently sweating his way through the presentation in front of a roomful of investors.

The roadshows prove to be a great excuse for the bankers to get together. But too often, it's the same crew of guys from the most active bond houses. To broaden the group, one of the syndicate bankers will organize a big lunch every couple of weeks inviting every syndicate banker (minus a few of the softer souls) from Goldman Sachs and Morgan Stanley to Nomura and BNP Paribas. That poor chick at Bank of America still doesn't get an invite, but there is a female exception rule for hot interns.

It's not a function of the odd depraved personality here or there; it's systemic across the industry.

These gatherings are typically one large day-drinking session. Unfortunately for me, given our prominence in the fixed-income world, I usually head back to the office around 2 P.M. I'm busy executing Asian deals, while also trying to help my US and European counterparts sell their deals into the region. Many of the other bankers carry these festivities deep into the afternoon, or longer.

Despite my best intentions, it's a real challenge to get to the gym during the lunch break—too many bad influences. A typical example: I'm packing up my standard-issue canvas bag for the gym when my dealerboard lights up. It's Adam Mitchell. "Hey, boy-o, had a client booked for lunch, but he just bailed. Don't make me eat by myself." Adam, aka Mitch, is a close friend of mine from the investment bank. He is the definition of FILTH: a boisterous, energetic, British lager lout who had a few missteps early in his career in London, so he decided to move to Asia, where he has subsequently done pretty well for himself. I love him.

That's what friends are for. "Okay, done. Lobby in two." We head up to the Lobster Bar and Grill at the Shangri-La, one of our go-to spots. Because the hotel also plays host to so many roadshow luncheons, it's impossible to go there and not run into other clients, colleagues, or competitors. It's not exactly the subtlest spot to misbehave, so I'm always anxious about going there with Mitch, even if it has been sold as a "quick, civilized lunch."

Today, it's absolutely jam-packed. We sit down; Mitch immediately orders a dozen oysters to share and a US$200 bottle of wine. That's when I spot Bob Morse, the CEO of Citigroup Asia, and Wisal Lari, at the entrance by the hostess stand. She sits them at the only remaining free table, right next to us. This isn't like the Four Seasons or the Regency dining rooms in New York; we're at these small, parallel, two-top tables that create a buffer between the more casual bar and the formal restaurant, where the seating is more spacious and private. Morse and Lari are so close that they might as well be joining us for lunch.

Bob Morse is a really nice guy, although I don't know him that well. Lari isn't my boss, but he thinks he is. He's a slippery used car salesman type who still feels the need to work the phrase "American Express Centurion Concierge" into almost every story he tells. Except for his inner circle of sycophants, people hate him.

He's predictably arrogant. Once, while we were waiting in the conference room for a client to show up, he sat there thumbing through a Ferrari brochure. He didn't even bother putting it away during introductions. Slightly bemused, the client asked him if he was in the market for a new car. Lari deadpanned, "Yes. Yes, I am."

I actually ran into him on the street one time. I pulled up next to him; I was in a taxi and he was in his Ferrari F430. I assumed he must have just taken delivery of it because it still had the plastic wrapping around the passenger seat.

I rolled down my window and got his attention. "Hey, Lari. Nice ride. I thought there was a credit crunch?"

He gave me this shit-eating grin that with his overbite made him look like a rat. "Not here there isn't." And then when the light changed, he sped off.

I later found out that he kept the plastic cover on the passenger seat for months, just so people would know that he received one of the first ones brand new, as opposed to having to pay above retail for a barely used model from someone who had been on the wait list and flipped it for a quick buck.

I also had another colorful encounter with him at the fixed-income Christmas party. A few of us from the trading floor were standing around making small talk with a couple of Lari's rather attractive subordinates. As soon as they walked away, Lari started telling a joke where the punch line was about how many mangos one of them could fit in her pussy. I was offended, but only because it was a shitty joke.

Back to lunch—as we are exchanging pleasantries, a waiter and waitress return to our table; she places a beautifully ornate tray of oysters in the middle, and he starts the process of ceremoniously presenting our bottle of wine.

Looking at this random display of decadence, Lari and Morse just give us this confused "what the fuck" look. It might be acceptable if there had been a client with us, or if it wasn't 12:15 P.M. on a Wednesday. It's clear that in their eyes, this is highly inappropriate, or, as Lari is probably thinking, "a bit homosexual."

Now, we have two options in terms of how to address this: we can get embarrassed and defensive, or we can embrace it.

I simply look over at Morse and say, "Don't worry, we're just getting warmed up."

I learned this lesson of not displaying weakness a long time ago in London. It was a nice summer day in Canary Wharf and I was having a leisurely alfresco lunch with a colleague of mine. It just so happened that we were enjoying a few beers. All of a sudden, Mark Watson, the head of fixed income, appeared from nowhere, looming over us. He stood there, in silence, and just shook his head like a disappointed father. As if that wasn't bad enough, our waitress appeared at exactly the same time. "Okay, gentlemen, one tiramisu, two spoons." I froze, turned bright red, and just sat there unable to speak. Sharing a dessert is pretty hard to live down on a trading floor.

As I get more and more comfortable in Asia, a small group of us start some of our own lunchtime rituals. Most of us single expats with generous housing allowances live in the Mid-Levels, so we'll often order food and have it sent to one of our apartments. We'll watch a movie or play video games, eat pizza, and drink a few beers. I've got my BlackBerry, Bloomberg Anywhere, and, in a pinch, can be back in the office in five minutes. We gradually begin to use these lunchtime sessions to participate in another prevalent investment banking hobby: doing cocaine.

There's nothing worse than doing coke while being anxious, uncomfortable, or rushed. Not that I have a problem with bathroom stalls or taxicabs, but it's a lot more fun and social when you're sitting on a couch, passing around a plate, and enjoying the process.

We meet downstairs in the lunchtime taxi line that we share with Merrill Lynch, Goldman Sachs, Barclays, and Deutsche Bank. People just see three or four bankers jumping into a cab and assume we're off to a client meeting. *Who knows what they're up to?* Five minutes later, we're at my place, watching *Chappelle's Show*, eating our Tokio Joe's, and passing around a plate. It also makes more sense to be at home because, too often, the coke gets cut up with baby laxative.

Two hours later, we head back down Garden Road to Central, fully charged for the afternoon. We use a strictly enforced buddy system for the remainder of the day—checking and reminding each other to look out for bloody noses.

Girlfriends and health kicks would occasionally push these sessions into hiatus, but the ability to spend a couple of hours relaxing at home midday never gets old.

When I later move into the Four Seasons, give up the drugs, and institute one of my many healthy "new leaf" initiatives, going home for lunch becomes even more enjoyable. I'll pick up some sushi takeout from City Super, change into my swim trunks, and lounge by the rooftop infinity pool, complete with an expansive view over all of Victoria Harbor. I swim laps, eat my sushi, take a nap, and get some sun. After an hour or so of that, I head back down to my room, rub one out, shower, put on fresh socks, clean boxers, and a crisp shirt—then head back to work feeling totally refreshed. It's like a minivacation.

As I get to know more and more people in the region, we form a monthly Friday lunch group at Ruth's Chris Steak House. The group includes an assortment of colleagues, competitors, and clients. Occasionally, we include a few nonfinance guys, but it's too annoying to watch them break down and split a check. "You had the tomahawk. You had the lobster. You had the filet with a crab cake. I just had the sirloin and no appetizer. And I didn't have any of the wine, just two beers." With the amount of money we spend there, we are treated like gods.

It's midmorning and I just got off the fourteen-hour red-eye from Los Angeles. I love these long flights, especially from L.A. It takes off just after midnight, which means I have ample time to have a nice dinner and plenty of drinks before making my way to the airport. I've got time to hit the Cathay lounge for a few more drinks before boarding my flight. I'll wait until we're allowed to recline our beds, pop a Xanax, put on a movie, and drink until I fall asleep. Six hours later, I wake up, rehydrate, and order some food. Then I can start drinking again, pick up where I left off on Denzel's *Man on Fire*, and fall back asleep. The flight is sufficiently long enough that I can get drunk, pass out, get drunk again, pass out again, and then still wake up feeling pretty good, just in time for landing.

I don't need to be a hero today and bother turning up at the office. It's the summer lull; the market is not only dead quiet, it's dead. People have effectively shut up shop until September.

I decide to spend the day detoxing by the pool at the Shangri-La. At some point in the early afternoon, my phone buzzes; it's Mitch. "Hey, boy-o. I thought you'd be back. Listen, I've been jammed all day. [Bankers are still busy when credit markets are dislocated.] I need some lunch. Meet me at Ruth's Chris in twenty minutes." *Click.*

I roll over and go back to sleep. Forty-five minutes later, he calls back. "Where the fuck are you?" He's tenacious to the point of being unstoppable.

"Sorry, man, I would if I could, but I'm at the pool, and I'm too lazy to go home and change."

He won't take no for an answer. "Listen, mate, I'm here by myself. Be a friend. Just come as you are. I'm buying. See you in ten." *Click.*

Reluctantly, I oblige. It's only a short walk through the shopping mall below the hotel. My only real issue is that I am wearing white Havaiana flip-flops, olive-colored reflective Prada swim trunks, and a fluorescent orange Vodafone Formula 1 racing shirt. This, along with my Persols and a baseball cap, is my go-to Eurotrash uniform when I feel like going incognito. It stands out so much that no one recognizes me.

Normally, I'd just stop in the mall and pick up some new clothes, but I figure, what the hell, why not flex some muscle at Ruth's Chris?

When I arrive, my swim trunks are still damp. I apologize to the general manager, the maître d', and my favorite bartender for my attire. They actually think it's pretty funny; it's also only 5 P.M. so they're pretty relaxed.

I find Mitch fully suited, jacket on, sitting at a suspiciously large table by himself, thumbing away on his BlackBerry. He's impressed. "Holy fuck. You weren't joking about not being dressed. Don't worry about it. But I wasn't sure that you were coming, so I've invited a few friends."

He's drinking whiskey, but I order a bottle of wine. A half hour later, we're still getting caught up. I'm telling him about my extended vacation and he's filling me in on some office politics; it's a wholesome conversation. That's when I see the maître d' leading three women in our direction. And by women, I mean prostitutes. And by prostitutes, I mean Indonesian girls from the bowels of Wan Chai—complete with Lucite heels, miniskirts, and halter tops.

The girls quickly polish off my bottle of wine, and Mitch, always the gracious host, reaches for the wine list. Seeing what he orders is always a great barometer of how drunk he is—HK$2,000, or $260 a bottle. That's not totally insane, but for three hookers, it's downright criminal.

I remind myself that he's paying but still guard the bottle as best I can. After an eternity of small talk, and three bottles later, we order food. It's now pushing 7 P.M., which means the dining room is slowly filling up for dinner.

Having spent all day detoxing at the pool, I have to make frequent trips to the bathroom. I don't know what people find more shocking: our companions, my attire, or my offensively small bladder. On one of my many trips, I notice that a group of Credit Suisse bankers I know reasonably well is gathering in one of the glass-walled private rooms. Fortunately, they don't see me.

Finally, our food arrives—on Ruth's Chris's world-famous piping-hot plates. With each plate, the waiter reminds us, "Please do not touch. Very, very hot." We get this every time we come here.

Today, this gives Mitch an idea. "Okay, ladies, you're going to play a game. We're going to have a contest to see which one of you can hold your finger on the plate the longest." He's not kidding. After a minute or so of explaining and coaxing, he says, "Hurry up. We're running out of time. Okay, ready, set, go."

It doesn't take much more than a single second before every person in the main dining room is treated to a chorus of "Ooooh. Aaahh. Eeeeeh," courtesy of the three hookers.

"That was pathetic. Let's go again."

The combination of the plates having cooled slightly and the nociceptors in their fingers shutting down makes round two slightly better. The winner almost makes it to three seconds before three more rapid-fire, piercing howls.

"Ooooh. Aaahh. Eeeeeh."

I can't take it; I excuse myself to the restroom.

"I'll join you." Mitch jumps up and pulls me into a tight embrace as we walk toward the bar. "What's wrong, mate? You seem off."

"Mitch, fuck you. Look who we're with. Look how I'm dressed. I mean Jesus Christ, Credit Suisse is having a client event right fucking there." I shouldn't have said that. Without hesitation, he releases me from his hold and pushes his way into the private room and yells, "What's up, Credit Suisse fag-gots." And then he runs out, giggling, into the bathroom.

That's when I pull a runner, right out the front door. I've had enough. Besides, I'm not risking Mitch sticking me with this fucking bill. That's the last time I dare to show my face at Ruth's Chris.

Money might not buy happiness, but I'll take my chances.

She's hot, but not "risk half my net worth" hot.

On Valentine's Day, I send my wife flowers with a card that says "Congratulations."

You don't feed wild animals because they become dependent and can't fend for themselves. How's it different for poor people?

In life, the boos always come from the cheap seats.

The Warren Buffett of Shanghai

"Lights." That's what we say on the trading floor when our phone rings. And by phone, I mean dealerboard—a large electronic panel with communal and direct phone lines, a squawk box (the hoot), and a small TV screen. If I need to pick up a trader, syndicate, sales, or research line, or even broadcast myself to the entire trading floors of Hong Kong, Singapore, Tokyo, London, and New York, it's all right in front of me. There are so many phones ringing at all times on a trading floor that we generally have the ringer volumes set at barely audible levels. For the uninitiated, it can be easy to miss a call unless you are paying attention. I have my dealerboard programmed so that the lines that I care about will flash in green and the lines that I don't care about will flash in red, hence the term "lights."

Chapter One of Trading Floor 101 for interns and analysts details how to answer the phones and operate the dealerboard. I have seen trainees reduced to actual tears for not answering the phone fast enough, accidentally dropping a line, or listening in on a call and forgetting to use the mute button. For a generation of kids who grew up without a home phone, basic telephone etiquette is increasingly an issue.

"Are you fucking retarded? How the fuck can I trust you to sell a bond if you can't even figure out how to answer the fucking phones?" I've said it many times. I've heard it many times. It's been said to me *once*.

The drawback of dealerboards at this time was they didn't have caller ID, so it was impossible for me to screen my calls.

"Hey, we've got a situation." It's Benny Lo, the head of the China coverage team, calling. "I'm hearing that ███████ is about to announce a deal away from us, mmm'kay? It's likely Morgan Stanley as sole bookrunner on the deal."

Missing a deal is not a very pleasant experience. You have to explain it to your boss and sometimes to his boss. And when you're sitting in Hong Kong, you also have to explain it to the product (emerging markets credit) boss in New York. The only thing worse than missing a deal is missing a deal and having your boss see it hit the tape before you do. *One of your clients is doing a deal and you don't even fucking know about it.* Fortunately, I am responsible for structuring, pricing, and selling the deals, so I don't have to worry too much about being accountable for the direct relationship. By that I mean I still get yelled at, but at least I won't get fired over it. That's on the coverage banker's head.

It's hard to imagine a scenario much worse than this. Morgan Stanley, one of our main rivals, is about to announce a sole-bookrunner deal for the first-ever high-yield corporate bond to come out of China.

"We need to get in this fucking deal," Benny whines. No shit, Einstein. He is one of the most annoying and notoriously pedantic bankers I've ever worked with, but in fairness, this is a bona fide fire drill. "I'm arranging a call with the chairman for this afternoon, and I'm going to need you to be on it. It seems that Morgan Stanley has been telling them they can get a deal done at 10% and is charging them two points in fees." (That means if the company raises $300 million, they keep $294 million as proceeds and the bankers get $6 million in fees.) For most of us, you need only a few of these deals under your belt each year to guarantee a decent six- or seven-figure bonus, depending on your rank.

Our strategy is fairly simple: lie through our fucking teeth. So with the help of our translator, I hop on to a conference call with Benny and Chairman Zhu, one of the richest men in China. Despite growing up in the shadow of the Cultural Revolution, without electricity or running water, Zhu has put together a conglomerate that spans real estate, pharmaceuticals, and commodities. To call him eccentric would be an understatement; he famously likes to remind people that he didn't own a pair of shoes until he was sixteen years old.

How I articulate myself is largely irrelevant because so much of whatever I say is lost in translation. So I go for melodic tones and short bursts that exude a sense of confidence and conviction. A few overpromises and outright lies also help. "Put us in this deal and, as the number one bond house in the world, we'll get you a better deal at a better price and at a lower fee." Despite having done zero credit analysis, I explain to him that we can get him a deal done at 9.5%, 50 basis points lower than what Morgan Stanley had told him. How is that possible? I tell him that we know more investors and have more leverage with them because we do more deals than any other bank. We also have a better read on the market because our trading desk is more aggressive and therefore sees more flow. It's impossible to quantify any of these points, so it's more of a confident assumption than an outright lie.

My only real concern is that everything I tell him will be further buoyed and exaggerated by our enthusiastic coverage bankers in translation. It's literally a game of high-stakes Chinese Whispers.

I feign surprise that Morgan Stanley is planning on charging him 2% in fees. What an outrage. For the privilege of helping deliver the first-ever high-yield corporate bond out of China, we'd happily do the deal for 1.5%. Chinese people are particularly sensitive to the thought of someone trying to rip them off.

It's also a good time to remind them that we are, and have been, active in lending to them. Part of providing low-margin services (loans) to clients implies that they reward us with higher-margin business. How do you say Glass-Steagall in Chinese?

Just like that, we're in.

Now, the fun part. I get to call up my counterpart at Morgan Stanley. "Hey, Chico, you know that deal you think you're announcing for ████████ next week?" (I use the term "Chico" as a generic and dismissive nickname [along with "Bubba" or "Fuckstick"] for people as a tribute to my former colleague in London.) Of course, he has to play coy; no banker would dream of discussing his nonpublic pipeline with a competitor. "Well, guess what? Now we're joint books. Since we're on the same team, we might as well get on the same page in terms of how we're going to get this deal done." That's just another way of saying, "Bring me up to speed on your months of hard work."

"Call you back." *Click.* He hangs up, presumably to call his own China coverage bankers to find out what the hell is going on. Five minutes later, he calls back. "You motherfucker. You guys pitched this at 1.5% fees and told him he could get a single-digit coupon." So now, they have gone from having a prestigious deal all to themselves, and looking at $6 million in fees, to having a fifty-fifty deal and only making $2.25 million. In terms of his bonus, and how we look at this situation, I've just taken a Patek Philippe off his wrist and put it on mine.

The next day is the kickoff meeting with the client to discuss market conditions, execution strategy, and deal logistics. If I can avoid these meetings, I do. It's the responsibility of the coverage bankers and execution team. My job is to stare at screens and talk to traders, salespeople, and investors and get the deal done, not to glad-hand the issuers. I'll typically call in to the meetings, say my part regarding markets and strategy, and then drop off; there's no point wasting my time sitting through a discussion on documentation and other legal formalities.

Ten minutes before the big meeting starts, my dealerboard lights up. It's Benny, panicking because he's stuck at the airport and not going to make it back in time. "We clawed our way into this deal; if we're not there, Morgan Stanley will try and get us kicked out. Since you spoke to the chairman, can you please go in my place, mmm'kay?"

Typically, it takes about fifteen minutes to leisurely walk from our offices to theirs, circuitously weaving through walkways that hover above the streets of Hong Kong, slowing down through the various connected office buildings along the way in order to enjoy a brief air-conditioned respite from the sticky, smoggy, heat. By comparison, a taxi would take about twenty minutes with the traffic.

I'm afforded no such luxury today; by the time I get there, I've got a serious *schvitz* going on. I steam into Morgan Stanley's office feeling like I'm walking into the funeral of the guy I murdered. At least the client is happy to see me; I'm the hero who saved him a bunch of money on fees and promised him a cheaper deal.

I look around for a place to sit at the conference room table. The way these meetings work in terms of etiquette is the client, the senior bankers, and the immediate deal team usually sit around the boardroom table, and then the analysts and other junior support staff sit in the chairs that line the walls of the room. If not, they stand.

At least Morgan Stanley is gracious enough to have saved me a seat. Actually they probably didn't save it for me. It's just one of those things that always happens, particularly within hierarchical cultures like Morgan Stanley; all the junior bankers are too terrified to take the last seat, for fear of someone more senior walking into the meeting. Having to relinquish a seat to a more senior colleague in the middle of a meeting is the banking version of the walk of shame.

However, I am now presented with one rather awkward dilemma. The only seat available is next to my ex-girlfriend, otherwise known as the Warden. Obviously I knew that she is still a banker at Morgan Stanley, but I had no idea that she would be on this deal team.

Unfazed and still thoroughly pleased with myself for getting into the deal, I grab that seat. In my mind, this is my movie scene moment and I am Ryan Gosling. In reality, I am more like Seth Rogen. I am drenched in sweat beyond the point of obvious discomfort. It's a good thing Chinese clients don't give a shit about personal hygiene.

Knowing that the stars will probably never align like this again—that we would be mandated with Morgan Stanley (it's usually us or them), that I'd be doing a high-yield corporate deal (not our traditional strength), that my ex-girlfriend would be the banker staffed on the deal (she does more traditional leveraged finance), that I would actually attend the kickoff meeting (which I never do), and that the only available seat would be next to her (I hate being late to meetings)—I have to do something to make it memorable. I have to.

During the meeting, there isn't much for me to do or say. On the assumption that they were going to be sole bookrunner, Morgan Stanley has the deal fully baked in terms of execution and roadshow strategy, and given the disparity of what we had each pitched the company on pricing, we avoid any kind of discussion on the topic. I throw out a few "I would agree with that" lines just to keep my voice fresh.

My ex-girlfriend, on the other hand, decides to use this opportunity to showcase her knowledge of the covenant package (the specific promises or stipulations listed in the indenture designed to protect lenders) and to demonstrate the depths of her relationship with the client, seemingly all for my benefit—as if I needed a reminder as to why things didn't work out between us. Just as she is repetitiously re-phrasing her boss's words—Morgan Stanley bankers are fa-mous for repeating each other, just using different phrases—I decide to take her down a notch and hopefully also expedite the meeting. Under the table, I remove my shoe and begin to gently caress her ankles. My disgusting, moist sock then glides up and down the back of her calf. Surprisingly, she's able to fight through it like a champ—even pausing to give me a friendly smirk.

I'm not going to let this deter me. The next time she opens her mouth, I decide to take my equally clammy hand and slowly slide it up from her knee, stopping just at the point where her thigh meets the seam of her skirt. Then I just leave my hand there, teasing the edge of her skirt with my index finger. That was enough. She doesn't speak for the rest of the meeting.

The deal hasn't even started yet, and already, I know it's going to be eventful. The roadshow includes stops in Hong Kong, Singapore, London, New York, Boston, and Los Angeles—in that order. The idea is that you whip up interest and momentum from anchor accounts in Asia, where the investor base is more familiar with the credit and the risk, such that by the time you are meeting European and US investors, you have the ability to convey a sense of momentum and strength. This also allows you to engage these typically larger and more influential investors in the context of the yield discussions (informal price guidance) derived from the early investor feedback out of Asia.

From the outset of the roadshow, it's very clear, and unsurprising, that investors do not care about this deal at all below 10%. The genesis of my recommendation to the company wasn't based off any roll-your-sleeves-up credit work or investor sounding; it was simply a function of saying, "Okay, what number do we need to show the client in order to get in on this deal."

Our roadshow efforts are not helped by the fact that Chairman Zhu is not your typical CEO. In one investor meeting, he is asked about the quality of construction in one of his real estate developments. "Stupid question," he says through a translator. "I don't want you to invest in my deal." Then he abruptly gets up and walks out of the meeting, leaving a potential $50 million anchor order behind.

In another meeting in New York, with one of the largest emerging market funds in the world, he lights a cigarette and just sits there puffing away. This is Mayor Bloomberg's New

York; you can't even smoke in a bar. The investor, a hard-core amateur triathlete, declines to participate in the deal.

Given his propensity to chain-smoke, Zhu also has the not-terribly-subtle habit of clearing the phlegm from his throat whenever he feels like it. It doesn't matter what's happening or who's talking.

European and US investors aren't accustomed to meeting a Chinese client like this. Each day, at the first meeting after lunch, he'll spend the entire hour aggressively picking at his teeth with a toothpick, which is clearly not at the advice of a dentist; he's never seen one. If Winston Churchill said Brits have "honest teeth," there's no adequate description for what this guy has going on inside his mouth.

I don't think he even cares about the meetings. His only stipulation, other than demanding that banks include young attractive females on their roadshow teams, is that they find the most authentic Chinese cuisine in each city because he refuses to eat Western food. He does make an exception in Boston, insisting that the entire roadshow team join him at Hooters. Imagine ten bankers in suits afraid to order beers, just because the chairman asked the translator to ask the Hooters manager to go find some Chinese tea.

This is the first-ever Chinese corporate high-yield deal so many investors have never seen anything like it. Of course, all the bankers are panicking, including Benny. I love it. I tell him to calm down: "Perfect, now we can blame the chairman when we have to tell the company that this deal is going to come in at least 50 basis points higher than what we promised."

Benny is not convinced. "I don't think you understand. This guy does not give a fuck. He'll walk, mmm'kay?"

That's what they all say, and then we have to go through this little song and dance where the client pretends to be unhappy with the outcome. But then they have no choice but to accept the terms as dictated by the market. The market is the market.

At the start of each day, the syndicate bankers lead the market update calls with the deal team, running through headlines, reviewing credit market conditions, and summarizing the day's schedule of investor meetings. We do the same thing at the end of each day, but with greater emphasis on specific deal-related investor feedback. This is our chance to gradually work the client's expectations back to reality with some negative feedback.

After several catastrophic days on the road, the relationship bankers delicately convince the chairman to come back to Hong Kong and allow the rest of the deal team—including his highly impressive, Western-educated CFO—to complete the remainder of the roadshow on the company's behalf.

Not only have we been telling the deal team that market conditions have weakened and investor appetite for risk has diminished for first-time issuers, things really have deteriorated. We're now looking at a market-clearing transaction in the context of 10.5%, or 100 basis points higher than what we promised—not an immaterial difference in the context of a $300 million deal.

The time has finally come for us to drop the hammer; we're already late on providing formal price guidance to the market. We've been whispering "low/mid-10s" to investors, and even that doesn't get them too excited. We now need the chairman's approval to go out to the market with official price guidance in the range of 10.5% area. This is by far the most aggressive we can be. Attempting anything tighter substantially increases our chances of having a failed deal.

Benny is a fucking idiot. He jumps at the chance to host the next meeting with the chairman in our office without really understanding that we will now have to deliver the bad news in person. Our counterparts at Morgan Stanley are more than content to listen in on a conference line—undoubtedly laughing as I get crucified as the bearer of bad news.

We meet the chairman and his entourage upstairs on our client reception floor. It's a fucking zoo. Once again, Benny has outdone himself. In a misguided attempt to demonstrate our support for the deal and for the client, he has teed up every senior banker imaginable to come out, shake hands, and say something about how committed we are personally to overseeing the success of this deal. It's known as the Citi Swarm. Not only that, since this is a new client relationship to the firm, everyone has crawled out of the woodwork— private bankers, commercial bankers, transaction and cash management professionals, aka the guys who wear the brown suits.

After brief introductions, I lead the parade downstairs to give them a tour of our impressive (by Asian standards) trading floor.

"Chairman Zhu, this is our team of credit traders, the largest team in Asia. They will be responsible for making a market in your bonds and supporting the deal." I pause for translation, while directing their gaze down a long row of bodies staring at screens, pounding away on keyboards, amid the energetic buzz of dealerboards lighting up. We get a polite acknowledgment from the desk head and then slowly move on to the next row. I don't even think the chairman gives a shit; he's already spotted the credit derivatives desk assistant. She's a 5, which is more like a 7 on a trading floor, but he doesn't appear to be quite so discerning when it comes to the talent.

"And this is the team of salespeople. They have been responsible for setting up the roadshow meetings for you and are
working with their clients to generate the orders and interest
in your deal." As I am waiting for translation, I pull the head
of hedge fund sales away from his desk and bring him over
to the group. "This is the head of the team. His number one
priority right now is selling your deal." The chairman nods;
they shake hands.

We finally work our way over to my boss's office, where
we'll be holding the meeting. Again, it's all very impressive.
It's a large glass office, prominently situated in the corner of
the trading floor. The only problem is that there are so many
people that we are literally overflowing out the door and onto
the trading floor.

I wait uncomfortably for everyone to dial in: the underlings
in Shanghai, the traveling roadshow team, and my dickhead
counterpart at Morgan Stanley sitting contentedly at his desk
a half mile away.

I dispense with the small talk and jump right into our issue:
there is a successful deal to be had; it's simply a function of
price. I'm confident in my ability to convince him that what
we're proposing is a deal he needs to take.

Typically, I prefer conducting these price guidance discussions from the comfort of my desk, where I am just a voice on
a conference call. I can read from prepared notes, instant message with my syndicate counterparts, and access any relevant
or supporting market information. Instead, I am completely
out of my comfort zone, huddled around a small conference
table, staring at a very rich, very powerful Chinese Steve Bus-
cemi. All I can hear is the sound of bankers fidgeting and the
clamor of the trading floor pouring through the open door. I'm
accustomed to tuning out distractions, but this is like taking

the SATs while sitting under an overworked air-conditioning unit, next to a window overlooking a football field during cheerleader tryouts.

I take the team point by point through every facet of the transaction to date, pausing every two sentences for translation. Typically, it's good to keep things succinct and simple for the sake of translation. But with so many senior bankers in the room, I have no choice but to articulate myself as if I'm talking to them as well, which is proving to be a bit of a challenge for the translator.

I talk about how comparable credit spreads have widened and market sentiment has weakened. I review each of the investor meetings they have had and some of the feedback that has come in, with particular emphasis on the price sensitivity of each investor, all of which is north of 10%. I remind everyone that initial price guidance is just the first step, a device to get investors enticed, to keep as many accounts as possible engaged and looking at the credit, and to generate momentum for a deal that will end up at a tighter level. "The best possible way for us to achieve a sub-10% final outcome is to start with an initial guidance that is substantially wider than that." Of course, there is no way we're ever getting below 10%, but I'm trying to work in baby steps here. "With that, it is our joint recommendation that we go out to the market with price guidance of 10.5% area." I pause there for translation.

And then I just sit back and listen. My words are not met with a warm embrace. A typical happy conversation in Mandarin Chinese sounds like a bunch of loud angry people yelling at each other. By comparison, these guys sound pissed. A couple of the more astute bankers who had been standing in the doorway quietly slink away; they don't want to be associated with this inevitable train wreck. There's a solid five minutes of aggressive back-and-forth between the chairman and various people on the phone, with everyone seemingly calling each other "nigga" over and over. (Phonetically, "nigga" is a crutch word in Mandarin, similar to "like" or "um.") The translator doesn't even bother.

Finally, one of the coverage bankers speaks up on behalf of the company. "The chairman is obviously very unhappy with this recommendation. He understands the strategy of starting at a number that is inclusive across the range of interest, with the hope of creating some price tension to achieve a better result. However, he cannot accept 10.5%, particularly as he had been told 9.5% just one week ago. He would like to propose price guidance at 10%, with the expectation that the final result will be closer to our target." Everything is a fucking negotiation with these guys. At this point, we're screwed. The chairman can't be seen as losing face in front of his team, and we simply have no room to budge.

Just as I am about to respond with a polite version of "no fucking way," an unfamiliar noise starts pulsating from our trading floor, like a malfunctioning squawk box. It gets gradually louder and then a little bit clearer; it sounds like a drumbeat and a cymbal. It can no longer be ignored. We collectively pause and look out across our trading floor just as it erupts into a full applause. Then the music starts; it's Outkast's "The Way You Move," which had only recently worked its way back into the zeitgeist after the Maury Povich "Not the Father" video went viral.

That's when we see him. Our head of hedge fund sales, the person I had introduced to the chairman as being responsible for selling his deal, is bouncing around the sales row with an impromptu, but remarkably well-choreographed, dance routine.

If this isn't strange enough, he also has KFC chicken skins stuck to his face. This becomes evident when, mid-routine, he starts eating one of the skins that is sliding down his cheek. I later find out it was the result of having lost a bet.

Suffice to say, we never got to lead the first-ever Chinese corporate high-yield bond. But then again, neither did Morgan Stanley.

It's not the lie that bothers me. It's the insult to my intelligence that I find offensive.

I never said I was better than anyone, just more successful.

If we don't sin, Jesus died for nothing.

I'm an 8 in a suit, a 5 without a shirt on, but a 10 with my card behind the bar.

I want a place in East Hampton, not history.

Bluetooth

The frosted glass doors separating the trading floor from capital markets glide open. It's Earpiece, the head of ██████████████. You wouldn't know it from his swagger, but he's responsible for one of the least sexy products in the entire bank, excluding whatever the fuck the brown suits do in repo, commercial paper, or cash management.

There is no clever backstory behind his nickname; he simply wears a Bluetooth earpiece in his ear at all times. It doesn't matter where he is or what he's doing; he keeps it in his ear.

Nobody knows if he's talking to them or someone on the phone. "That'll work," he said to me one day while we were standing side by side at the urinal. I'm pretty sure he was talking to someone on the phone. But he was staring at my cock, so I'm not entirely sure.

I have to admit it, Earpiece is a master of internal politics. It's hard to accuse someone of not working hard when he's got that earpiece as a constant reminder of how busy he might be. He also constantly shadows his bosses. If they're downstairs at Starbucks, he's there. If they're outside smoking, he's there smoking. In fact, he started smoking just so he can spend more time with his boss, ████ ███████. All the while, he keeps his earpiece in. Instead of being looked at as a sycophantic moron, he gets labeled as a dealmaker.

He can also name the best karaoke joint or massage parlor in every city in Asia, which comes in handy with his superiors, visiting colleagues from out of town, and clients.

One day, Earpiece doesn't show up. He doesn't respond to emails or texts; he's gone. Many hope he's dead. Rumors have it that he's resigned to go to Goldman Sachs and run the loan syndicate team over there (a team that is later supposed to report to me). Thank fucking Christ; they can have him. We're celebrating.

There are two problems. First, our degenerate head of ▮▮▮▮▮▮▮▮, Wisal Lari, misses having someone so dedicated to kissing his ass. Second, Goldman Sachs is famous for rigidly refusing to hire someone and promote them at the same time. For example, if there's a well-regarded associate or VP at a real bank, a second-tier house can easily come in and steal them away with the promise of a guarantee and an immediate promotion in rank. Morgan Stanley poached our main high-yield guru like this by making him a managing director. Goldman would never dream of doing that.

Since Earpiece was a director at Citi, there is zero chance that Goldman is going to bring him in as a managing director. This leaves the door open for Citi to bid him back by matching Goldman's guarantee and then promoting him. We call that a battlefield promotion. A lot of people try to do this—they leave with the expectation of being bid back with a matching guarantee and a promotion.

Earpiece pulls it off. Now, all of a sudden, he's back and bigger than ever. Of course, we all hate him even more and resent what he's done, effectively carving out a piece of our bonus pool and locking it in for himself. No one would give a shit if he were some big hitter who added a lot of value, but he's a fucking coordinator—with Citigroup's behemoth balance sheet. His few successful deals only happen because of the franchise, not because of him.

Now, he's a managing director. Worse, as a concession, senior management has allowed him to expand his empire to include the private placement business. It's one of the most lucrative pieces of the Asian franchise outside of distressed and structured credit. These fluid deals reside in a gray area that we all want a piece of. What might start out as a straight bond deal can easily evolve into a loan, straight equity, or any kind of combination or hybrid structure. So now, Earpiece is eating my lunch.

He's gone from lifeguarding the most plain-vanilla business to lording over one of the sexiest, fastest-growing, and highest-profile products. More important, it's the most fun. I suffer through dogshit breakeven deals for Korean bureaucrats and Indian scumbags so I can enjoy a boondoggle due diligence trip to Ho Chi Minh City with some hedge fund and sales guys, looking at a secured real estate deal that will pay us three points in fees.

He instantly becomes an even bigger prick. The only thing that doesn't change is his earpiece.

One day, I see him hanging out three rows over, holding court over a few people in our credit sales team. I show up, and he immediately clams up. He doesn't want to let me in on anything he's working on in the event that it infringes on my mandate. Everything goes awkwardly silent. But I'm not going anywhere. I pull up a seat. "What's up, kid?" He's more senior than me, so of fucking course, he hates being talked to like that.

He stands. "I gotta go." He continues speaking to the sales team, purposefully ignoring me. "Thanks for the feedback,

I'll have my guys send you a couple of teasers for these deals, and then we can get some NDAs in place and show them out." And then he's gone. The frosted glass doors slide shut behind him as he disappears back to the private side.

Lester, one of the senior sales guys, starts going off. "Jesus fucking Christ, I hate that fucking piece of shit. He wants us to wall cross [where investors agree to receive nonpublic information, keep it confidential, and not trade on it] every fucking hedge fund on every fucking theoretical deal, get them to sign NDAs, and then he just wants to start throwing shit against the wall to see what sticks. This is not how you run a fucking business."

Having worked in New York before coming to Asia, Lester has an impeccable reputation and is generally regarded as one of the most important salespeople on the trading floor. "There is no way in fuck I'm showing any of these deals to my clients; they'll laugh me out of the room. This fucking ass clown has no fucking clue what he's doing. There is zero value added here."

We are listening to one of the most epic trading-floor rants I have ever heard. Lester has the attention of the entire row, not just the credit sales desk, but also the entire Asian sales team. One row over, the credit trading and credit derivatives guys are standing up and staring at him. These outbursts happen in New York relatively frequently, but no one in Asia has ever seen anything like this.

I interrupt. "Holy fuck."

Lester stops ranting, somewhat confused, but waiting for me to continue. I get the sense that he thinks I want to take the baton and continue his rant for him.

"Holy fuck." I say it again, legitimately in shock. "Holy fuck." This time I am able to focus my excitement and point

to a stack of papers on his desk that say PRIVATE AND CONFI-
DENTIAL. I don't even notice the papers (a huge compliance
breach on his part); I'm looking at what's on top of them. It's
Earpiece's earpiece.

In all of our days, weeks, and years working together in Asia,
no one has ever seen Earpiece without his earpiece. And here it
is, sitting on top of Lester's desk. He must have been so flustered
by my presence that he left it behind when he scurried away.

Lester doesn't even hesitate. Who knows how long it'll be
before Earpiece comes racing back, not just for his earpiece,
but also for the nonpublic term sheets and pipeline information that he's recklessly left sitting out on the sales desk. Lester
grabs the Bluetooth earpiece, immediately jams it down his
pants, and then begins a play-by-play commentary, while danc-
ing, bouncing, and jostling around.

"Ohh yeaaah. The earpiece is on my cock . . . Now, it's touching my balls. Back to my cock. Tongue'n my pee hole. Back
to my balls . . . Oooh, yeah. Juggle those nuts. Now, it's flirt-
ing with my asshole. You naughty earpiece. It's near the anus.
Oooh yeaah." We're frozen, as he continues. "Hey, earpiece, at
least buy me a drink first. It's . . . it's . . . it's gonna . . . it's gonna
penetrate . . . penetrate . . . my anu—oooh yeah."

Lester doesn't stop there. He starts jumping up and down.
"Now, it's inside my asshole. Out. In. Out. In. Out. In. Is it bad
that I like this? Don't judge me; this feels soooo good."

"Now it's racing back and forth between my asshole and my
ball sack. Oooh, the friction. I feel like a Boy Scout building
a fire in my pants. Ooh, my fiery loins." The entire row is in
hysterics. Finally, seemingly exhausted, Lester sits back down.
I assume he is done.

Did I mention that Lester is a managing director who turned
down a job offer from Goldman Sachs?

But he's not finished yet. Leaning back in his Herman Miller chair, Lester hoists his feet high into the air, pulling his knees up until they are almost touching his ears. With his hand still buried deep into his pants, nothing is left to the imagination as he pretends to finger himself with Earpiece's earpiece.

"Stop it. I can't take it. Please," I cry. Finally, we all settle down. Lester finds and removes the earpiece and sets it back on the table where he found it.

No more than three seconds later, the frosted glass doors open again. It's Earpiece. He hurriedly paces back over to us. "Oh shit, I forgot my stuff."

He grabs his papers and walks away, slotting the earpiece firmly into his ear before disappearing back through the sliding doors. As the doors close, the entire credit sales and trading rows erupt.

From that day forth, we never saw him remove that earpiece from his ear again.

Most people wouldn't even be the main character in a movie about their own lives.

I say "keep the change" purely for my own convenience.

Talent is the only thing that stands between most people and their dreams.

My first wife was vehemently pro-life until my girlfriend got pregnant.

One of the biggest problems with today's society is that we've run out of colonies to send our undesirables to.

The Stakeout

When I first move to Hong Kong in 2004, I'm seated in the middle of the trading floor, across from the credit traders and flanked by salespeople. This proximity is insane; everything I work on all day is the very definition of non-public, market-sensitive information. Everyone around me can see my screens and hear me on the phone; they can even listen in on my calls if they want.

Generally, I'm encouraged to take nonpublic conversations off the desk—either into a conference room or to the other side of the Chinese Wall, which in this case is an actual glass wall separating banking from sales and trading. But that's simply not practical all the time.

No one seems to really care that it's illegal, so I don't worry about it. Besides, salespeople and traders are more fun to be around than investment bankers. Being in the middle of the action allows me to stay in tune with markets in real time, helping me provide more thoughtful and relevant advice to our clients. Traditionally, that's always been part of the argument for keeping syndicate desks on the trading floor.

Typical scenario, I'm allocating a deal and I sense Jimmy (a sales guy) looking over my shoulder. "Whoa, whoa. You can't give Roo's client more bonds than mine." Or, I hear a sales guy talking to a client: "Hey, I'm hearing that there's a big Hutch deal coming next week." He's obviously heard this from listening to me on the phone, and it is the kind of sensitive information that a client could use to trade on. That's when I know that I need to change seats.

I move to the very corner of the trading floor, sitting among the IT guys and the business unit managers. The BUMs are the people who are responsible for managing the expenses of the trading floor—from Herman Miller chairs and extra screens to stationery and color ink cartridges, it all runs through them. Most important, they sign off on our T&E, or travel and entertainment.

My new seat gives me an expansive view of the entire trading floor. Across from me is the credit research and strategy row, and then trading and credit derivatives, then credit sales, and then interest rate products and structured credit. There are another ten rows of people beyond that, but I only really care about my direct universe.

Sitting among the BUMs and IT guys feels like being at the lunch table with all the kids I made fun of in high school. I have more interesting conversations with my dentist. However, it does come with a few perks.

I no longer have to worry about expensing my numerous dodgy receipts. My new buddy, the BUM, will handle that. In fact, one of my colleagues, Peter, is so tight with the BUM (they both have and love a certain brand of German automobile) that he's able to expense his dirty karaoke trips, no questions asked.

Peter's a hero to the Latin American borrowers and New York coverage bankers who come through on their fake road-shows, under the guise of flogging subordinated perpetual non-call ten-year hybrid Tier 1 notes to Asian retail investors (mom and pop). These coupon-hungry "investors" know about as much about these structures as they do the Lehman mini-bonds they've dumped their retirement savings into.

Many of these issuers don't really need to do a roadshow, but there's an entire team of bankers in New York calling them, saying, "Hey, how would you like to go on a one-week tour of Asia? I'll go with you."

By day, they meet with private banking sales teams who care more about their own commissions than the underlying credits they're selling. Invariably, the issuers and bankers carve out ample time for suit fittings and watch shopping. At night, they want Peter to take them for a nice Chinese seafood dinner followed by a visit to an exclusive karaoke bar, where they charge hot-dog-at-Yankee-Stadium prices for hookers.

At the end of the night, Peter receives a bill that says something nonsensical like Kyoto Toro Fuji Sushi Restaurant, which of course is what makes it possible to expense. Being best friends with the office BUM also helps.

Another great benefit of sitting among the guys in short-sleeved dress shirts and square-toed shoes is that we get a heads-up on the fire drills—the actual fire drills, not the circle-jerk bake-off pitches that junior investment bankers refer to as fire drills. This sounds trivial, except for the fact that for many of our fire drills, they shut down the elevators—and we're up on the forty-eighth fucking floor.

I'll get a five-minute heads-up, which is just enough time to discreetly and selectively spread the word to my friends. We'll be on our third beer at the bar in Hong Kong Park by the time everyone else, exhausted and sweating, is spilling out of the ground-floor stairwell.

One day, Ken, the IT guy, spins his chair around. "Oi, gee-zah. I saw yer mate last night at Fenwick's. Bloomin' three o'clock in the morning. He was there. Clear as mud, I saw him. He was by 'imself. Fookin' big cigar, he 'ad. Talkin' to some bird. Didn't leave by 'imself though, did he. Fookin' Dirty Sanchez."

It's taken me almost a year to learn how to understand how Ken speaks. "Ken, are you trying to tell me that you saw Dirty Sanchez at Fenwick's, by himself, smoking a cigar, and that he left with a hooker?"

"Is wot I said, innit?"

I have to repeat myself. "Ken, are you saying that you saw Dirty Sanchez do a late-night solo Fennie's smash-'n'-grab at three A.M. on a Tuesday?"

"Are you retarded? Yeah, I saw it wif me own eyes."

I still don't really believe him. I believe that he believes it, but I don't believe it. Fenwick's is a dark and dingy basement firetrap of a bar in Wan Chai, and is probably the most famous and least discreet stop on every depraved tourist's Hong Kong whore tour. There is no way that this guy, who has hundreds of subordinates and is known to every major buy-side client in the region, can be so blatantly injudicious, if for no other reason than that his own wife works in the industry—banking, not whoring.

Dirty Sanchez is our regional head of ████████████. He lives in Singapore but makes very frequent trips to Hong Kong, always opting for the "management flight." The management flight is when you intentionally pick flight times in the middle of the day, so that you can have a leisurely morning, then lounge, drink, eat, and sleep your way through the meat of the day, finally arriving at your destination just in time for late-afternoon team drinks.

The genesis of his nickname, Dirty Sanchez, or Filthy for short, has nothing to do with any deviant proclivity; it's simply a reference to the pet ferret he keeps above his upper lip. This nickname, which he is not aware of, was actually given to him by a prominent hedge fund manager.

What makes the Tom Selleck homage even more ridiculous is his pairing of this voluminous womb broom with the worst comb-over any of us have ever seen. It's so bad that if you ever have to walk with him to a meeting on a windy day, he forces you to keep changing directions as he attempts to prevent his homemade hair hat from flapping up and saying hello.

Of course, no one is really surprised by the idea of infidelity or carnal indiscretion. It's a fairly standard industry practice and certainly not an aberration exclusive to Asia. One of my bosses in London lived in a palatial home on Holland Park but also owned a flat in Mayfair that his wife didn't know about. He was well known for arranging an FBT (Fake Business Trip) and staying in Mayfair with one of his side chicks. The issue with Filthy is that he is so sanctimonious that having a solo Fenwick's game would be off the charts.

A few weeks later, I'm at my desk when Ken strolls in mid-morning, looking rough and smelling like stale beer and two-week-old sheets.

"Fookin' ruff night, it was. Killed two birds wif one stone, if u get me drift. Was leavin' wif one and 'ere comes walkin' anovah wif massive tits. 'Ello, luv, right, ur comin' 'ome wif me. Shagged 'em bof in tha bum. Mate, when I woke up, me bed looked like a butchah's block. Was afraid I might'ave committ'd a murdah."

If I spun around every time I heard him say something like that, I'd never get any work done; so I just ignore him. Ken keeps going. "Oi, u 'earin' me? Saw ur mate again. two o'clock in tha mornin' this time. I was cunt'd, maybe fif'een lagers in me. But it was definitely 'im olrite. I'd bet me mum's life on it. And I like me mum very mutch."

We can settle this right now. It just so happens that Filthy is in the office, standing three rows across from me, talking to a few of his salespeople. "Ken, stand up. Come over here." I pull him closer to me and point across the floor. "Ken, first of all, he's not my mate. But I just want to be clear. You saw him, that guy right there, by himself at Fenwick's again last night?"

"Too right, mate. I'm not a fookin' id-i-ut."

I immediately start firing off Bloomberg messages to some syndicate and sales colleagues and friends, as well as to a few clients—all of whom are well aware of the running joke that is Dirty Sanchez. "It's confirmed. Filthy has a filthy solo Fennie's game." The problem is that without definitive proof, there is still this lingering doubt. A close friend and former colleague turned competitor proposes a solution: a stakeout.

The chances of success seem slim—the plan is to camp out the next time he's in town and try to catch him in the act—but regardless of the outcome, we're going to have some fun trying.

A couple of weeks go by, and there's been no sign of Filthy in the office. Finally, I call his secretary. "Hey, Debbie. Listen, I want to take [Filthy] to see a few key clients." (He insists on only seeing "top-priority clients.") "Can you check his diary and let me know when he's back in Hong Kong?"

I report back: "Okay, next Wednesday, Filthy's in town, but only for one night. He's got a client dinner, so it's gonna be tight. But I'm willing to give it a shot if you guys are." Of course, everyone is up for it.

There's a Mexican place across the street from Fenwick's—the perfect vantage point. We plan on getting there around ten o'clock just to be safe, which means we meet up in Central at six in order to start drinking.

Most of us don't actually expect to see him there; it's just a funny premise and a silly excuse for a group of us to get together and drink. One of our friends at Credit Suisse is paying 12-to-1 on a Filthy sighting; I go in for $100, but it's not a bet I'm expecting to win. There are a few other side bets that involve Tommy Bahama shirts (his signature look at management off-sites) and cigars.

The big day finally arrives. There are eight of us, with representation from JPMorgan, Credit Suisse, Deutsche Bank, Citi, and a couple of buy-side clients. Irrespective of Filthy, this is an amazing idea—a group of friends sitting outside in the heart of the red-light district, people-watching and burning through pitchers of Patrón margaritas as quickly as they can make them.

Ten o'clock might have been a bit too ambitious of a start because there is no sign of Filthy and a few us are already pretty hammered. Eleven P.M. and still no Filthy; surely his client dinner is over by now. I check in with a friend of mine across town at Bar George in Lan Kwai Fong, a notorious Filthy hangout; he's not there, which bodes well for us. Just to make sure we haven't missed him, we take turns making solo recon trips—running into Fenwick's and doing a quick lap around the bar. Some of us take longer than others.

At midnight, we run into some guys we know from Barclays and HSBC. One of our junior hedge fund sales guys, Smithers, gets scared. "Dude, that guy's wife is friends with my wife. I told her I was at Cipriani with my boss tonight." It would be impossible for a person to look and act any more like the *Simpsons* character than he does.

"Don't be a bitch. He's not going to say anything. What's he gonna say, 'Hey, I saw your husband in Wan Chai'? He's here too."

At one o'clock, Smithers and two other guys give up. I double down with another $100, this time at 15-to-1. While it would be nice to win some cash, I don't really care if Filthy shows up or not; it's fascinating watching the different types of people who go in and out of Fenwick's: young, old, skinny, fat, handsome, ugly, rich, poor. Some guys walk in only to come back out immediately with a look of total shock and disgust on their faces. Other guys walk out unashamedly with a girl under each arm. Others are sheepish and cautious, holding hands like they're on a first date. Some people are so drunk that they stagger out using a hooker like a seeing-eye dog. I can only assume that she is taking them to the nearest ATM—good for her.

Don't get me wrong; I see this all the time. But tonight, with our eyes vigilantly glued to the door, it becomes more of a case study in human behavior, with each of us providing commentary, play-by-play analysis, and drunken theories on the exploitation and dehumanization of sex workers.

Just before 2 A.M., our numbers have dwindled down to four guys. We've long since made the necessary switch to beer just for the sake of our own survival. Losing focus and interest, we're just about ready to pack it in when we spot a shadowy figure slowly getting out of a taxi.

Holy shit, it's him. The Tommy Bahama shirt and cigar confirm it. Lester just scored $5,000 and I have a decent payday coming my way as well.

Hours of dedication have paid off. Laughter, high fives, and table slapping ensues. Filthy is proceeding cautiously, looking around and over his shoulder as he is forced to yield to a drunken *gweilo* and his plus one who are angling for Filthy's taxi. This is when he spots us; a clear, uninterrupted line of sight to four drunken bankers, celebrating and jumping around like buffoons. Instinctively, he looks away, clearly contemplating what to do. But there is nothing that he can do; he's been busted and he knows it.

He nods in acknowledgment and heads our way, weaving through the other two lanes of oncoming traffic. He greets us like a dog that just shit in your living room and knows it's only a matter of time before you discover it. "You guys got me, huh?" He takes a seat at our table. "So, what are we drinking?" We flag down the waitress and order another round of beers.

We never fess up to the stakeout, simply chalking it up to a coincidence, but he has a suspicion we're here for him. Mission fucking accomplished; it's time for me to head home.

"Okay, guys, I'm out. I need to be up in four hours." I chug my beer and signal the waitress for our check.

"Don't worry, this one's on me." Filthy inspects the bill. "Wow, I see you guys have been here for a while," and then he slaps down a card. I'm almost positive he uses the corporate card.

We all walk across to the taxi stand and join the queue of johns with their takeout. One of our friends is married and his wife has been blowing up his phone, so we let him take the first cab. The remaining three of us all live right near one another, so we agree to share a taxi back up to the Mid-Levels.

After a few minutes, the next cab approaches. Filthy graciously offers to let us take this one. "There are three of you; you guys go ahead. I'll get the next one." As we drive away, we crane our necks around to see Filthy doubling back across the street and heading into Fenwick's.

Some of the best moments in life are the ones you can't tell anyone about.

When you're rich, "crazy" is just "eccentric."

Imagine the feeling of winning the lottery and then losing everything. I know a few ex-girlfriends who can.

I doubt alcohol kills more people than it creates.

My wife would leave me if I lost my money. And I'll trade her in if she gets fat.

Princelings
and Dumplings

"Hey, dude, are you coming down to Singapore later this week?" I say to Justin, the new first-year analyst rotating through our desk.

"I don't think so. They told me that it's already over budget, there's nothing of value I can do while I am there, and that I need to stick around here to man the desk."

"Okay. Just have Connie book you a flight and a hotel room anyway, and I'll sort out the rest for you."

It's our annual credit conference—the largest in Asia: four hundred investors; fifty bond issuers; three days of presentations, workshops, and meetings; and three blurry nights of total debauchery. It's a boondoggle for most people, but for me, an event of this magnitude designed to bring investors and issuers together is right in my wheelhouse. I'm supposed to take it very seriously.

I usually go down a couple of days early and kick off an entire week of meetings, pitches, golf outings, and drinking with clients. I also get to play host to the countless colleagues and senior management who fly in from London and New York and, having heard the stories about what bankers get up to in Asia, are here to have a good time. Wedding rings are optional.

My problem this year is that I am in the middle of executing two live deals, one for a Korean utility and the other for an Indian bank, which means much of my time is spent sitting in the Ritz-Carlton lobby or upstairs in my room, stuck on tedious internal and client conference calls. My entire week is shaping up to be an endless stream of these calls, mostly listening on mute as bankers from the various bookrunners take turns fluffing the client and saying the same things over and over.

I call Justin's staffer—the half-wit in charge of overseeing the pool of new analysts who rotate around fixed income for six months before finding a permanent seat on a desk. I make up some shit about how I need an analyst to help me coordinate the schedule of investor and issuer meetings, and explain how it's good exposure for Justin to shadow me for a few days.

I remember the feeling of being the only analyst chosen to attend conferences in Lisbon and Madrid. Now it's time for me to pay it forward. I could pick any one of the new analysts to come down and help me, including the hot Taiwanese chick who likes to party, but I choose Justin because he has a very specific skill set.

I call Justin back. "You're all set. You can come down tomorrow and hang out for the rest of the week. But I need you to do one thing first. Go to my apartment, pack up my PlayStation with *Madden* and *FIFA*, and bring it with you." Principally, I am having Justin fly down to play PlayStation with me.

"EASports . . . It's in the game. Hell yeah, baby." I can tell he's excited.

We spend the next three days holed up in my room, shades drawn, beer bottles everywhere, DO NOT DISTURB sign strictly enforced—with only fleeting, yet highly strategic, appearances at the conference. The only thing most people see is me pacing around, looking tired and stressed, barking into an earpiece. Am I hungover? Yes, of course. Is the burden of balancing a hectic schedule of investor meetings, networking with senior management, and executing multiple live deals weighing me down? Perhaps. Am I still seen as taking the time to selflessly mentor a junior banker, taking him under my wing, showing him the ropes, and introducing him to as many people as possible? Fucking right; he's almost out of business cards. Although, in reality, to the extent that I appear frazzled and stressed out, it's because I am struggling to contain Justin's shotgun Philadelphia Eagles offense with my Swiss cheese Dallas Cowboys defense.

Prime Minister Thaksin Shinawatra is downstairs giving a keynote address; who gives a shit? I just hit Terrell Owens on a play-action deep post route to win the game and $500. I've got no problem taking money from my first-year analyst; his family is loaded.

After five consecutive hours of intensely competitive football (the first game kicked off with my 9 A.M. Korean client market update call), we decide to celebrate down at the bar by the pool. Venturing outside feels like walking out of a movie theater on a hot sunny day, having forgotten that it's the middle of the afternoon.

The conference is business casual, but of course, we're in suits. Our fake message is clear: we are obviously just coming from an important meeting. We loosen our ties, roll up our sleeves, and order a round of beers.

"See, dude? Aren't you glad I picked you? Right now, all of your peers are stuck in the office doing dogshit work, running on fumes, and you're here with me, sitting under a fucking palm tree with a beer in your hand."

"I'll drink to that." He gives me this big goofy Malaysian grin. "Cheers."

I look across and point out all those suckers in the hotel gym (which at the Singapore Ritz-Carlton overlooks the pool), pounding away on the treadmills. Immediately, we both make direct and unavoidable eye contact with my boss, the head of fixed income. Not only is he one of those "suckers" on a tread-mill, but he is famous for his no-nonsense intensity—and for his ability to maintain a seven-minute-mile pace while typing on his BlackBerry.

He acknowledges us a with a purse-lipped, sarcastic slow nod, without breaking his stride. There is probably nothing worse that we could be seen doing right now. We're not work-ing. We're not attending the conference. We're not entertain-ing clients. The cardinal sin of any boondoggle is cliquing together and fraternizing without actual clients. Here we are drinking beers for no justifiable reason at two o'clock in the afternoon.

I don't really give a shit. I'm executing two lucrative deals this week, while still being the life of the party at the evening festivities and always the first one to appear at the morning breakfasts, staying just long enough to get noticed, principally by him.

I do feel bad for Justin; I'm the one who dragged him out for beers in the middle of a conference, in the middle of the afternoon. There's no scenario in which he comes out looking good. But then I remember that he's untouchable. A Princeling.

Princelings, or as we affectionately call them, Dumplings, are the children of regional tycoons, captains of industry, and gov-ernment officials. Of course, we're no strangers to nepotism. We all understand and expect that Chelsea Clinton can walk into a job at McKinsey or at Marc Lasry's hedge fund. But in

Asia, it has increasingly become the rule and not the exception. All banks hire a disproportionate number of Princelings, and not just the ones who graduated from Stanford or Harvard, with the implicit expectation that it comes with benefits in the form of business from their influential families.

When I started as an analyst, all the hiring was centralized through New York so that the firm could control and maintain a consistent and high standard of talent. We all trained together in New York, along with the European and Asian analysts. With this came a fair degree of mobility, such that if someone wanted to move to Asia from the US, or to the US from Europe or Asia, there were opportunities, particularly at the junior level—which of course is what enabled me to work in London and Hong Kong with relative ease.

When I first got to Hong Kong in 2004, the hiring protocols were more or less the same as when I had started. We'd get friends or clients asking us to help them out with internships or analyst positions for their kids or relatives, and we'd simply pass them on to New York with a kind word and a nudge for special consideration that we knew would typically go ignored. New York didn't give a shit at all. They didn't want or need to do us, or our clients, any favors; Asia was still a rounding error in terms of revenue for most of the larger global banks.

But by 2006, everything had changed. We started recruiting many of the new analysts for Asia from the pool of résumés that were sent in to the private bank by their ultra-high-net-worth clients looking for favors. JPMorgan, Goldman Sachs, HSBC, UBS, Morgan Stanley, and most other firms would do the same thing through their respective private wealth management divisions. It became the running joke any time one of our counterparts at another bank brought a new analyst to a meeting or roadshow luncheon. "So, who is his [or her] father?" was the first question, unless she was hot, then it was "Is she single?"

Many of the kids we hired were so dumb and undeserving (there are plenty of Princelings from Harvard, but they only want the cachet of Morgan Stanley or Goldman Sachs) and it frustrated New York so much so that they "coincidentally" decentralized recruiting and training, so that the hiring for Asia was done out of Asia.

I chose Justin from a pool of eight kids in Hong Kong specifically assigned to fixed-income sales and syndicate. Of these eight kids, only one of them came from a target recruiting school. None of them particularly excelled on paper or in person. None of them would have made it beyond the first round of interviews in New York. But two of them were kids of well-known billionaire families, and the rest were just superrich—all of them.

In some cases, these kids didn't even want to be there; all their family wanted was to be able to say that their kid worked as an "investment banker" for a prestigious firm for a few years before joining the family business or going to business school. It didn't matter what the job was. In one instance, the structured credit trading desk hired the son of a billionaire Hong Kong tycoon as the desk assistant. The kid was remarkably down-to-earth, but it was hilarious watching people tiptoe around him ever so politely, prefacing mundane requests with "Hey, if it's not too much trouble . . ." as opposed to the typical "Hey, fuckstick."

At the end of the day, we'd all get in the same long taxi line to go home, and these kids would discreetly slink away to the chauffeured cars waiting for them.

When I started, I was not fully cognizant of the extent to which many of these kids are untouchable. In my world, bullying and hazing are an important trading-floor tradition and a valuable training tool. Being sent an hour away to pick up the "best roast beef sandwiches in the city" is just one of many ways I was reminded of my lowly status when I was an analyst. The tough love and usually good-natured antics are part of the maturation process of learning how to thrive on a trading floor. As I saw it, I had an obligation to pass this ethos down to the next generation.

When they had been out of training for only a week, I called each of the new analysts pretending to be from HR—my effeminate Cantonese-English accent is amazing. I told them to come down later that week at a set time for the prerequisite new employee drug test. The HR rep for fixed income had no idea what to do with them when they randomly and nervously turned up at her cubicle. Seven of the eight showed up. One kid called in sick that day; I liked him immediately.

My harmless gag wasn't well received by HR or the analyst staffer, who himself had been a banker (obviously not a good one) prior to his current administrative position. "Trust me, this isn't New York and you're not Lewis Ranieri. You don't want to mess with these kids here."

This message was quietly reinforced a few weeks later when the errant toss of a Nerf football smacked a girl named Shalom right in the face. Besides the fact that it's not kosher to hit a girl, some of the local Chinese guys were in complete shock. "Do you know who her dad is?"

"No, I didn't know her dad is the CEO of some Taiwanese conglomerate that I've never fucking heard of. But more important, why the fuck is her name Shalom?"

In Asia, many Mainland Chinese and Taiwanese assign themselves or their children completely arbitrary English names. This is why there are so many kids in Chengdu and Shenzhen who call themselves Monica, Rachel, Phoebe, or Joey. (Even they can't bring themselves to go by Ross.) It turns out that Shalom had spent a year in California as a foreign exchange student to learn English. The very Jewish family that hosted her graciously assigned her the name Shalom. The language barrier proved insurmountable when we tried explaining to her why we thought this was hilarious. *Oy vey iz mir!*

It wasn't simply that the hiring of Princelings was good for winning future business; there were times when we would explicitly draw from these resources. "Hey, you know we're pitching X bank next week for a bond deal. Does your dad know the CEO? Maybe he can remind them that you'd be on the deal team if we're mandated."

There were even times when we weren't above asking one of these analysts to help us out on a deal. For one notable Indonesian high-yield bond, we were so close to getting it over the line that, having exhausted all institutional avenues, we decided any little bump in interest from retail investors via the private banks could make a difference. "Hey, why don't you show this deal to your dad? It's got an 11% coupon."

As far as Princelings go, Justin is a great guy. Personally, he's very likable. Professionally, he's probably the best of a bad bunch. And after our adventure at the Singapore conference, I decide that he's got potential—so I offer him the opportunity to step out of the analyst rotation and join my desk full-time. Of course he jumps at the chance.

I don't care about the silk glove treatment that these kids expect; if Justin's going to join my desk, he's going to have to toughen up fast. The syndicate desk is a balancing act between managing the demands of investment bankers and their corporate clients and the needs of salespeople and their buy-side clients.

Upon seeing Justin fumble over the difference between a bid and an offer when tasked with the simple assignment of updating some trading levels, Andy decides that he is still too green and unsure of himself for the trading floor. "Dude, don't send your boy back over here to waste my time until he knows what the fuck he's doing."

So we devise a plan to help give Justin some confidence and toughen him up for the trading floor.

Andy taps him on the shoulder. "You learned PowerPoint and Excel in training, right?"

Justin nods unassertively.

"Good. I want you to make a slide for me. Do you think you can handle that?"

Once again, Justin gives a tentative nod.

"I want you to take a survey of the guys on the trading floor—only the guys. Then I want you to chart it up, make a one-page PowerPoint summarizing the results, and then present it to us.

"It'll be good for you. It's a great chance for you to walk around the trading floor and introduce yourself to everybody. Trust me, when this is over, everyone will know who you are. And they'll know, unequivocally, that you can be trusted.

"Here's the survey question you are going to answer for me: There are five women in the credit sales team. Rank them in the order of most fuckable."

"Are you kidding me?" Finally, Justin says something with a hint of conviction.

"I'm dead fucking serious. You'll present your results at six P.M. today. Ticktock, motherfucker." With that, Andy walks away.

I assure Justin that this no joke and that if he expects to ever get any assistance from the trading desk in the future, he should probably comply with the request. It's also my job as his mentor to help get him started with some advice. "Try not to write anything down, but if you have to, just don't use real names; you don't want to get in trouble or cause unnecessary offense."

I bring Justin up to speed on the importance of nicknames on the trading floor. Computer screens are visible to anyone with an inquisitive eye. Phone lines are shared. Bloomberg messages are often auto-forwarded. Chat rooms are monitored. We have nicknames for everybody, unless they are completely irrelevant. Each of the five women he has been tasked with ranking has a nickname—Roo, Fudd, Wally, Corky, and BF.

Roo has a FUPA that a marsupial would be envious of, hence the derivative of kangaroo. Fudd has body odor issues. If Elmer Fudd were a real person, I imagine he'd smell like her. Wally has a terrific and playful personality, but as her boss says, "She's about ten weeks of dedicated anorexia away from being hot." Hence, she reminds us of a walrus. Corky has an extra chromosome, and BF is your classic Butter Face.

Despite his initial reluctance, I can tell that Justin feels somewhat privileged that we have decided to share this information with him. And with that, he dutifully and discreetly sets off on his way.

It takes him all afternoon, but he completes the assignment as directed—much to our amusement. We watch him go row by row, introduce himself, and then turn completely scarlet as he poses the question. This of course evokes a wide array of reactions from the participants, ranging from "Get the fuck out of here" to "Dude, who put you up to this?" Only in a few cases did he get a hostile or negative response: "This is not funny or appropriate." We were careful to steer him away from the other pussies.

Despite not every person being willing to participate, Justin still manages to get enough data points for the results to be statistically meaningful. He then proceeds to chart up his findings in Excel and then format it into a succinct PowerPoint slide.

Just after 6 P.M., as things are winding down and people are starting to head home, Andy parades over with his cronies from the trading desk, two hedge fund sales guys, and even a few random survey participants.

The head of the hedge fund sales desk is seemingly apprehensive. "Okay, this is ridiculous. Someone could get fired for this. We can't do shit like this in the middle of the fucking trading floor." Before anyone can protest, he continues. "Justin, print out a few copies, and let's take this into the conference room so that we can enjoy it."

Not only is Justin's presentation excellent, we're all quite surprised by the results. Roo, who was ranked fourth on my list, has emerged as the clear winner, receiving nearly double the votes as the runner-up, Wally. Trying to put Justin on the spot, Andy asks him to explain how it's even possible for Roo to have been voted so much more fuckable than everyone else.

Once again, Justin blows us away with his analysis. "That's an excellent question, and frankly, it surprised me as well. So I decided to follow up with each person who listed Roo first. Hence, you will see the asterisk next to her ranking. It seems that quite a few people listed her first with an assumed stipulation that it's strictly a hate fuck and in no way meant as a compliment. If I make an adjustment for this dynamic, we end up in a statistical tie between Roo and Wally."

The other fascinating tidbit to emerge from this study is that 100% of the people surveyed have Corky listed as dead last. As such, from that moment on, she is referred to simply as

Five. After all, a nickname that stems from a Down syndrome reference is totally inappropriate.

Andy's equally impressed. "Beers on me for a job well done." He hands the presentations back to Justin. "Now, shred these fuckers and let's get out of here."

With that, we give a Justin a small round of applause; he's unable to hide his elation. I feel like a proud father; the torch had been passed.

Hermes ties are like Air Jordans for white people.

I already know I'm going to Hell. So at this point, it's go big or go home.

Don't get married until you're at least 35. You want a Trophy wife not a Participation Medal wife.

Only idiots get bored when we've all got handheld devices containing infinite knowledge at our fingertips.

I'd watch a TV show where teens describe their most popular Instagrams to WW2 veterans.

The First Day of School

One of our key hedge fund sales guys has just resigned to join a direct competitor of ours. Considering he's been the driving force in placing the majority of my bond deals, it's a crushing blow for my business. But as a friend, I'm very happy for him.

Not only am I happy for him, I'm also very proud of him. I remember vividly when he first joined the sales desk in Hong Kong. He arrived in Asia, MBA and CFA in hand, not only because he saw career opportunity, but because he has a fetish for Asian girls.

At first, he was overeager to the point of being annoying, answering every line before the end of the first ring. But we saw potential in him. He just needed to be toughened up a little bit. After some careful planning, scripting, and coordination, we decided to tee him up for one of the great trading-floor prank calls of all time.

It's not just about pranking him; it's also a test to see how he handles himself under pressure, and essentially if he's ready for greater responsibilities beyond simply answering phones and getting coffee.

A hedge fund manager, who runs a multibillion-dollar credit fund and is one of our biggest clients, calls in to the sales desk. He's in on it, of course, and has already been given a script I outlined for him. The rest of us are listening on mute from our respective dealerboards.

One ring in: "Citi. This is Charlie."

The client is curt and intimidating, not a stretch role for him to play. "I need Lipton." Dennis Lipton is Charlie's direct boss. Of course he's off the desk because he's crouched over next to me, hiding behind a wall of screens, listening in on the call.

"I'm sorry. He's off the desk. May I ask who's . . . can I help with something?" Charlie is already tripping over himself.

"You know who the fuck this is. This is [intentionally inaudible]."

"I'm sorry. I didn't catch that. Whom may I ask is speaking?" Charlie again exudes reticence, despite the confident, but still grammatically incorrect, emphasis of the word "whom."

Sensing the weakness, the client turns up the heat. "Dude. It's David motherfucking Lim, only your biggest fucking customer. Listen, I need a firm offer on Hutch 33s." This means that he is looking to buy some Hutchison Whampoa bonds maturing in 2033. "Can you help me or do I need to call Deutsche?"

In theory, this should be like taking an order at McDonald's— not that complicated. All Charlie has to do is get the pertinent information and communicate it to the trading desk, and if the price is right, they'll execute the trade; it's simply a function of coordinating the dialogue. Charlie gets a little excited at the prospect of executing his first trade. He composes himself, stands up, and shouts across to our head of trading. "Hey, Joel, where would you offer Hutch 33s for ████████?"

Of course, he fails to inquire as to the size and neglects to tell the trader he needs a firm (tradable) price. Normally, a trader would take his wheels off for being so sloppy. But our trader is also in on the joke, so he quotes Charlie an offer, which is then immediately relayed back to the client.

"Okay. Done. I'll sell you thirty million there. Send me a ticket." *Click.*

We can feel Charlie standing there, trying to process everything that has just happened, thinking, *Okay, a client asked for a firm offer. That means he wants to buy. But when I quoted him the spread, he told me he was selling. So I guess we just bought $30 million bonds from him. But if we bought from him, then shouldn't I have given him a bid instead of an offer? But he said he wanted an offer. Oh well, I have to assume that the client knows what he's doing.*

Charlie shouts back across to the head trader. "Hey, Joel, you bought $30 million Hutch 33s from ████████ at that spread."

"No I fucking didn't." Then he goes back to doing whatever he had been pretending to do, leaving Charlie standing there staring blankly, without a clue as to what he should say or do next.

After a few painful seconds, Joel looks back up at Charlie. "First of all, fucktard, you just asked me for an indication only. But more important, you asked me for an offer, not a fucking bid. And certainly not a firm bid for $30 million . . . What's your name again, and where the fuck is Lipton?"

On cue, Lipton casually walks back over to the desk. "Hey, man, I miss anything?"

Charlie, visibly flustered, relays everything that has just happened. This is a nightmare situation for a new sales guy— making a terrible first impression with the head of credit trading and potentially fucking up a trade with your boss's biggest client. Lipton, playing the part of supportive boss and mentor, remains calm. "No big deal. So just call him back and clarify what he wants to do. He's cool."

Based on the length of time it takes Charlie to nervously retrieve the client's phone number from his Bloomberg header and dial it, we already know this isn't going to end well.

"Hey, David, this is Charlie."

"Who?"

Charlie attempts to explain the mix-up, that David had asked for an offer, but that if he wanted to sell bonds, he'd be happy to now quote him a firm bid price.

David just starts screaming at him. Meanwhile, I'm three rows over, listening in, with my tie rolled up and stuffed in my mouth just to keep from laughing.

"Fuck you. Who the fuck are you to tell me I made a mistake? I told you I needed a firm bid, not a fucking offer. Are you fucking retarded? You own 'em, sucka." *Click.*

Poor Charlie, he's drowning. But Lipton insists that he call back.

"Dude, don't call me again. Send me a fucking ticket for the $30 million I sold you, at the level you quoted me, or I'll never fucking trade with you again."

Lipton sticks to the script. "Fuck, man. What did you do? This is my number one account. If he puts us in the box for this, I'm fucked."

Now Charlie's head is spinning. He's starting to question his own memory of the events to the point where he now thinks that he might have been completely at fault.

"Hey, Joel, I guess I screwed up. Is there anything—"

"Are you fucking stupid? Are you about to ask me to buy $30 million of thirty-year paper at the offered side of the market?"

Between Lipton's and Joel's yelling at him, the entire trading floor is just staring at him thinking, *Holy shit. The new kid must be fucking incompetent.*

There's blood in the water. Charlie's voice is cracking; his eyes are welling up with tears. So naturally, Joel keeps pushing and starts grilling him on the difference between "bid" and "offer" and asking him to calculate how much money he just lost the firm if they have to honor the trade. When Charlie's unable to do the bond math in his head, Joel yells at him even more. "Can you even spell the word 'duration'?"

If it were me, I'd just say, "Fuck this, pull the tapes." But when you're new to the trading floor, it just doesn't occur to you that all the lines are recorded.

Finally, Lipton says, "Look, just go downstairs, get some air, and take a walk and think about what you did. I'll call David back and try to sort this out. If he doesn't let you off the hook, the trading desk is going to take a $400,000 hit, and they're going to hate you for a long fucking time. Do you understand that?"

Thirty minutes later, Charlie comes back, still looking sullen and sickly. We give him a small standing ovation. He is so shell-shocked that he is unable to comprehend how and why we would even do such a thing to him. "Wait, so the client was in on it too? I don't understand."

As things settle down, Charlie admits that he came very close to never coming back upstairs and just calling in and quitting out of shame on the spot. That night, I take him out and we get blackout wasted, and we've been good friends ever since.

He's come a long way since that memorable day. Now he's leaving, heading over to a clean slate and a seven-figure guarantee, with three months' gardening leave—a legally required paid vacation to prevent conflicts of interest or sensitive information from passing from one bank to another.

The next three months breeze by for him in a drunken haze. I do my best to keep up. On the last day before he starts the new job, we meet up and decide to make it a lazy Sunday of brunch followed by some healthy day drinking. We're more aggressive than usual, ordering drinks two at a time. Charlie's still clinging on to the last days of summer; he's trying not to accept that sinking feeling—the reality of going back to school.

Six hours into our brunch, we still haven't left our table. That's when I remember that it's the day of my on-again, off-again girlfriend's birthday party barbecue. I had been invited, probably because the Warden knows I give amazing gifts. Since we're currently on a nasty break, sober me had zero intention of showing up, but all of a sudden it seems like a hilarious idea for drunk me to attend with Charlie as my date.

As expected, the barbecue is almost entirely investment bankers and their *tai tai* wives. It's what we'd call a ski conference, everybody just standing around jerking each other off, as in the same hand motion you make pushing yourself with the ski poles. The conversation is tedious. It revolves around new yoga studios, "NOBU versus Zuma? Discuss!", a ranking of the best airport lounges in the region, a review of the latest Aman resort, and the controversy over the new herringbone seat configuration on Cathay Pacific's business class.

I want to kill myself, but it helps that Charlie and I are shit-faced.

Somehow, I get cornered by Becky, the wife of a mid-ranking, harmless equity syndicate banker. "So, who are you reading?"

"Excuse me?" It's not just that I am hammered; I heard her. I just want to hear her say that one more time.

"Who are you reading?" And then before I can even say a word, she keeps going. "I just finished Niall Ferguson's *The Ascent of Money*, and while I think stylistically, it's similar to his earlier work, I continue to be amazed by his insight, given that he has the perspective of both a historian and an economist."

Now I know why the jerk-off hand motion was invented. While she's talking, I'm making eye contact with Charlie, using my tongue to visibly molest the inside of my cheek. With that masterfully insightful comment, she stops and stares at me, letting me know it's my turn to try to impress her. Just as I am about to call her a pretentious cunt, Charlie pulls me back. "Okay, I think it's time for us to leave."

With that, we catch a taxi down to Lan Kwai Fong. The beautiful thing about Hong Kong, and LKF in particular, is that it's so diverse and transient that every night is Friday night for somebody—even on a Sunday. There are always people out, and there's always an excuse to be out. We make our way to Lux, a bar midway down the hill and right in the middle of the action.

It doesn't take us long to strike up a conversation with a group of six reasonably attractive young, apparently single white girls, a Halley's Comet–caliber event in Asia. Our luck could not be better. We have just stumbled into a girls' night out for the cast of the Hong Kong Disneyland production of *Sleeping Beauty*. Young, bright blue eyes, blond hair, curves. What more could you ask for? Now, these aren't A-list models, of course; it's even better. They are struggling B- and C-list models who get shipped out to Asia for short-term gigs. Most of them come from places like Cincinnati or Tulsa. If they have any other stamps on their passports, I'm guessing they say Cancún.

A few rounds of shots and a few exotic tales of our Asian experience, and we're in. It's such a layup trade. Would they rather spend their free time in some Disney dormitory budgeting their per diem, or living it up with some bankers on an unlimited budget, jetting off to Bali or Phuket on a whim?

The only foreseeable problem tonight is that we're so heavily outnumbered, we'll have to contend with the usual girl pact to stick together and their tendency to look out for their weakest (ugliest or drunkest) link. If the ratio is too far off, you can't peel any of them away from the herd. Even if I do, there's too great a risk that, by the numbers, the majority of them will feel left out and pull the rip cord for the entire group before I have time to close.

I decide to wave in another friend of ours to help even things out. I text Andy, "LKF now. Need wingman. Layup."

Twenty minutes later, he's there. It doesn't matter that it's 10 P.M. on a Sunday night, or that, as someone who manages hundreds of millions of dollars of the bank's capital, he should probably be falling asleep reading *Barron's*. When I remind him of this fact he laughs it off. "Sheeeit, ain't my money, nigga."

Our goal is to convince all of them to come back to my apartment and keep the party going. It takes us a couple of hours to get them comfortable, but they finally agree. "You can see the Great Wall of China from my living room." Just as we're ready to wrap things up, close out the tab, and head back to my place, the biggest cock block in human history appears before us: the Hong Kong Disneyland cast of *The Lion King*. Just as these girls personify everything that you think of when you imagine corn-fed beauty pageant runner-ups, these guys are exactly what one would expect from the all-male cast of *The Lion King*. I thought the NBA was the black ballet; apparently there's a real one too. And these guys are jacked, even the guy who plays the warthog. I had no idea the rigors of theater could be so physically demanding. It's also very clear that these guys are already acquainted with our girls and have been waiting for their opportunity to try and score.

The first thing they do is convince the girls to stick around and have a few more drinks with them. Our perfectly executed plan starts to fall apart. Maleficent changes tack (she wouldn't have a fucking clue what that means): "Let's just all stay here a bit longer."

It's immediately clear that these guys hate us and everything that we represent. They love our bar tab, but they hate us. We try to be cool without being condescending, but that's nearly impossible on a sober day, let alone when some random guys are using my bar tab to talk to girls that I've already teed up.

Not only are they mooches, they're coming in swinging— huge chips on their shoulders. They know they can't compete on Hong Kong's terms (cash and cachet), so they just try to box us out physically, literally putting themselves between the girls and us. Hakuna matata my ass.

After watching Mufasa order round after round of shots on my tab, I glance over at Andy in disgust. He's also been edged out away from the girl he had been talking to. That's when he decides to let them have it.

"Hey, guys. Hey, guys." He speaks up loud enough to get the attention of the core group of girls. "I have a joke for you. What is orange, burgundy, yellow, blue, violet, candy-apple green, magenta, turquoise, fire-engine red, teal, and ivory . . . and tied up in my backyard?" He pauses, and then drops a punch line that is so angry and offensive that even I'm appalled—and that's hard to do. Sharing and collecting racist and mean-spirited jokes is a long-standing banking tradition.

BANG. POW. BOOM.

The next thing I know, I come to in a taxi sitting next to Charlie. Blood is streaming down my face. "What the fuck happened?"

Charlie's laughing. "Sorry, dude. I guess you were standing next to the wrong guy. He just sucker punched you. And then the girls broke up the fight and told us to leave." We're both so drunk it's funny. "Man, you got knocked da fuck out."

Somehow Andy escaped injury, and upon seeing that Charlie and I made it into a cab safely, pulled the trader card. "Dude, I can't believe you dragged me out of the house for this shit. I need to get some sleep. You got this?"

Several hours and twelve stiches across the bridge of my nose later, we're finally leaving the hospital. Already after 5 A.M., I head home to get cleaned up for work. And to think all of this started with an innocuous Sunday morning text from Charlie: "Brunch?" What a way for him to start a new job—still drunk and on zero sleep.

As soon as our morning market update call ends, I walk over to the trading desk to confront Andy.

He sees me coming and quickly covers his tracks. "Hey, man. What the fuck happened to your face?"

"Took an elbow playing basketball." I don't want to throw him under the bus in front of his boss, so I lean in close. "How does a skinny pretty boy like you learn a fucking joke like that?"

He just laughs. "When I was in college, I dated this chick from Mississippi. Want to hear another one?"

"Fuck you."

What I lack in social skills, I make up in wallet.

If I only wanted one drink, I'd go for Communion.

Too many people are smart enough to be angry, but not smart enough to be successful.

If riding the bus doesn't incentivize you to improve your station in life, nothing will.

"Just be yourself" is good advice to probably 5% of people.

Because They
Are Muppets

"The Duke is coming in for $50 million at reoffer," Smithers shouts across the trading floor in my general direction. I hold a thumbs-up above my wall of screens to acknowledge the order, without bothering to look up.

The Duke is ███████ ██████. He's an EM (emerging markets) credit portfolio manager at a $2 billion hedge fund. We call him the Duke because he is a pompous, unjustifiably egotistical, high-maintenance, pain-in-the-ass client. Also, he calls everyone "dude" but says it in a way that sounds so retarded, like he's saying "doo"—which is close enough to "duke" in my book.

It's June 2007, and I'm doing a $300 million subordinated hybrid perpetual bond for the State Bank of India with UBS as my joint bookrunner. There's no point in even explaining what this means from a structural point of view, or highlighting the regulatory and strategic accounting implications of issuing subordinated debt, because that's the entire point—many of the investors who are participating in these deals don't understand or care to know what they are buying.

The process of selling a deal like this is actually fairly easy, provided that markets will cooperate. The State Bank of India is a well-known name, and there are enough similar bonds

226 STRAIGHT TO HELL

out there that the success of this deal is simply a function of price—the premium that the investor will receive on top of where comparable bonds are trading.

Markets have generally been constructive, and when we announce the deal, it looks like we have a clear execution window. However, just after we release the official price guidance, rumors begin to circulate about possible massive subprime CDO-related losses at a couple of Bear Stearns hedge funds (Lehman and BNP are also wrapped up in the rumors). No one's panicking, but there's definitely a sense of skittishness. As a result, the market tone turns instantly cautious, credit spreads widen, and risk appetite diminishes, especially for new issues. In the face of rumors and uncertainty, many investors move to the sidelines, put their hands in their pockets, and wait for clarity.

My real concern is that having to postpone or cancel this deal will only further impair investors' confidence, making it more challenging to execute some of the more lucrative deals in our near-term pipeline. We could revise the price guidance higher to reflect the deterioration in market conditions and diminished risk appetite, but there is no chance the client will agree to that.

A $50 million order from the Duke is a welcome respite. But deep down, I know his order doesn't mean shit. The Duke's modus operandi is to jump into deals he thinks are going to be hot and then flip them back to some other trading desk a couple of days later, thinking we won't find out about it. He doesn't understand credit and is a classic example of the axiom "Don't confuse brains with a bull market."

He usually comes into deals early with a grossly inflated order. Then, if he doesn't get a good allocation, he throws a temper tantrum. "Hey, doo, I came in early to support the deal.

I came in size. And now I hear the deal is four times oversubscribed, but I only got $2 million bonds on a $20 million order."

The response in my head is something like, *Listen here, fuckhead. The only reason you gave us the order early is because you don't even bother opening the prospectus. And I allocated you on the basis of what I thought to be your real demand—which isn't anything close $20 million.* My actual response is more like, "That sucks, bro. I fought for you. But [insert joint bookrunner's name here] didn't want to allocate you; they said you flipped their last deal. I'll try and hook you up next time."

The Duke tends to let what he hears about the size of the order book dictate how big (and inflated) his order is going to be. For some unknown reason, he must have been told that this is a really hot deal, despite the obviously weaker market backdrop. Part of the reason he might think that the deal is still in good shape is that's what we're telling our sales force to say: that the order book is comfortably oversubscribed with key anchor orders and high-quality, real money (buy-and-hold) investors with little price sensitivity.

Smithers yells back across the three rows that separate us. "By the way, you know the Duke is Roo's client. Can you put the order in for her? She's not around and I can't access any of her clients in the system." I put the order in for Roo and then shoot her a quick email so that she knows to confirm it when we launch final deal terms.

Roo is the head of ███████████. I wouldn't say that she is ugly, but she certainly isn't hot—a trading-floor 6. She's a nasty piece of work: insincere, two-faced, and manipulative. Her first husband inadvertently summed her up best during his toast at their wedding reception when he said one of the things he loves most about her is that even when she's mad or yelling at him, she still has a smile on her face. I gave them two

Baccarat wineglasses and a Frette sheet set from their registry, along with a card that said, "I hope you like the glasses and the sheets. So when you're getting drunk and fucking, you can think of me." I wasn't invited to her second wedding.

Given the broader market weakness, some investors are downsizing their orders, setting higher limits, or even pulling their orders altogether. The size and quality of the book is shrinking every time I refresh my screen. We manage to twist a few arms to stay in the deal, essentially calling in favors or giving out markers. "Support me here, and I'll take care of you the next couple of times you need a favor."

As I am trying to salvage this deal, I also have to be mindful of my own reputation. There are a few priority accounts, mostly hedge funds, whom I rely on regularly for anchor orders, information about private deals and our competitors' pipelines, or even for seemingly innocuous favors like taking meetings for me when I need to fill out a roadshow schedule. For the sake of my business going forward, I cannot afford to burn these guys. Beyond that, many of them are my good friends.

I jump into a conference room with my cell phone. "Hey, man. Real quick. You didn't hear it from me, but you don't want to be in this deal. Just do me a favor and call your UBS coverage and cancel your order through them. If you still want bonds this time tomorrow, I'll get them to you at the reoffer price."

It's not uncommon for syndicate bankers to do this. I learned it from ▮▮▮▮▮▮ ▮▮▮▮▮▮▮ on the EM syndicate desk in New York. I'm shooting myself in the foot on this deal, but the long-term benefits to me certainly outweigh any short-term pain. Now these people owe me a favor, and I look good compared with my counterpart at UBS, assuming he isn't doing the same thing.

Following an arduous call with the issuer, we finally have their reluctant approval to launch and price the transaction—a (smaller) $250 million deal at the wider end of the price guidance. On the face of it, it's a massive failure. But from where I'm sitting, it's a fucking miracle that we have a deal at all.

The message that we deliver to the market is that, while the book is strong enough to support a larger deal, we're downsizing because the issuer's price expectations have not been met, making it appear to be a decision made from a position of strength. This reassuringly implies that this unmet demand will be looking to scoop up loose bonds in the secondary market. This could not be further from the truth.

Now, all we have to do is agree on the final allocations with UBS and price the deal. When we get to the Duke's order, I ask UBS, "What do you want to do? But before you answer that, know that my salesperson has reassured me that not only is the order good, it's all real interest, and that we should give him a priority allocation."

He just starts laughing. "Oh really . . . Well, in that case, I guess we have to fill it, right?"

"Fuck him—full fill. If we don't, I'm not even sure we can get to 250 without being long ourselves."

By filling the Duke, and pretty much everyone else in the book, we're able to allocate $254 million, leaving ourselves with a small $4 million short position. We're short, not to make money, but to be slightly better positioned to support the deal, by buying back paper in the secondary market. I would have liked to have been even more short, but it is physically impossible to stuff anyone else with any more bonds.

Any time we price a new deal, our trading desk is obligated to make a market and to help us support it, i.e., keep the price at or above reoffer for a reasonable period of time (until we can blame broader market weakness for any sell-off). If we don't make aggressive markets and show a willingness to buy back bonds, investors aren't going to want to participate in our deals. In this case, I've shown the order book to the trading desk, and they're scared shitless. We all know as soon as it prices, and investors see that they've been allocated in full on a deal we've been touting as oversubscribed, they're going to be calling up asking for firm bids. This is particularly true for accounts who inflated their orders; now, they're sitting on bonds they never wanted to begin with.

We've pounded the pavement for three days; there is not a single person out there who's still a buyer and isn't getting at least as many bonds as they want. In other words, the trading desk knows that if they get stuck owning paper, there's nowhere to go with it, regardless of any bid/offer spread.

The technicals of this deal aside, our trading desk has also taken a very bearish view on credit in general; they don't want to be long paper trying to help me support a shitty deal. "Dude, do me a favor. Don't price this now; wait for most guys to go home for the day. And then, when you price, let me know fifteen minutes ahead of time, and we'll clear out for the day so no one can trade with us until tomorrow. Let fucking UBS make a market in this pig."

That's what we do. We spin our wheels, announcing to the Asian sales force and to investors that in order to accommodate important European accounts that need more time to get approvals, pricing will be delayed. Implying that some key European investors are coming into the deal is a confident message to send, and it's a total lie.

At 7 p.m., we price the deal. Only a handful of salespeople have hung around for their clients' allocations; thank God. Typically, I'll stick around for a couple of hours after we price a deal to ensure that everything is smooth, particularly as it relates to the hedges. I also like to make the rounds calling the financial media, talking up the success of the deal and running through relevant terms, market color, and deal statistics.

Tonight, fifteen minutes after we price, I'm out the door—with just a quick Bloomberg message to the sales force: "Out of pocket, in a client dinner. Any State Bank of India issues to be dealt with tomorrow."

Walking out, I am joined by Smithers in the elevator bank, one of the few guys who had hung back for the allocations. Even though most of his clients had gone home, he was able to send them a Bloomberg ticket so they'd have it when they get in the next day.

"This is the worst deal I have ever been a part of." He's totally deflated and I think genuinely remorseful about having put some of his clients in this deal.

"Fuck them. Do you know how bad we would have looked if we had a failed deal?"

"I think we could look worse tomorrow if this thing trades down two or three points."

"If this trades down two points tomorrow, it'll be because the entire market sells off, and then our entire pipeline will be on hold anyway. So who gives a shit?" Besides being amazed that we got the deal done at all, deep down, I do feel a twinge of guilt. At the same time, many of these investors have only themselves, their greed, and their complacency to blame.

It's a bull market; they jump in every new issue without doing their homework. I once had a hedge fund manager call me up saying, "Hey, I really like this Magnatron story. Can you put me in for $20 million?" My response was simply "No problem, but are you referring to the MagnaChip deal?" Of course, he wants to be in on it after he heard it's eight times oversubscribed.

Smithers really came through for me this week; without him pounding the phones, there would have been no deal. "Come on, man. Let me buy you a quick beer."

He gives me this look of total lifelessness. "You know my wife is eight months pregnant, right? And if you had priced this deal when you should have, we would have been out of here two fucking hours ago—which is when I told her I'd be done."

I've got forty-eight floors until we reach the lobby in order to convince him. "So you're two hours late. What's the difference between that and two and a half hours?"

A few minutes later, we're trekking up the hill through Hong Kong Park and over to the Lobster Bar at the Shangri-La hotel for a quick drink. Although I have many second homes in Asia, the Shangri-La is one of my favorites; I lived there for almost a month when I was having some domestic troubles with the Warden. It has the only hotel pool in the city with unobstructed sunlight all day long.

Many a memorable night out begins with the idea of having one quick drink, although from the get-go, it's certainly not my intention to stop at one. Knowing full well what misery lies ahead of me tomorrow morning, I am fully committed to not remembering how I'm going to get home.

We grab a couple of seats on the couch, order two Peronis, and then just sit in silence. After a couple of minutes, I'm ordering another drink; Smithers has barely touched his. "What are you going to do about the Duke?" he asks. "Come tomorrow morning, he's going to shit his pants, and when he does, he's going to be calling Roo, and you, demanding that you take the bonds off his hands."

"Smithers, he placed an order for $50 million. I confirmed the order. I even had Roo confirm the order after you gave it to me. Do you know what she did? She sent me this obnoxious email, saying that it's not inflated and he should be given a priority allocation, particularly because he's looking at a couple of structured credit trades."

The thought of her being so stupid finally makes him smile. He hates her as much as I do. She was promoted to managing director ahead of him, coincidentally the same year when there were complaints about the firm not having enough senior women in sales. She had new business cards printed the next day.

Out of nowhere, a bottle of Dom Pérignon appears. Before the waiter can say a word about its origin, Mitch plops his considerable weight next to us on the couch and gives Smithers a huge slap across the thigh. "Hey, boy-o." He's hammered, all six feet four inches of him. He's not alone either; Grace is with him. Grace is a part-time prostitute (presumably due to lack of demand) from the Philippines. She's on Mitch's roster of rotating companions, all of whom are either professionals or semipros.

I wouldn't mind Mitch joining us for drinks tonight if it weren't for the fact that Grace is so hideous—way too ugly to be in this bar. What's the point of paying and spending time with hookers if they aren't smoking hot? Mitch likes to say that he has a well-balanced portfolio, but Grace is definitely sub-investment grade—by far the worst credit in his stable of nags. I look around and count at least three other prostitutes in the bar who put her to shame. This is the Shang, after all.

Using trading-floor vernacular in reference to women is douchey but fairly common; I remember having a female desk assistant in London whom everyone called Hooks. (When a bond is downgraded one notch below single-B, it's referred to as getting "triple hooks," or a CCC rating.) There are also garden-variety sayings like "buyer" and "mine" when you see a hot chick, and "no bid" and "yours" when you see a pig. Grace is an illiquid distressed asset that trades by appointment.

Mitch is like a cartoon character. "Come on, lads. Let's 'ave a drink." He is built like a professional wrestler and has the same attitude. He's famous for sneaking up behind one of his dinner companions in restaurants, pulling his cock out, and then resting it on their shoulder to see how long it takes them to notice. Smithers can see where tonight is going; he chugs his room temperature beer, stands up, and reaches for his jacket.

"Fuck off, cunt." Mitch pulls his jacket away and throws it onto the ground. When he's wasted, he is notoriously aggressive and belligerent. "You're not fucking going anywhere; I just bought you a fucking bottle of champagne."

Smithers surrenders, as if he has a choice. "Okay, okay. I'll stay for a little while longer."

Even that response is a bit too hesitant for Mitch to accept. He shoots his hand into the air and yells, "Mhgòi, mhgòi." Our waiter has only just started to walk away from having poured the first bottle. "Go ahead and bring us another bottle, please. I'm thirsty."

The service at the Shangri-La is impeccable; the second bottle of champagne arrives just as we finish the first, or three minutes later. Mitch is on fire tonight. "We're going to need one more bottle, and then also a table for four for dinner on the restaurant side.

"Smithers, I am treating you as my special guest for dinner, and I'm not taking no for an answer."

Welcome to the Hotel California, Smithers. A few minutes later, they politely inform us that our table is ready. Mitch leads the way, holding a bottle of champagne with one hand and Grace the hooker with the other. I'm mortified; who knows how many people around here recognize me? Smithers, I

imagine, is simply numb as we are escorted to our table, prominently located in the middle of the dining room.

Mitch points to the maître d'. "Excuse me, I'm terribly
sorry. But I've got no idea where my mouth has been, and
it's touched this bottle. Can you please bring some more
champagne?" Grace blushes and flashes a whitish snaggle-
toothed grin. So she does comprehend English after all—
good to know.

Mitch continues. "Oh wait, Fred [not his name]. We're pretty
hungry, especially this girl." Mitch gestures to Grace by grabbing her breast. "May we also please order four surf and turfs?
Medium rare for everyone. And another bottle of champagne.
Thank you so much, Ted." At this point, in what is an otherwise completely full restaurant of Hong Kong society types
and regional business people, we have graduated from being
an offensive disturbance to an outright spectacle.

I make a toast. "Only in Asia can one quick drink cascade
into who-knows-how-many bottles of Dom and a nice steak
and lobster dinner with old friends and new. Here's to just
another Thursday night in Asia."

We cheers. Grace the hooker chugs her entire glass of champagne. Mitch, ever the big-hearted gentleman, attentively fills
it back up to the brim. Instead of seeing her holding a flute
of Dom Pérignon, I imagine her kids back in the Philippines
living with their grandmother, drinking dirty water from old
Gatorade bottles. Up to this point, she hasn't said a word. I
count myself lucky.

After the meal, I make the switch to Macallan, ordering a
double twelve neat. Mitch orders a double thirty neat. Given
how drunk he is and how I suspect he's going to drink it—
by slamming it—ordering the more expensive thirty-year-old
Macallan seems a bit extravagant and wasteful to me.

The bill comes; Smithers's response is priceless. He just looks at it and laughs. "Have fun with this one, guys." In theory, Mitch should pick up the tab. But when he says, "Do you think you can jam this through [expense it]?," it's clear to me that this one stings. So as a face-saving gesture, I propose a wager: if he can tell the difference in a blind test between a Macallan 12, 18, 20, and 30, then I will pick up the check.

I order the drinks (regular size, not samples) from Anthony, the bartender, and ask him to write the correct years underneath the corresponding beverage napkin beneath each glass. He then ceremoniously brings them over to our table and hangs around to watch. He still remembers me from when I lived upstairs.

Mitch doesn't waste any time smelling or tasting each one several times. He looks at each glass, downs it, and moves on to the next one without hesitation. "Okay, it's eighteen, thirty, twelve, and twenty." Anthony is our game show host, dramatically turning over each napkin to reveal the results. Motherfucker. Mitch nails it.

The fact that the staff is not only pleasant but friendly with us is indicative of how much money we spend there, and also the fact that in Asia, you can get away with pretty much whatever you want, especially as a white guy with a corporate credit card.

"Fuck it. Now it's my turn. If I'm paying for this, I might as well try it too."

I attempt to be slightly more deliberate, not that I have much experience doing this. I sniff and smell, taste and taste again. It's a stab in the dark; I miss two of the four and, in an attempt to bring closure to the evening, offer my concession and reach for the check. "What are you doing?" Mitch shouts. "Let's go again."

We go a few more times, even managing to coax people at an adjacent table to get involved. Finally, Mitch says, "Anthony, you might as well just bring us a bottle of the Macallan 30." As we polish that off, he slurs his way through explaining to me how and why it's so easy to tell the difference—from what I remember, for Macallan, it's mostly in the color. It's an expensive lesson.

So in the process of determining who's going to pay for dinner, my original bill almost doubles. Without saying a word or even looking at the new total, I pay our tab. For good measure, Mitch tips an obscenely generous amount and signs my credit card receipt "CUNT" in giant block letters.

He's using my own move against me. I've always found it irritating to see guys pick up tabs pretending like they're being generous when you know damn well that they're just going to expense it. So, as a joke, when we're out drinking, I sometimes scribble "CUNT" or "CUMFACE" across the signature line of the receipt, so that they can't expense it, or if they do, they'll have some explaining to do. It's a good thing I'm tight with my business unit manager.

What a night. Mitch probably won't remember it. Smithers will want to forget it. Grace the hooker won't appreciate it. And I get stuck with a fucking monster bill. But it's worth it: I managed to drink just enough to remember getting back to my apartment but without any recollection of how I made it into my bed.

Thank Christ my maid wakes me up the next morning with a blow job—that's the name of my morning detox: apple, carrot, pear, ginger, and a pinch of cayenne pepper.

Walking into the office, I notice that Roo is in before me for the first time in her miserable existence. Normally, I would be in no mood to deal with her, but in this case, I already know exactly how it's going to play out, so I'm looking forward to it.

My dealerboard lights up as soon as I sit down; it's the Duke calling. It's either my green dot status on Bloomberg or Roo who's alerted him that I'm in the office; I suspect the latter. My position is really simple: "Well, the color we have from UBS and from Roo is that your $50 million was all real interest. You can't expect me to take the bonds back just because the market sold off." He starts talking about how supportive he has been of our deals and that this is a misunderstanding, and he really needs a favor out of us. "Sorry, mate, there's nothing I can do. Gotta hop." *Click.* I can't imagine how he can explain to his bosses that he owns 20% of this pig of a deal.

Ten seconds later, I can see one of the credit sales lines lighting up. It's the Duke calling Roo; I don't bother listening in because my comprehension of Cantonese is terrible.

The bullshit that follows is exactly as I had anticipated. Roo first tries sweet-talking me into buying the bonds back. I say, "Fuck no." Then she throws Smithers under the bus and says that he made a mistake when he took the order by not making a note of the actual demand. Then she tries explaining how the client left a $50 million order when he wanted only $10 million, purely as a favor to us, so that we could advertise a greater level of oversubscription on the deal. It's as if she has no recollection of our email exchange; not only is she totally insincere, she's also a sociopath.

"He can go shit in his hat. He fucking owns them. If he wants to sell them back to us, tell him I'll bid 99.5 for 5 million, and that's it."

I know what's going to happen next. She's going to escalate this to Dirty Sanchez (her boss) and to BJ (my boss). Like clockwork, two hours later, I see the three of them in BJ's office. Once she's had time to make her bullshit case, Dirty calls me in there. "Hey, it sounds like there's been some miscommunication, and there's no point placing blame [that means she blamed me], but in the interests of preserving this relationship, we want you to buy back $25 million and then ask UBS to buy back the other $25 million."

I casually produce a copy of the email. "What's the miscommunication?"

Having clearly forgotten about the email, and having tried to throw every possible person under the bus, Roo's completely out of options—well, almost. She can still throw her client under the bus. "That's right. Sorry. I've been so busy that I must have mixed this up with something else. Let him eat these. That'll teach him a lesson for inflating his order. And if we have any blowback, I'm very close to his bosses—so we won't have any franchise repercussions."

By the end of the week, the Duke has lost over $1 million on that position alone. He owns 20% of the deal; there is no-where to go and nothing to do but sit and wait for markets to stabilize. Like they say, "Hope is a poor hedge." By the next week, we're guessing that figure has grown to $2 million, or more. The following week, he gets fired.

The news of his demise is met with cheers across the close-knit community of syndicate and sales bankers. "You got the Duke shit-canned? Allow me to be the first to buy you a drink."

This deal, and the fact that the rumors about Bear Stearns are true, closes the Asian public bond market for four months, until October, when we reopen it with a jumbo US$ bench-mark for an Indian bank.

It takes a while, but Roo is eventually fired a couple of years later. It would have been much, much sooner, except that she keeps getting pregnant. And she fucking hates kids.

I wish I loved anything as much as I hate almost everything.

If you abstain from smoking, drinking, and using drugs, you don't actually live longer. It just seems longer.

The fact that most people are too stupid to know how dumb they really are is the fabric holding our society together.

If you love something, set it free. If it comes back, it tried to do better, but decided to just settle with you.

Getting rich isn't hard. Any hot girl with questionable morals can do it.

The Minibar

I come to, my head fucking pounding; I'm still drunk, but at least I'm in my bed. Make that a bed. That's a relief. How I got there, I have no clue. It's probably something like six o'clock in the morning. I've got no idea why or how I wake up so early, especially since my first meeting isn't until 9 A.M.

Lying in bed next to me, sound asleep, is the naked body of a smoking hot chick. I lift the covers further for a more detailed inspection. Holy shit. Nice. Still alive? Nice. She is amazingly proportioned, quite curvy for an Asian chick. Clearly surgically enhanced, but what the fuck do I care? I poke the ass to see if the rest rolls over. Damn, I want its autograph.

Now for the life of me, I have no recollection of where the fuck she came from, where I met her, and how she ended up in my hotel room. More important, I have no clue if she is a professional or not. I reach over and grab a tit, a fucking awesome tit. Okay, this might be a little creepy, but fuck it.

But she is definitely hot. *Is she a whore?* I ask myself. We were out with some legit girls for a while, but then again, I'm in Singapore. I remember being out with a bunch of clients and colleagues. We went to karaoke; there were some pretty good-looking chicks there. I remember being the big hit, owning

"It's Not Unusual" by Tom Jones. *I must've hooked up with one of those chicks. I am the man.* This discourse continues in my head. *She's probably legit, maybe a junior client, or an analyst from the Singapore office,* I tell myself hopefully.

Having exhausted my capacity to debate with myself, I pull back the covers again and give her a gentle tap on the ass. Nothing happens. She doesn't even budge. So I go back for the double tap, this time a little bit harder. Again, nothing happens. So finally, I wind up and come down with the full-out spank. Instantaneously, she jumps up—wide-awake—and immediately starts blowing me.

I'm now getting the best blow job I've ever had. Not the best blow job you've ever had, the best blow job I've ever had.

At this point, I don't know what's going on and I don't care. She finishes. "Okay. I go shower now." Not sure how I should play this. I'm hungover and some chick who just gave me the best head ever, who I still hope might be a client or colleague, just spoke to me in Tarzan English.

I do my best to go back to sleep.

The next thing I know, she's looming over me, dressed in a cheap cocktail dress. Okay, how do I play this? "Okay, hon, you have to go, and I have to go back to sleep for an hour. So give me your business card and we'll hook up again next time I'm in town." I knew it wouldn't work, but I try.

"You pay me money; everybody pay; you owe me S$200. Nobody fuck for free." What a profound statement: "Nobody fuck for free." I think back to everyone I can ever remember fucking, especially my current girlfriend. But then again, my girlfriend's probably more expensive than a thousand hookers and still never gives heartfelt head, at least not to me.

I know the drill. "I paid Mama-san last night, otherwise you wouldn't be here. It's already taken care of." The events of the previous evening hadn't actually come back to me, but it's worth a shot. That fails immediately; this clearly ain't her first rodeo.

"What? You crazy, la? Who fuck for free? You pay, you fucking fuck." She reiterates in increasingly broken English. "Nobody fuck free, you fuck."

I get out of bed and scrounge around for my wallet. No cash. I find my pants from last night. No cash. My suit jacket. No cash. All I can find are a few illegible credit card receipts. It must have been a fun night.

Bottom line, I have no fucking cash anywhere. Now, the last thing I am going to do is the reverse walk of shame with some love monkey down to the nearest cash machine.

Before I can even start to pitch a layaway plan, she grabs the phone and presses 0. "I call hotel security," she says while holding the phone out like a gun. "Or you come with me to ATM and pay me S$200. Okay, fuck, you pay me S$200. No one fuck for free. You pay S$200."

My survival instincts immediately take over. I leap across, slam the phone down, and gently lead her over to the closet. I pull out the hotel laundry bag, shake it open, and hand it to her. I then pull her over to the minibar, open it up, and start stuffing the bag as she holds it open. Two Diet Cokes, two Heinekens, two small bottles of Pellegrino. Boom. A handful of the airplane-sized Grey Goose and Bacardi bottles and then some. I pause for only a matter of seconds before I hear, "No. No. S$200. More. More." Next go the Pringles, M&Ms, and Twizzlers. "More," she barks. In go the Oreos, Junior Mints, and the mini Jim Beam.

I reach up to the countertop—the half bottle of cabernet sauvignon, the Jack Daniel's, the pistachios, the Toblerone. And the fucking Moët.

Finally. She looks into the bag, surveying her loot. "Stop. Now too much." She then reaches in and pulls out the Pringles and the Toblerone, pauses for a few seconds, and then pulls out a mini Bacardi, sets them back down on the countertop gently, and says, "Okay, this good, la."

And then just like that, she goes off on her way, stuffed laundry bag of loot over her shoulder like some kind of Singaporean Ritz-Carlton Santa Claus/whore prancing along in her four-inch Lucite hooves, marching to the drumbeat of the damned.

I shower, suit up, and head downstairs for day two of our Asian investor conference, and then successfully forget all about the experience.

That is, until two weeks later, when my secretary hands me my expenses and reminds me the minibar is not covered under T&E. The minibar bill? S$198. I owe her S$2.

Flowers and an apology are a lot easier than actually changing.

I spent $2,000 on a suit I don't need, just to impress a sales chick I didn't find attractive.

How easily someone is offended is directly proportional to how stupid they are.

Most girls cannot pull off their attitude. They need to either get hotter or be nicer.

Watching how someone behaves at an open bar tells you everything you need to know about them.

Conference Call Etiquette

The audible sound of Mase rapping "What You Want" is faintly yet unmistakably playing over what is an otherwise intensely challenging conference call. We all try to avoid acknowledging the obvious, but there is an overriding sense of "Are you fucking hearing this too?"

Finally, I speak up. "Hey, Henry, can you please turn down the music in your car. We're having a hard time hearing you." I'm generally well composed on client calls, but it's hard to get the words out without cracking up.

We are approaching the end of the Asian investor roadshow for a high-yield deal for a Thai telecom provider, and the reception isn't exactly what we had promised the client. Surprise, surprise.

"What? I'm not even in—"

Before Henry can complete his defense, I cut him off with "Oooo-kay. Well, let's just try and continue." Right on cue, the music fades away.

Now begins the process of moonwalking the client back to the reality that their funding cost is going to be at least 25 basis points higher than what we had been guiding them just a few weeks before. Normally, this wouldn't be a huge problem; we'd just blame "adverse market conditions" or imply that the company's performance on the roadshow is not instilling sufficient confidence in the minds of investors. However, these guys are experienced in the realm of investor relations and capital markets, and they have already been getting feedback from their other relationship banks with respect to overall market conditions that vary from "robust" to "highly receptive to new issues."

I'm quick to point out that our competitors are simply upset at not being included in the deal and are just trying to sabotage the execution process. None of this changes the fact that we have a very unhappy client.

My priority at this point is to make sure that all blame gets shifted away from us and onto our joint bookrunner, so that we aren't put in the box and excluded from their future deals. Looking at the company's debt maturity profile, I know they've got to come back to the capital markets each of the next two years, and they have a long list of lending relationships, all of which represent mouths that expect to be fed in the form of bond mandates. Fucking up this deal provides the perfect excuse to leave us out of the next deal and rotate another bank in. This is always the big test for banks when it comes to repeat issuers—seeing which banks they retain from the previous deal and which they replace.

"Market conditions have continued to deteriorate overnight; it's less evident in quantifiable data, but we're definitely seeing diminished investor risk appetite on the heels of some modest weakness in credit spreads as well as some poor-performing new issues over the course of the last few days. In fact, a few key investors who have been looking closely as this deal, doing their homework and getting approvals internally, have now moved firmly to the sidelines."

We say more or less the exact same thing any time we are trying to work an issuer's expectations back from where we set them when we were trying to convince them to announce the transaction. "I realize we had told you to expect an outcome in the context of 9%; however, it is now quite evident that printing a trade at 9.25% would be a fantastic result in the current market environment."

This is never an easy call to have. They need $500 million, and now after they get halfway through a roadshow, which required board-level approvals predicated on specific funding targets, we're shifting the goalposts. But they're already pregnant; they know it and we know it. Walking away from a deal at this point in the process would be disastrous, for them and us.

It seems masochistic to develop a habit of overpromising clients, but that's often what it takes to fight for and win these sought-after mandates. Even after the mandate is secured, it's another battle trying to convince some issuers to get off the sidelines. "Do you think the market conditions will be better if we wait until January?" If I've made my P&L for the year and our compensation numbers have already been submitted, then the answer is an emphatic: "Yes, sit tight. You'll get a better deal printed in January." If it's early October and it's been a rough year, then the answer is even more emphatic: "The clear window for optimal execution is right now." Irrespective of what's in the client's best interests, there's no point in bringing a really lucrative deal to market once bonus numbers have been set; come January 1, everything resets to zero. Not only would you not get paid for it, but having a strong pipeline going into year-end also provides good job security.

In our defense, we've done a phenomenal job to produce a transaction at this level; the only issue is that it's just slightly short of the client's target. Once we get them over this hump, they'll be very pleased with the outcome and, more important, the way that the deal is perceived and talked about in the financial press.

Henry from Deutsche Bank goes to speak. "Listen, just to re-affirm what John said, we're all working and pushing our sales forces to get guys to commit and to remove their price sensitivity. We're going to continue to push until London opens, but that's when we'll need the green light from you to refine the price guidance. And as John said, right now, it's looking like the right price is not going to be at the tight end of the range. What I would suggest is . . ."

Mase's "What You Want" mysteriously starts in again, this time not quite as subtly as before.

"Hey, Henry, we can't hear you again. Can you please turn down the radio in your car again?" This is the ultimate sin. It's now almost 10 A.M. and I have implied to the client that Deutsche Bank is obviously not taking this deal very seriously. I've already made it clear that I have been glued to my desk since 7 A.M., calling investors and whipping salespeople to try to pull this deal together.

As I am holding my iPod earphone up to my alternate receiver, I have to mute my own headset to prevent people from hearing me laughing. I can barely keep it together.

Henry can't really protest too much without coming off as overly defensive. He tries to reassure everyone that he's not the source, is glued to his desk, and is equally focused on this deal. My hope is that there is some doubt lingering in the client's mind and that it's still there in six months when they are thinking about which of us to include in the next deal.

I wish I could take full credit for having thought of this trick. ██████ ███████████, my counterpart at Goldman Sachs, whom I would later be hired to replace, is credited with having invented it. Typically, we'd just play music on the internal bookrunner-only calls as a means of stopping bankers from speaking for the sake of speaking. However, I've just taken it up to a whole new level—doing it on a client call in an attempt to undermine a competitor.

Within seconds, I get an instant message from Henry, "FU(K YOU, DIKHEAD." He's typing like a twelve-year-old because Bloomberg explicitly prevents the use of most swear words on its platform. It is physically impossible to send a Bloomberg message with an identifiable swear word in it; hence, no one on Wall Street was surprised by Mayor Bloomberg's subsequent Big Gulp ban.

Later that day, I get a call from Henry, who also happens to be a close friend of mine. "Well fucking played. I'm going to have to add that move to my arsenal." This wasn't the first time dirty tricks like this have been employed and it wouldn't be the last.

Undermining our competitors on deals that we're working together on isn't even the primary motivation for conference call antics. We're just trying to overcome the monotony and tediousness of the vast majority of these calls by entertaining ourselves and each other.

The most painful conference calls are for the deals where there are more than three bookrunners, because it means there will be a minimum of fifteen or twenty bankers on every single call; the good news is that these are the perfect environment for relative anonymity with virtually zero accountability.

In 2005, we get mandated along with six other banks for a rare and prestigious US$ benchmark deal for the China Development Bank, the state-owned Chinese bank. This deal is a nightmare, starting with the fact that the fees are virtually zero—so it's purely a franchise trade. With so many bankers involved, and each one of them trying to distinguish themselves in front of the client, the conference calls carry on endlessly.

Deals like this are incredibly boring. We don't actually have to do anything—like when no one noticed when you lip synced in choir as a kid. With seven bookrunners, we take turns leading the calls, with one person delivering the message that has already been discussed and agreed on as a group, prior to the client call. This means I have to speak only once every seven calls, or every three days or so.

The anointed syndicate desk will provide an update on the deal, and in the interest of saving time, each bank will take turns simply saying, "JPMorgan agrees," or "Citi agrees." This tacit agreement whereby people shut the fuck up works relatively well, until it comes to this douche at UBS, Ewan Hunt. "UBS agrees; however, I'd also like to reiterate . . ." and then he drones on for a full five minutes, providing absolutely no new information. This of course snowballs, compelling other bankers, not to be outdone in front of the client, to also take turns rehashing the recommendation. A simple ten-minute client update turns into an hour-long dick-waving contest.

When it's not my turn to lead the call, I don't even bother. I'll dial in, say something to make my presence known to the client, and then just grab an analyst. "Listen in and let me know if I need to hop back on."

The price guidance discussion is going to be a shitshow. We need to get our price guidance recommendation signed off on by the client and then release it as early as possible during the

Asian morning, so that we can confirm as many Asian orders as possible to generate momentum for the European open, in order to confirm those orders and keep the momentum going into the US open. It's imperative to communicate this number as early as possible.

On the morning of the big call, I purposefully dial in to the call ten minutes early and am prompted by the automated operator to record my name. Standard protocol dictates that you simply state the name of the bank, saying only "Citi." This morning, for my name, I say "UBS" in the most obnoxiously nasally sounding accent I can think of. Then I put that line on hold. When the call is due to start, I dial back in as myself using a new line.

In the middle of the call, it becomes expectedly contentious. Bankers are turning on one another and undermining the process by asking loaded questions on the client's behalf. "I understand that the syndicate recommendation is +100 basis points over the ten-year US Treasury, but what if we modified to a range of +90 to +100?"

As Madame Wu Li, a senior China Development Bank executive, is finishing an impassioned speech about why she will not accept our recommendation, I release the holding line that's been blinking away on my dealerboard for the last hour. The automated voice interrupts her: "Now exiting the call: UBS."

The timing is perfect. After a few seconds of stunned silence, Madame Wu responds to this great insult with a simple "Hello? Are you still there?," leaving the UBS team scrambling to reassure her that they are all still on the line.

For the rest of the deal, on every single conference call, someone from one of the other banks would wait for a tense or pivotal moment on the call and say, "I would just like to confirm if UBS are still on the line."

Another common method of overcoming the boredom of conference calls is to play Conference Call Bingo. The way we play it—with one person tasked with saying certain words on a client call—doesn't really have anything to do with actual Bingo, but that's just what we call it.

Our version of the game is hardly an original idea, but it's hilarious to hear guys who are getting paid so much money attempting to say ridiculous things to an important client while discussing their billion-dollar bond offering. For the most part, we generally only play Bingo on layup trades, which were the majority of deals up until June 2007. For challenging deals, or in the face of difficult market conditions, we don't mess around. You don't fuck with your own bonus.

All of this is coordinated and communicated in the Bloomberg chat rooms that are set up for each deal. The chat rooms are the center of our universe. They are a fundamental component of being able to get deals done and are an essential distraction when markets are quiet and things are slow. If the transcripts of some of these chat rooms are ever published, plenty of people will end up fired, divorced, or in jail.

Before a call, the bookrunners collectively put together a list of five terms that the banker leading the call has to work into the client update. For example: "chrysanthemum," "elephantiasis," "hemorrhoid," "Nostradamus," "butt plug."

Those examples are actually pretty easy to work into a discussion about the investment grade credit spreads. The client just thinks you're eccentric, silly, or slightly vulgar. An amateur might get flustered by the prospect of saying "butt plug," but it's actually the easiest one on the list—"Investors are currently starved of new telecom paper, but plug that demand we will."

I prefer trying to make people look stupid with derivatives of words that don't exist, like "overfantasticality" or

"sentimentosity" or "hedgeasaurus," until a rule was introduced outlawing this strategy.

For morning calls, the stakes will typically be a round of
drinks for each missed word, payable at a syndicate deal team
lunch later that day. Not that we need an excuse to go day
drinking, but that's exactly what it is.

The guys at Credit Suisse and Deutsche Bank are far and away
the best at Bingo—totally fearless and amazingly creative. I am
definitely an all-star contender but have a colleague who is so
bad that he can't get more than one or two done. He is notorious for trying to whisper his way through the list, which, of
course, is a rule violation, punishable by having to buy an extra
round of drinks.

One of the more inane deals I've worked on was for the Socialist
Republic of Vietnam, along with Deutsche Bank and Barclays.
The Vietnamese are so dysfunctional and bureaucratic that we
carried the mandate for almost two years. During this time,
they insisted on weekly market update calls, even though they
clearly had zero intention of any kind of imminent launch.
They would set a theoretical execution window for two months
out and then insist on discussing it each week as if they were
ready to pull the trigger. And then a few weeks before the scheduled announcement date, they'd decide to postpone the deal
and set a new date for two months out, leaving some poor
analyst scrambling to cancel flights, visas, and hotels.

They just needed to fill up their diaries with meetings and
conference calls in order to appear busy on paper, just in case
some other government official decided to inquire what the
hell they did with their time. After about six months, it became
very clear that they wanted to work on this deal in perpetuity.

Because of growing retail and commercial banking activity (meaning more revenue channels) in Vietnam, we were forced by our senior management to participate in this charade and at least pretend to take it seriously—and take it seriously we did.

Sometimes, I'd adopt a ridiculous accent and lead the call pretending to be the guy from Deutsche Bank, or put on an exceptionally lispy, effeminate Cantonese voice and pose as the guy from Barclays. At one point, the guy from Deutsche Bank took it too far when he pretended to be me, opening the call with what sounded like a terrible Matthew McConaughey impersonation: "Dudes, guuud mornin'. Gotta tell ya, tha markit is lookin' and feelin' guud. Investors are rock hard for emerging market sovereign paper right now. Tha bases are loaded; it's time to take that pigskin and go in for the slam dunk." After that, some of the relationship bankers asked us to dial it back a notch, but somewhere, a recording of that call still exists.

Despite the request to tone down the antics, we continued to fuck around on the calls. A syndicate banker at Deutsche Bank even downloaded a soundboard of barnyard animal sounds. He started the next call off by apologizing profusely, saying, "I'm sorry if you can't hear me very well; I'm on the road today on a due diligence trip in Indonesia." Then he interrupted himself with the sounds of cows mooing and pigs oinking and apologized again. "I'm sorry about the noise."

The next week, it was my turn. I started off by apologizing for being on my mobile, even though I was sitting at my desk. Then, as I went through an update on market conditions, Deutsche would pipe in a rooster crowing, faintly at first, and then repeating it over and over, slightly louder each time. Part of the game was that I had to play along and come up with an elaborate explanation for whatever sound was played.

When I was interrupted by the sound of an aggressive dog barking, I politely explained that I was at the New Delhi airport and a wild animal had snuck into the terminal. "It looks rabid and is menacing this poor lady and her baby. Anyway, market conditions remain receptive to new issues as evidenced by the tight pricing and strong after-market performance of recent deals."

$20's are change, bro.

If you need an alarm clock, you need a new job.

Relationships are like a seesaw. If one of you gets too bored or too fat, the fun is over.

Why should I respect poor people? We live in a world that rewards achievement.

Hot girls will never know if they are actually interesting or not.

Letting the Bad Out

"**G**et the fuck out! Get the fuck out!" I am screaming at the top of my lungs. An intruder has me painfully chicken-winged with one arm twisted behind my back while he punches me in the head with his other hand. I manage to block most of his punches with my right hand, but my left arm feels like it is about to snap in half.

Some guy has broken into my apartment. This is Hong Kong, one of the safest cities in the world. Shock. Pain. Panic.

I scream out again, "Get the fuck out! Get the fuck out!" I try to pull away, but he's definitely got the upper hand. This is when I first realize that I'm also completely nude.

The intruder yells back, "Fuck you! Fuck you!" I manage to extend my left arm far enough to swing around with my right hand and clock this guy right in the temple. He doesn't go down, but he staggers back, releasing his hold of my left wrist in the process.

Now, it's a fair fight—at least fairer. I'm still a little bit wasted and, of course, somewhat exposed with my cock and balls flapping around. As I square up to fight, I notice that there

264   STRAIGHT TO HELL

are two of them, with the second intruder enjoying the show. This is probably not going to end well for me.

I throw another punch at the first guy and then retreat around to the other side of my dining room table. My punch has proven to be not particularly effective; I'm now cornered as they close in on me from both sides of the table.

"Fuck you. Take what you want and get out," I try to reason with them. They continue to converge on me. There's really no point in screaming because the typhoon-proof walls are made of concrete.

I decide to go on the offensive and lower my shoulder and barrel at the smaller of the two intruders, taking him out with a highlight-reel hit. From there, I race down the hallway toward my master bedroom. My plan is to lock myself in there and phone for help.

My apartment hallway isn't that long so the other guy is right on my heels. I make it inside, but right before I can slam the door shut behind me, he manages to wedge his arm inside the doorframe. I'm pushing and slamming the door against his arm; he's pushing with his shoulder to minimize the force, while also trying to muscle his way in. At this point, it's clear to me that these guys want more than my valuables. I have never experienced a feeling of such terror.

I'm fighting a losing battle, especially now that there are two of them pushing against the door. I relinquish my tenuous control of the doorway and jump across the bed to create some separation. Once again, they have me cornered.

"Fuck you. Get out!" one of the guys yells at me. Holy shit, are these guys on drugs?

"Fuck YOU! Get out!" I yell back.

One of the guys inches his way around the bed while the other one guards the doorway; I'm totally trapped. I grab the only defense I can find—a pillow—and launch it at the guy bearing down on me. It doesn't do shit. I throw the second and only remaining pillow within reach. But again, its impact is negligible, if not laughable. Finally, I grab the duvet with both hands and flip it up like a cartoon character casting a net, flinging it directly at his head.

This move is not entirely ineffective; the distraction gives me enough time to jump back across the bed and make my escape. Now I'm on the offensive once again, bounding over the bed, ready to launch myself at the guy standing in the doorway. I have already leveled this fucker once. There's no way he can handle another piece of me—a strong man, naked and fighting for his life, using the bed as a springboard to launch my escape right through him.

He offers little resistance as I lunge through the doorway and run back down the hallway. As I am running, my concept of time slows to a virtual halt and I am overcome by this epiphanous moment of clarity. *Hang on. That duvet cover that I just threw, that tasteless pattern . . . I'd never own sheets that disgusting. That can't be my bed.*

I make my way out to the living room. Holy shit, there's a leather couch and a bookshelf straight from an IKEA catalog. *Who decorated this fucking place? That dining table, what is that, wood veneer?* This is when it finally takes—this is not my apartment. The layout is identical, but I am definitely not in my apartment.

I head straight for the front door without stopping to collect my clothes, my wallet, my cell phone, anything. I make it out into the corridor; it looks familiar. *Okay, so I'm in my own apartment building.* I'm not sure if this is a good thing or a bad thing. I look across the hallway and see a familiar doormat and Chinese porcelain umbrella stand. *Not only am I in my building, I'm on my floor.*

I manage to make it into my apartment and bolt the door behind me before my neighbors make it out into the corridor—assuming they even followed me at all. I retreat to the safety and comfort of my own bed and considerably nicer sheets. It takes quite a long time for the foreign chemicals in my body to overcome the adrenaline of my misadventure. But eventually, I pass out.

The next morning, the bruises to my head, shoulder, arm, and wrist tell me that none of this was a dream. I lie in bed for hours, dreading the idea of having to go back across the hall, apologize, and ask for my clothes, wallet, and BlackBerry back.

Once I'm ready to face the music, I drag myself out of bed and head into a spare bedroom that I've converted into a walk-in closet. There I see yesterday's suit jacket hanging from my valet stand, my tie deliberately placed on top, with my BlackBerry and wallet neatly arranged on the adjacent dresser.

I have to remind myself that it couldn't have been just a dream; my head is about to explode and these bruises don't lie. The only conceivable explanation is that I must have come home, gone to bed purposely, and then had some kind of unfortunate drunken sleep-walking escapade. So it's not entirely my fault—this is back before anyone really understood the dangers of mixing alcohol, cocaine, Klonopin, Xanax, and Ambien.

After about a month of sneaking in and out of my apartment, I finally run into my neighbors in the lobby—two Australian guys I'd never met prior to the night of the incident. They recognize me right away. "Mate, fuck me, it was you after all?" But they're pretty cool about it—nothing a case of wine and an apology can't smooth over. All in all, I consider myself to be pretty lucky. If a Chinese family had lived there,

I'd probably be dead. If a woman had lived there alone, I'd probably be in jail.

I need someone to save me from myself, a grounding force in my life. I need a girlfriend.

The timing works out perfectly. Soon after this incident, an ex-girlfriend "coincidentally" transfers from New York to Hong Kong just a few months after finding out that I had moved here from London the year before. Her plan works, and just a month later, we're back together. I couldn't be happier or healthier. We have rekindled a volatile relationship and seemingly made it perfect.

Capital markets are booming in the post-SARS Asia; our jobs keep us busy and feeling satisfied and fulfilled. She works traditional investment banking hours, which means long nights, frequent business trips, and the occasional weekend in the office. I'm working sales and trading hours, which means 7:30 A.M. to around 7 P.M., or whenever we can hand over to New York. Occasionally, I'll have evening conference calls or will work late into the night if I am pricing a deal during New York hours.

We understand each other perfectly—the canceled plans, the late nights, the interrupted dinners, the stresses of a high-intensity job, and the priorities associated with being career focused and ambitious.

We're the perfect power couple, two mid-twenties bankers pulling down solid six-figure incomes. Life is good. The Four Seasons Langkawi only has a $2,500-per-night suite available over Easter? No problem. We don't like our main course entrées at L'Atelier de Joël Robuchon? Bring the menu back. The Armani bar won't let me in wearing shorts? There's an Armani store downstairs. My maid is stealing my $200 La Mer moisturizer? Good for her; skin care is important.

One of the best aspects of our relationship is that, given our respective schedules, we spend time with each other only two or three nights a week. There's always plenty to talk about and we generally don't get sick of each other. A quiet night at home watching a romantic comedy, something most guys dread, is a welcome respite for me after three or four nights in a row of wining and dining clients, or going out with colleagues and friends while she's working late.

Most nights, I am able to do as I please. I can have drinks and dinner with clients or friends and I'll still get home before she does. As long as I get home first, it doesn't even count as a night out.

Or, after a really rough day at the office, I might just be too exhausted to go out after work, or simply not be in the mood to be social with anybody. Thankfully, she's still at work, so I can play *Mario Kart* in peace while I blast my way through a six-pack.

A simple text from me saying, "Long day. Quick gym. Then home to wait for you," is all I need to pave the way for an unregistered night out. The only thing I need to watch out for is the occasional surprise text back, "Got out earlier than I thought," or "Gonna head home and do my conference call from there."

That's when I'll pound my drink, pay my tab, deflect the verbal abuse from my friends, grab a cab, race home, shower, brush, rinse, and then jump safely into bed with a prop—something weighty like Ron Chernow's biography of Alexander Hamilton—right before I hear her key in the front door. Perfect timing. This scenario's playing out time and time again is actually the genesis of the Warden nickname.

Of course, mistakes are bound to happen. It's not always possible to keep these worlds entirely separate. In fact, in Hong

Kong, it's impossible. The universe of expatriate bankers is exceptionally small. We all drink and eat at the same places, hang out at the same clubs, and live in the same neighborhoods. Despite Hong Kong being a city of seven million people, it's impossible to go out on any given evening and not run into someone you know.

The downside of living this dangerously is that I risk getting busted constantly, particular if I run into any of the Warden's colleagues. There are a couple of them who obviously want to sleep with her, so they've become famous for ratting me out. Other times, some half-wit will innocuously mention to her that they saw me out. Just like that, I'm in Château Bowwow. Thank God for spare bedrooms.

She constantly hears stories about me from her colleagues, and not just about debaucherous late-night exploits. Since I'm competing with them for business and sometimes even working with them on deals, our worlds are inescapably intertwined. This dynamic can go both ways. I'll be out with some hedge fund client, and he'll say, "Yo, I took a roadshow one-on-one for this Morgan Stanley high-yield deal. I want to bang that blond China coverage chick that came to the meeting," or I'll hear a colleague or another competitor say, "We're doing this property deal with Morgan Stanley. Man, that bitch is a cunt."

For the most part, I enjoy the few evenings and weekends that we do get to spend together. I just also enjoy my freedom and enough time to let some bad out. In addition to having a date night once or twice a week, we also try to meet for lunch every now and then.

Lunch dates are a dangerous precedent to set. I should have learned my lesson in London when I had a girlfriend from my analyst class who couldn't comprehend the notion of separation of work life and social life. Granted, I was sleeping with the girl who sat twenty feet away from me on the trading floor, so I guess I didn't either. Every time I'd come back to my desk from grabbing a sandwich with a colleague, there would be a message waiting from her: "I saw that. So you have time to have lunch with Kamal, but when I ask, you say you're too busy?"

Lunch dates with the Warden aren't any better. There's nothing fun about it, sitting there for an hour listening to her vent about coworkers I don't know or give a fuck about. *Listen, I don't give a shit if Andrew, some random fucktard on your execution team whom I've never met, gets AIDS and dies, let alone that he had the "audacity" to circulate a draft offering circular and list you last on the CC line of the email, even though you are the self-described "point person" on the deal. Not only is your story ten minutes too long, it's not even story worthy in the first place.*

On one such day, about thirty minutes before my dreaded Warden lunch, I get a Bloomberg from Ewan Hunt, the head of syndicate at UBS, inviting me out for a liquid lunch. I can either go meet my girlfriend and listen to her drone on about how great and underappreciated she is at her job, or I can share two or three bottles of wine with Ewan, a slightly irritating prick.

Ewan is undeniably smart and articulate, but he takes himself far too seriously. He once gave an interview to the *Wall Street Journal* about the quality of business hotel gyms and demanded that he be quoted. That's also what makes him so easy to fuck with.

If I'm on a client conference call with him on a deal, I'll refer to him as a vice president because I know he has this compulsion to immediately interrupt and clarify that he's an executive director. Or if I know he's dialing in to a call from an airport (which he likes to announce in an attempt to highlight his importance), I'll tell him to go on mute because we're getting a lot of terminal background noise. "That's not from me; it's quiet here in the first-class lounge." The entire syndicate community is well aware of the origin of the massive chip on Ewan's shoulder: his first wife left him for another woman.

I'm not really in the mood to have lunch with him today. "Sorry, dude. Short notice. No can do. Insufferable lunch with the bird already on the books." More important, if I cancel on her, I'll have to make it up to her tonight—and I already have plans.

After a bit of back-and-forth on Bloomberg chat, Ewan guilt-trips me into canceling on the Warden and joining him. "Okay, for fuck's sake." I feel bad for him. "See you at Dot Cod in twenty. I'll tell her that I have back-to-back conference calls and can't leave the desk. If you get there first, order a bottle of something decent."

We have a delightful lunch; as I said, aside from being completely self-absorbed, he is charming, well read, and intellectually curious. Three bottles of wine later, we reach the point of either staying out all afternoon and getting shit-faced, or going back to the office and finishing out the day. I choose the latter.

In the ten minutes it takes me to walk back to my desk, I have a Bloomberg message waiting from Ewan: "Good times. Any preference on what client I list you as when I expense it? ;)" I'd rather someone not treat me to a meal if they're just going to mention the fact that they paid for it. But that's typical Ewan.

Twenty minutes later, I get an email from my girlfriend with "FWD" in the subject line that simply says "WTF?" Ewan had forwarded her our entire Bloomberg conversation where I'm bemoaning my lunch dates with her and joking about lying to get out of it. "Is this really the guy you want to be with?" he wrote, and added, "I'm in town until tomorrow if you want to grab a drink. ;)"

Now, I've always known that he's had a thing for my girl-friend, but I never expected him to go this low. I do the only sensible thing I can do: I forward that email to every senior syndicate counterpart in Asia, introducing it with "FYI . . . Just in case you ever thought you could trust Ewan Hunt."

When it comes to relationships, sometimes other people are out to fuck me over. And sometimes, I just do it to myself. But in investment banking, it's often the job that fucks me over. Socializing with colleagues and clients is an important ingredient to having a successful career. Decadent dinners and alcohol- and drug-fueled nights out are a sell-side job requirement.

On one such innocuous evening, the Warden sends me an email letting me know that she's working late and has to can-cel our date night. Perfect. I respond with feigned disappoint-ment and tell her that I'll probably head to the gym and then have a quiet night at home. I'm in decent shape, but based on the number of times I use the gym as an alibi, I should be a swimsuit model.

I make plans to meet a client and a few friends for drinks and dinner. It's a fairly simple plan—a free pass to eat and drink as much as I want and then go home, shower, and pass out. As long as I can do this before she finishes work, it's like it never happened.

It works like a charm—drink, eat, drink, pass out. The next morning, I wake up at 6:45 A.M. and tiptoe out of the bed so as to not disturb her. I'm usually out the door around 7:15 A.M., whereas she generally doesn't head to the office until about 9:30. If she's stirring after I've showered and suited up, I'll kiss her good morning.

"Just fucking go. Do you remember last night?"

Normally, I know better than to respond to this question. There's no upside in volunteering information that is potentially more damaging than what she might already know. However, this vague recollection of having texted her comes back to me. A simple message, "Exhausted. Off to bed. 143." I specifically remember sending her this text before I got too wasted, even though my night was just getting started.

This recollection gives me enough confidence to roll the dice. "What? I went to the gym and ran into a friend on my way out. He convinced me to grab a few drinks and then I was so exhausted that I came home early and went to bed."

"Okay. So you don't remember me, having worked all fucking night, coming home at two A.M.? Then I guess you don't remember me being bolted out of the apartment and knocking and banging on the door and calling your phone for thirty minutes? So then, I guess you don't remember the doorman having to call a locksmith who didn't show up for another hour? Only for me to come in and find you passed the fuck out?"

Mistakes are bound to happen from time to time. The remarkable thing is that despite this kind of reckless and selfish behavior being the norm, it's really a testament to how much I care about her that I am able to avoid incidents like this from occurring more often.

An almost identical scenario occurs just a few months later. After a particularly challenging deal, I head out early for drinks with a hedge fund client and Charlie, our sales guy who covers him.

After a few drinks, the client heads home. The Warden is working late again so Charlie and I decide to grab dinner at a tapas bar in SoHo. Over the next couple of hours, we have five bottles of wine between the two of us. We contemplate going out after dinner, but I want to get home before the Warden to avoid another slipup. Cutting a night short is way better than adding to her scorecard of how many nights out I've had in any given week. And after five bottles of wine, we're both dangerously close to flipping the switch, from which there is no turning back.

Walking out of the restaurant, Charlie trips and falls down the stairs. He's out cold, totally lifeless, other than the blood slowly pooling around his head. I don't know what to do; he's not moving and I'm incapable of providing any kind of assistance. Anybody entering or exiting from the restaurant is forced to step over his motionless body. Even though he's my good friend, it's fucking hilarious.

Within a few minutes, the police have arrived along with the paramedics in an ambulance. They manage to drag Charlie outside, prop him against the curb, and then wake him up with some smelling salts. He is adamant about refusing treatment and becomes increasingly belligerent with the paramedics and the cops.

The shouting escalates and evolves into pushing and shoving as they attempt to restrain Charlie. He looks over at me. "Dude, let's fucking bolt." With that, we sprint down the steep cobblestone alleyway and slip into the darkness before finding a taxi a few blocks down. Worried that he might pass out and never wake up, I convince him to stay over at my place.

The next morning, like clockwork, 7 A.M. comes and I'm showering and suiting up. Charlie's still passed out on my couch. "Yo, you gotta go home. You're gonna be late." I don't even bother to slow down on my way out; there's no time for a recap. But I do notice that there's no sign of the Warden. *Damn, did she pull an all-nighter in the office? I might be totally in the clear.*

By 7:30 A.M., I am in my seat leading the syndicate portion of the daily credit sales call. I'm impressed to see that Charlie, sitting three rows over, has managed to make it in on time, even if he is unshaven and glassy-eyed.

Around 9 A.M., I get a call from the Warden. "I just want to let you know that I am going to be late for work because I'm sitting here trying to scrub blood out of the cashmere throw that my grandmother gave me." Fuck, I forgot to check the spare bedroom before I left my apartment, although that's probably a good thing.

"Listen, baby, I'm really sorry but I can't have this conversation right now—"

She cuts me off and continues her tirade. "Do you realize that I came home at one A.M., exhausted, only to find a half-dressed bloody corpse on our couch? I guess I should have expected it after the bloody handprints on the door and the trail of blood that greeted me once I got inside. What a fucking fantastic way for me to get home."

The fire in my ear is matched only by the commotion of people now standing behind Charlie. He's either numb or still too drunk to have noticed, but it would appear, based on the reactions around him, that the wound on his head has split open again and blood is oozing down his neck and soaking the back of his shirt.

I interrupt the Warden. "Is my Minotti couch stained?"

"Fuck you." *Click.* I look up again to see Charlie being led out of the trading floor and off to the hospital.

Despite all of these ups and downs, my relationship with the Warden survives. One of the primary benefits to me is that she saves me from myself. Who knows what would happen if I didn't spend so much time trying to adhere to the image of me that she wants to believe in. The wheels would probably come off, as they certainly tended to do whenever she took a business trip.

Since we always vacation together, I never really enjoy the benefit of any extended freedom. Very occasionally, I'll hit the jackpot with her getting sent on a two-week global roadshow. Warden-free weekends are rare, but to have two in a row, that's a cause for celebration.

On one such eclipse, I make some plans with a few friends for Sunday brunch and some day drinking. A typical Sunday with the Warden is dreadful by comparison—a long hike followed by a sober brunch, a foot massage, and an afternoon shopping. The vibe is so much more laid-back without her mimosa counting. We're having a blast and drinking every drink like it's almost last call. One of our friends, whom we had arranged to meet up with, pulls up in a new BMW M3 convertible. He won't shut the fuck up about the new car. "Yeah, man, like I've been thinking about pulling the trigger on a 3 Series for months. But when I went down to the dealership yesterday, they had this baby, so I just said fuck it, and I lifted the offer on the spot. How fucking crazy is that?"

Four hours of drinking later, I can't take it anymore. "Dude, shut the fuck up about buying a car every Asian kid in college drives." I pay my tab, walk out, hail a cab, and head over to the street in Wan Chai where most of the car dealerships are located. I wasn't doing it out of spite; I simply realized that Hong Kong, as a tropical island, would be a pretty awesome place to have a convertible.

I stumble into a dealership, grab a sales guy, and point at the only convertible in the showroom. "If you can connect me with an insurance agent, and if I can take it home today, I'll take it."

Twenty minutes of paperwork later, I am the owner of a cherry-red Maserati convertible. To honor his end of the agreement, the sales guy drives me home in my new car; he knows I am in no shape to get behind the wheel.

I justify the impulse purchase by convincing myself that driving is going to become a new hobby of mine—it's more fun than going out drinking and, over the long run, costs substantially less. In college, I used similar logic to rationalize why a PlayStation was a phenomenal investment.

I decide to start off day one as a car owner by driving to the office. Typically, a taxi takes five minutes from my apartment building. Today, it takes five minutes just to get out of my parking garage, five minutes to drive, and another five minutes to park below Citi Tower. It turns out that the paddle shifters, a novelty at the time, aren't really that much fun in heavy traffic.

That evening, I've got client drinks, a dinner, and more drinks, which forces me to abandon the idea of driving home. The following evening, I decide to drive out to the Black Sheep, a restaurant in Shek O, a sleepy fishing village on the opposite side of Hong Kong Island. Two of my friends want to join, but I've got room for only one. We have a great time, but I don't really enjoy watching other people get wasted, especially when the Warden is out of town.

The week rolls by and I love the car, but so far, I don't think I've even been out of third gear. That Saturday night, I get home from a reasonably low-key night out around 2 A.M.; it's low-key in the sense that I remember getting home. Come 4 A.M., I can't sleep. I know if I pop a Xanax and Ambien now, my entire Sunday will be fucked, and I've already made plans to meet some friends at the beach.

I decide to greet the day with an early-morning drive. I start off in the Mid-Levels and head down through Central toward the Harbor Tunnel, which connects Hong Kong Island with the New Territories and Mainland China. As soon as I blow through the Autotoll lane without stopping, I'm on the clock to see how long it will take me to drive from Hong Kong to China. This trip usually takes just under an hour without traffic. I make it in twenty-four minutes. Once I get to the China border, I turn around and come back, this time making it in twenty-two minutes.

I'm gradually getting more and more confident. I'm passing what few cars are on the road like they're standing still. It's like I'm playing a video game. Having beat the highway level, now it's time for the mountain course.

It sounds dangerous—I'm not used to driving on the left side of the road while sitting on the right side of a car. I'm still getting used to using the paddles. I've been up all night. It's after 5 A.M. at this point so more and more cars are starting to come out. And now, it's starting to rain. But racing along the winding mountainous roads is actually pretty easy. There's not much traffic so I can live in the middle of the road, which makes taking the corners at high speed exhilarating.

After an hour or so of this, it's getting light out and the roads are starting to get busy; it's time to head home. I make my way down from the mountain track and back to the highway. Even though I'm heading home, I still have this race car driver mentality, aggressively weaving in and out of the traffic.

I'm coming up fast in the middle lane on what looks like a Mercedes C-Class. No need to slow down; I move across into the left lane in order to blow by this guy. As I make my move to pass him, I shift into fourth gear and accelerate to really put an exclamation point on it. In Hong Kong, since you drive on the left side, you should pass on the right, their fast lane. Not smart on my part—all the rainwater has run off the road to the left side. So as I attempt to accelerate by him, I lose all traction on the left tires and just start spinning out of control.

All this guy sees as I blow by him is my taillights, then my headlights, then my taillights, and then my headlights. I have no idea how many times I spin around, but it's not enough to slow me down that much. I careen across all three lanes right in front of him, hit the concrete divider head-on, and bounce back into the middle of the road.

None of this happens with any sense of clarity. All I can remember is losing control and starting to spin. The next thing I know I'm staring at an air bag and the entire car is filled with smoke. My car is a smoking, crumpled heap, sitting in the middle of the road, with debris strewn across all three lanes.

Mr. C-Class slows down, probably to make sure that I'm not dead. But when I look over at him, he sneers, offers a wave that is unequivocally sarcastic, rolls down his window, yells, "Ma fan gweilo!" (troublesome white devil), and speeds off.

I get out without a scratch, fortunate to have hit the concrete divider head-on. I walk around and inspect the damage; the car is fucked. At this point, there's not really much I can do about it.

The three lanes of traffic now have to converge into a single makeshift lane along the shoulder in order to get around me. Up until the accident, I hadn't recalled there being this many cars out on the road. That's when I see a taxi waiting in the line of cars trying to get by. He doesn't want to stop for me so I physically stand in front of his cab to prevent him, and everyone behind him, from moving.

As I jump in, I give him my home address in polite Cantonese.

"No hospital?" he says.

I shake my head. He says, "You drink? I call police."

"No. No. No drink."

"I call police anyway." There is no chance he believes me.

"No. No. No police. One thousand Hong Kong dollars okay?"

Fifteen minutes later, I'm asleep in my bed. A few hours after that, I'm at the beach, beer in hand, with a new story to tell. At this point, there's nothing I can do to change what happened so no point in spoiling the rest of my weekend.

Monday morning, I call the sales guy at the dealership. "Dude, I need your help. I need you to find my car."

"Okay. Where is it?"

"I had some engine trouble early Sunday morning. I left it on the side of the road. But I'm not sure where. Can you just find it for me?" I'm at my desk on the trading floor, so I'm trying to be discreet.

"Okay. Okay. I find it for you." About three hours later, he calls me back. "Okay. Okay. I think you crash your car, yes? It is in police impound. You have to go there with ID and fill out a police report. Do you know leaving the scene of accident is a criminal offense in Hong Kong? You very lucky this not in *Apple Daily* [the Hong Kong equivalent of the *New York Post*]."

This proposed solution doesn't really work for me. "I can't do that. I'm too busy. Just do me a favor and figure it out. I don't care what it takes, but I'm not going there in person, and I'm not filling out a police report. I paid you a lot of money for this car. Just figure it out."

About an hour later, he calls me back. "Hey, I don't know if you are going to like this but think I might have found a solution. Just between us."

"Hold up. Hold up. Lemme call you back from my cell." I hang up the recorded line, grab a spare conference room, and call him back from my cell phone. This is where my Maserati story has to come to an abrupt end. Suffice to say, despite having heard all about my new car, my girlfriend never gets to see it. And she definitely never gets the real story. It would be disastrous to arm the Warden with this kind of ammunition to throw back in my face.

The warning signs are all there for both of us—objectively, this is a terribly dysfunctional relationship. She wants the person I am 20% of the time 100% of the time. I find myself getting increasingly excited every time she works late or goes out of town.

Even when we go out together for drinks or dinner with my friends, it becomes a game. Any time she goes to the bathroom or steps outside to take a work call, my friends and I will all do a quick shot. Of course, at the end of the night, after six or seven off-the-record shots, I'll have to put up with her saying, "Jesus, you're this wasted from two glasses of wine. I told you you're allergic to alcohol." But it's worth it. She already thinks I have a slow metabolism. Now she also thinks I'm a lightweight.

The trouble is that it's just so convenient and comfortable. We're both too busy with our jobs to worry about any major changes in our personal lives. Sometimes, it's just nice to have this part of life figured out, even if it's not perfect.

Replacement is also a real issue for me. I have no problem dating Asian girls; God knows I'm an equal opportunity employer. But historically speaking, nature has seemingly instilled in me a specific affinity for buxom blondes. Nearly all the white women in Asia are married. The rest are older thirtysomething Europeans, transient Americans, or big-boned Australian rugby chicks who'd violate my adherence to the Mickey Mantle Rule—*I only date broads with small hands. Makes my cock look bigger.* There's a small group of second-rate eastern European models who are sent to Asia for short-term modeling gigs, but they're just one roofie away from waking up as hookers in Dubai or North Korea.

So the Warden and I persevere. With adequate time to let the bad out, I can enjoy a vacation from myself and happily pretend to be the person she wants me to be when we are together.

Then Barney Frank's financial crisis comes along and destroys everything. Credit markets become completely dysfunctional. We are faced with shorter and shorter windows to get deals done, followed by prolonged periods, weeks and months, where absolutely nothing happens.

I'm spinning my wheels in the office, finding the end of the Internet every morning by 10 A.M., taking a long lunch to hit the gym or drink with my equally bored and frustrated colleagues and counterparts. We'll then spend the afternoon playing Bloomberg chat room trivia (a game I invented), or doing inane things like syndicate-wide haiku contests.

The only productive thing I can do when markets are completely frozen is develop stronger relationships with my buy-side clients. This means longer lunches, boozier dinners, more frequent nights out, and the occasional golfing trip to Macau.

Other causalities of the crisis are my girlfriend's weekly trips to Korea or China, the frequent global roadshows, and the all-nighters in the office. Now, she wants to plan dinners every night and romantic getaways every weekend.

We liked each other so much more when it was just two or three days a week. Now, I find myself waiting for her to fall asleep so that I can sneak out of bed, play *Madden* on the PlayStation, and enjoy a few beers.

She's getting to see the person I am the other 80% of the time, and I'm getting to know the person she is 100% of the time. And we hate each other.

Finally, neither of us can take it anymore. We decide that the best thing to do is try yet another trial separation. The next day, I move out of the apartment we recently moved into together and into the Four Seasons.

The Four Seasons is amazing. I can walk to work. I've got a rooftop infinity pool overlooking all of Hong Kong harbor and Kowloon. I can get Michelin-starred room service. I don't have a midweek curfew or need to worry about alibis and having to make apologies in the form of Graff earrings. Best of all, "I live in the Four Seasons" is an amazing pickup line for Cantonese girls.

The Warden retains full-time custody of my maid, who meets me in the lobby every Monday morning at 7 A.M. to pick up all of my dirty laundry and to give me a suitcase full of clean clothes. I might be living in one of the nicest hotels in the world, but I'm not going to pay for their laundry services. Amazingly, I'm not alone in this ritual. I see several other maids in the lobby, suitcases in tow, also waiting for their respective employers. Hong Kong truly is a destroyer of *gweilo* marriages.

Apparently, I still had a lot more bad to get out of my system. After nearly six months of living the life of a touring rock star, I receive this email from Four Seasons management:

From: ██████@██████.com

To: John Lefevre

Date: Tue, Jul 20, 2010 at 5:59 PM

Subject: Four Seasons Place—Room 4827

Importance: High

Dear Mr. Lefevre,
Hope this email finds you well.

As per our previous communication through phone, I am very sorry to inform you that our management would not like to consider your extension of Room 4827 because we have received six serious complaints during your current stay with us. Please be so kind to understand that you will have to check-out on 26 July 2010 according to your current contract. According to your previous request, please find the following details of the glitch report for your information.

Date of incident: 07/16/2010

Time of incident: 08:37 PM

Location of incident: FSP 48/f guest lift lobby

Details of incident: Guest from Room 4827 walked out from taxi and shouting to the taxi driver in the FSP entrance. Security accompanied the guest to his room. Upon arrival on 48/F, the guest was over react and kept yelling in the corridor by using foul language. Security tried to stopped the guest but not success. After 15 minutes, guest went back to his room.

Date of incident: 07/09/2010

Time of incident: 01:45 AM

Location of incident: FSP concierge

Details of incident: At 0145 hrs, Mr Lefevre was intoxicated. Security escorted Mr Lefevre to Rm 4827. When Mr Lefevre opened the Rm 4827 door, he refused to stay and said he was bored, started to use foul language to talk to Security Team. Mr Lefevre attempted to assault security personnel. Security Team suppressed Mr Lefevre and brought him to FSP lobby. At 0245hrs, Mr Lefevre was chased by three police officers and two IFC securities from IFC escalator to FSP concierge gate. Mr Lefevre was using foul language to talk to the police officers with physical contact. AM speak to calm police officers. The guest returned to room 4827.

Date of incident: 06/17/2010

Time of incident: 10:25 PM

Location of incident: FSP 59/F Swimming pool area

Details of incident: At 2225 hrs, Mr Lefevre was found sleeping on the beach chair. Security tried to wake him up, however he had no response.

Date of incident: 05/29/2010

Time of incident: 09:20 PM

Location of incident: Hotel Driveway

Details of incident: At around 2120 hrs, Security was informed that guest is in Hotel driveway. FSP guest Mr. Lefevre, who seems to be intoxicated was inside the taxi

(JS2953) but didn't settle the taxi fare. FSP AM settled the taxi fare and Mr Lefevre was escorted to the room by Security.

Date of incident: 05/21/2010

Time of incident: 09:15 PM

Location of incident: FSP 59/F Swimming Pool

Details of incident: At 2208 hrs, guest from FSP Rm 4827 (Mr. Lefevre) was eating sushi and drinking with female guest in the swimming pool on 59/F.

Date of incident: 05/16/2010

Time of incident: 06:15 PM

Location of incident: FSP Lobby and 59/F

Details of incident: At 1815 hrs, Security was informed a intoxicated guest who was showing up at the FSP lobby with no shirt. FSP AM stopped the guest and advised him return and put a shirt on before to the IFC mall. The guest obliged and returned to room 4827—(Mr Lefevre) who was escorted by AM.

If you have any enquiries, please feel free to contact me at any time.

Thank you for your kind understanding!

———————————————

Best Regards,
Vicky ▓▓▓
Four Seasons Place Hong Kong / Leasing Executive

Not only are they banning me for being a terrible human being, they have politely complied with my request to prove it in writing. My favorite part of the email is that they begin it with "Hope this email finds you well" and end it with "Thank you for your kind understanding!"

One month after being expelled from the Four Seasons, I was offered the job of head of Asia debt syndicate at Goldman Sachs.

Listening is part waiting for your turn to speak and part reminding yourself to change facial expressions every 10 seconds.

The greatest nicknames for people are the ones they have no idea that they have.

On Valentine's Day, send your girl flowers anonymously. If she doesn't mention anything, dump her.

I am not inappropriate. You are just fucking boring.

"Vegetarian" is an ancient derogatory term for an idiot who couldn't fish or hunt.

A Long Day

From about the middle of 2007, the cracks are really starting to emerge. Credit markets are completely dislocated and dysfunctional, with market execution windows opening and closing violently and with little provocation. New deals are few and far between. I am able to get a contentious deal done in June but then nothing again until September, when I hit an improbable home run with a Chinese high-yield private placement that nets us $6 million in fees.

And then, just like that, the market slams shut again. Come October, the contagion finally reaches equities, and investor risk appetite evaporates overnight. It's lights out; we might as well shut up shop for the rest of the year.

I don't really care. I've more than made my budget for the year, so a few more deals won't really move the needle on my number (bonus) much anyway. I'm happy to kill the rest of Q4 taking longer lunches, arranging client meetings at bars, making unnecessary trips to Jakarta and Seoul, or simply playing Bloomberg chat room trivia with my equally bored counterparts at rival firms.

Everything is fairly calm, except for the fact that we all know "it" is coming.

The way things work with layoffs or redundancies on a trading floor is that once team heads have been asked to update revenue estimates (budgets) for the purpose of evaluating head counts, rumors and fear start to spread and people will obsessively speculate on how long it will be before a few unfortunate souls get "the tap" on the shoulder or "the call" to go meet HR in a conference room upstairs.

Information and rumors travel at light speed on a trading floor, across Wall Street, and then around the globe; after the first tap and formal confirmation, everyone knows. Occasionally, there's a false alarm. By the time poor Jignesh comes back upstairs from an all-too-leisurely trip to Starbucks, someone has already called dibs on the HP financial calculator he left on his desk, and people as far away as London and Tokyo are reading his obituary. "Sorry, dude, I thought you got shit-canned" has to be one of my favorite all-time apologies.

Usually, we don't make mistakes, and when the real day comes, it's no joke—the typical banter between guys making millions of dollars quickly disappears. It's probably the only day when there are no minifootballs being tossed at analysts' heads, no prank phone calls being made, and no bets being wagered on how many push-ups the Muslim research analyst can do while he's fasting for Ramadan. (That motherfucker cost me $800.)

Heading into year-end, the gossip proliferates, the speculation builds, and the tension swells. Every morning we'll come in to rumors that the bloodbath has started overnight in New York and a few names will get tossed around. "But he's still on Bloomberg," one guy will say, or "I can still see him in the system."

The quickest way to confirm the rumor is to send the person in question an email, because as soon as someone is fired, the IT guys swoop in and suspend their account. If the email bounces back as undeliverable, then you have your verification. So we invent stupid reasons to email our friends (and foes) in the New York office. It's almost like a game, trying to be the first person to confirm that so-and-so got canned. My strategy is always to send out a mass email to a distribution list, an entire department, sales desk, or deal team. Fishing with dynamite.

News of this magnitude is met with the full gamut of emotion, or sometimes just complete indifference: "Fuck him" or "That's too bad" or "Sweet, our share of the bonus pool's getting bigger" or even "Do you think I could get a good deal on his GT3?"

I get my first "undeliverable" message back. Fuck me. It's my good friend Dennis Lipton. He gave up one of the hottest fixed-income seats in Asia to take a job back in New York on the mortgage desk—of all places to be when 2008 rolls around. And boom, just like that, he gets fired, just a few weeks before bonus communication day, all for being at the wrong place at the wrong time.

So it's confirmed. The great RIF (Reduction in Force) of 2007–2008 has started. And from everything we are hearing out of New York, it's fucking bad.

One of the first things I do to get confirmation in Asia is to have my secretary call and try to make a conference room reservation on the fiftieth floor, which is where we have most of our formal client meetings. If there is going to be a big RIF, HR will book the entire block of rooms to prevent bankers from inadvertently holding a client meeting close by. It's not good for business for a client to see a teary-eyed banker turning in his BlackBerry on his way out.

The entire process is always a bit shrouded in mystery, given the seriousness and sensitivities involved. Even many MDs

294 STRAIGHT TO HELL

don't have a clue what's going to happen. Also, banks don't like it when the media find out about big layoffs because it sends the wrong message to the market and to shareholders. "This is a normal part of our annual process where we cull the bottom 10%" is our party line, which is obviously better than the reality, that revenue is down, and going forward, we're way overstaffed for the business that we expect to generate in the next few years.

My secretary confirms that all the conference rooms upstairs are blocked off all afternoon.

For the most part, everyone is nervous, primarily because we've all seen our share of injustice when it comes to redundancies. Beyond revenue production and performance reviews, sometimes it just comes down to sheer numbers and politics. Guys will get fired for being too senior, aka FIFO (First In, First Out). Or a guy might have just come across from Morgan Stanley with a fat guarantee the previous year and now has nothing but a big target on his back, aka LIFO (Last In, Fuck Off).

In the case of Dennis, there's plain bad luck. In tough times, if the powers that be in New York have an opinion, informed or otherwise, that certain areas of a traditionally lucrative business are going to be down the following year or two, they'll arbitrarily cull a large chunk of an entire team, rock stars included, just to satisfy head count pressure and ultimately to protect their own bonuses.

Everyone (myself included) is nervous and, to the extent possible, empathetic. The phones still ring. The dealerboards still light up. But people tend to be a bit slower and more apprehensive picking up the lines today. It's not even 10 A.M. and I've had five coffees, just because people can't sit still and keep volunteering to make Starbucks runs.

Inequity aside, people on Wall Street generally know where they stand. They know how much revenue they've generated; they know what they got paid last year, and they hear about what Mr. Aston-Martin-in-the-Parking-Garage got paid. Most guys are smart and objective enough to be mentally prepared for the ax. They have their wallet and keys in their pocket instead of in their drawer, their jacket is close by, and they've forwarded their email contacts to their personal account weeks ago.

And then it starts. The first guy leaves and doesn't come back. Another guy, youthful and exuberant, disappears looking like Tom Hanks from *Big*, only to come back thirty minutes later looking like Tom Hanks from *Philadelphia*. He collects his things, quietly nods, and walks out.

Time drags on. Other than on 9/11, I've rarely heard a trading floor with two hundred people so quiet; the unfamiliar patter of nervous fingers on keyboards has never been so irritating. That's when I hear Tony Paolini, our head of structured products, screeching into the phone with his high-pitched Italian accent, "Listen." But the way he says it, it sounds more like "Leeesin."

"Leeesin . . . Leeesin . . . No, you leeesin to me . . . Does it have the black seats with the red stitching, or the red seats with the black stitching?"

Everybody hears him, and most people are a bit confused and bewildered, but I know exactly what he's talking about. All I can do is make eye contact with a couple of guys three rows over to see if they are getting this too. Yes, they are. We exchange glances, shaking our heads and laughing silently to each other in disbelief.

I consider Tony to be a friend and a likable person—intelligent, funny, condescending and arrogant for a reason, and yet also oblivious to the feelings of others, totally unapologetic, and seemingly quite proud of all of this. So I'm not surprised by his obtuseness to the situation. He's just one of those guys who is missing a sensitivity chip, and maybe that's what makes him a good trader. Over the summer, almost on a daily basis, he would shout over at any intern, "Hey, Rick [there was no Rick], how about a Starbucks run." He'd then announce to anyone within earshot that he was buying coffees and then, without even thinking about it, dismissively throw the intern a HK$100 bill [US$13]: "Coffees are on me, guys." This poor kid would then have to take orders that would often total three times that amount and just have to eat the difference himself. Imagine being some lowly college kid, losing US$20–30 a day on coffee runs, just because some guy who gets paid comfortably in the seven figures doesn't give a shit. They're fighting to secure one of a handful of full-time offers into the analyst program, so of course none of them has the balls to say or do anything about it, and rightly so. But, for the record, and to my credit, once this was brought to my attention, a few of us started quietly subsidizing the interns on Paolini's coffee runs.

Today, assuming (and probably knowing) that he's not getting fired, Tony Paolini is just being himself. He continues into the phone, at this point practically yelling, "I ordered this fucking car six months ago. I was very clear. I want black suede seats with the red stitching." In case people still didn't get it, he slams his receiver down on the desk. "Fucking Ferrari. Man, I can't believe this shit."

His having caused a small disruption, the trading floor, four rows in every direction, is now standing and staring right at him. Five seconds later, a young VP sitting two seats down from Tony, having just received "the call," puts on his jacket,

gives a half-wave acknowledgment (now that everyone's looking in his direction), and then walks out, never to return.

"Oh . . . Fuck . . . Sorry, dude," Paolini says in a slow, drawn-
out, intentionally loud whisper. And then he just laughs, clearly
proud of what he considers to be perfect, albeit coincidental,
comedic timing.

Aside from a few times in 2001, when we were still reeling
from the aftermath of the dot-com bubble and in the midst
of the Enron and WorldCom debacles, I don't recall any other
days that have come even remotely close to being as bad as
this one.

I make it through the day without incident. Most of us decide to head out pretty early for a few well-deserved drinks,
and by that I mean to get shit-faced.

It's not uncommon for some of the fired employees to throw
themselves an impromptu party that same day by heading to
the nearest bar, opening up a tab, and spreading word that
they're buying drinks for anyone who cares to join them. It's
almost a point of pride, as a way of demonstrating that they
are taking the news like a champ, and are confident and secure
enough that it doesn't bother them too much. I assume they
don't want to go straight home and face their Warden equivalent. I know I wouldn't.

After a few hours of solid drinking, I decide to go back upstairs to my desk and catch up on a few things. After all, I hadn't
done shit all day. And Friday nights out aren't really my thing; I
much prefer a big night out on a Tuesday or Wednesday when
the amateurs and weekend riffraff are all at home or at work.

Around 9 P.M., the glass doors that separate the private side
(investment banking) of the Chinese Wall and the public side
(sales and trading) open and a young banking analyst, Carol,
walks onto the deserted trading floor and over to me. She is

working on a last-minute presentation and needs me to opine on pricing for a specific credit, provide recommendations in terms of a theoretical deal structure, and highlight what anchor investors we'd target—a fairly standard pitch for a company looking to raise money via the public bond market. How she knew I was still in the office, God only knows.

Truth be told, Carol is a pathetic specimen, so much so that even I have always felt sorry for her. She works at least six days a week, usually sixteen-plus-hour days, and sometimes through the night. Naturally unattractive and metabolically challenged, it doesn't help that she is forced to eat most of her meals at her desk and clearly never has time for the gym. On top of her having the body of an indolent hippo, her morose demeanor reminds me of a severely depressed zoo primate. Moreover, she is slow-witted and annoying and always seems to need something at the worst possible times, like trying to talk to me when I'm on a pricing call, or pestering Andy for trading levels in the middle of a some credit event shit-storm.

One day, she's hovering behind right as I'm cramming for an imminent client update call. "Not now, Carol. I'm busy," I say to the enormous shadow, without bothering to look away from my screens. Yet, she doesn't fucking move. That's when my dealerboard lights up; it's Andy.

"Hey dude, I know you're busy, but I've got a quick question: What do you call a fat Chinese person?" He pauses, stands up two rows over to make eye contact and flash me a big grin. Oh boy, here it comes. "A chunk." *Click.* I can still hear him laughing across the floor.

I frequently wonder how and why Carol manages to carry on living. Adding to her miserable existence is the fact that her boss, Benny Lo, is a tyrannical, abusive sociopath. He is such a pedantic piece of shit that most good analysts refuse to work for him. He is famous for taking a red pen to pitch books, making unnecessary changes, and then three hours and five iterations of the draft later, screaming, "What's wrong with you? This is all fucking wrong," and then changing it back to what the analyst had put in the first draft.

Fortunately for her, it's been a rough day, so I'm feeling particularly sympathetic. I'm a little drunk, and on a Friday night alone in the office, I've got nothing else to do. I handhold her through a few slides, marking up changes, reviewing a theoretical roadshow and marketing strategy, and explaining the optimal way to position the credit versus its peers. This is probably the nicest and most helpful I can remember being to any of the pitch-book monkeys from the origination team.

As she goes to leave, she says, "Thank you. Thank you so so much." And then she just breaks down and starts to cry. Oh fuck. I don't even like to put up with this shit from my girlfriend, and she's hot. And fucks me. Sometimes.

"Jesus. What's wrong? Is everything okay?" On a day like today, I'm being sincere.

"I'm sorry," she says while trying to exhale a sigh of relief from her mouth and simultaneously inhale through her nose as if to retract the tears and mucus and whatever else has been welling up inside of her. Whatever it is, it's not pretty. "It's just that I really thought I was going to get fired today. I know I make a lot of mistakes and people don't think very highly of me. But I just don't deal well with pressure, and I've been working pretty much nonstop. It's been really really hard."

She pauses, proceeds to sit down next to me, and then continues.

"But I'm trying and I'm getting better, and I'm going to keep getting better. So I guess I am just really relieved that I didn't get fired today, because I'm not even really sure what I'd do if I did get fired. I'm sorry. I'm just so relieved that I made it. Thanks again for all of your help." And with that she walks away, this poor, lonely girl.

I am genuinely moved. But as things go in this world, this would be the last time I would ever see her. First thing on Monday morning, she is fired.

It turns out that she was supposed to be fired with everyone else on Friday. But her boss didn't want to pull the trigger then because he had a hugely important pitch on Monday morning that he needed her to put together for him, which is why she was coming to me for help in the first place. So her boss made her work late into the night Friday and all day Saturday and Sunday in order to finish the presentation. With her new-found determination and reinvigorated spirit, she even pulled an all-nighter on Saturday night. And that's rarely supposed to happen.

So then, come Monday, her gutless boss called into the office from the road, asked to speak to another managing director, and said, "Hey, it's Benny. I'm not going to be able to make it back from this bake-off in time to come into the office. So can you please do me a favor and just go ahead and touch base with HR and then fire Carol for me, mmm'kay? Thanks."

And that was the end of it.

Fuck you, Benny. Mmm'kay? You're lucky the lawyers made me change your name.

If you're not dead to at least one person, you're not living right.

This morning's green tea cancels out last night's fifteen beers.

You shouldn't retire until your money starts making more money than you made in your best year.

I would agree with you, but then we'd both be wrong.

Every guy I know has paid for sex. One way or the other.

Making It Rain

The expatriate banking community in Asia is exceptionally close, with huge overlap between professional and personal relationships. Most of my good friends work in finance and are colleagues, competitors, or clients.

When one of the more notorious hedge fund managers announces that he's getting married, it's a big deal. The wedding party is a competition and demonstration of influence. I remember our boss saying, "Hey, Smithers, I hear your counterpart at Deutsche Bank is one of the groomsmen. Where the fuck are you?" That's a fairly aggressive way of insinuating that our client must be giving a lot more business to one of our main competitors.

With the Warden, I was never allowed to go to bachelor parties, missing out on trips to Taiwan, Vegas, Bangkok, Jakarta, and a few other "golf weekends." I did manage to sneak in a Macau stag party under the umbrella of a FBT.

The weekend is a big deal. Bankers and hedge fund managers are flying in from Singapore, Hong Kong, Sydney, London, and New York. Our home base for the weekend is the Shangri-La hotel in Makati City, an area of metro Manila and the main financial hub of the Philippines. Why would someone want to have a bachelor party in a landlocked swamp turned financial district outside of downtown Manila? The place is crawling with love monkeys.

It's my first time there. I have a colleague who usually calls dibs on the Manila business trips. Given his infatuation with love monkeys and the fact that he still lives with his parents, I don't object.

The weekend festivities kick off in local style—a private jitney from the hotel to the Hobbit House. Not to be confused with the Hampton Jitney, a Manila jitney is a semi-open-air hybrid between a taxi and a bus, constructed from old World War II vehicles that the US government abandoned in the Philippines at the end of the war. They have become a ubiquitous symbol of the local culture and tend to be ornately painted and operated by colorful street entrepreneurs. Typically, they are used to haul lower-class people long distances to their soul-crushing jobs, while crammed into an aluminum cattle car and forced to endure sweltering heat, shocking pollution, and agonizing traffic. Tonight, the jitney is like a Disney ride tour of the Valley of Ashes for a dozen investment bankers, most of whom clear seven-figure bonuses.

When our driver pulls into the Shangri-La and sees our group standing there, his eyes light up. He knows he's in for a night of abuse and torture, but he'll come away with more than an extra month's salary in his pocket. After a quick inspection, the first thing we do is send him back out with a handful of pesos to pick up a large cooler, bags of ice, and as many cases of beer as he can carry.

The Hobbit House is a mediocre steak house and bar with live music and performances. Started by a former Peace Corps volunteer, its mission is to provide dignified employment for "little people," while at the same time creating an homage to and celebrating its founder's love of J. R. R. Tolkien. There's been a bit of revisionist history applied to the actual benevolence factor following some local protests and calls for it to be closed down for exploiting and demeaning its employees. Their intentions may be good now—giving dwarfs a place to work and meet other little people in a country where they would otherwise be ostracized—but it hasn't always been the case, and it doesn't mean that their customers' intentions are equally noble.

According to our supposedly well-informed organizer and team leader, this is the place where midgets wear drink trays on their heads and drunken after-hours midget tossing is a nightly occurrence. When our waitress is not amused by our comments about midgets giving blow jobs while standing up, we begin to question his due diligence, as well as our expectations for the evening ahead of us.

As she is taking our drink orders, we test the waters once again. "Check out that pen in her hand. Wow. Let me see that," a guy shouts while grabbing at her. "No, not the pen. Give me your hand." He then proceeds to hold it up. "Wow, do you know how ginormous this would make my cock look?" Check please!

Apparently, the Hobbit House isn't what it once might have been, or perhaps never was. It's quite possible that we have mistaken it for the Ringside Bar in Makati, home (to this day) of midget wrestling, boxing, tossing and all-around belittling.

Having been abruptly asked to leave, it's time to jitney over to Burgos Street, the reddest street in the red-light district that is Manila. This is primarily the reason we're staying in Makati— Burgos Street is a strip of provocative neon lights and poorly lit bars for expats who seek the company of exotic Filipina girls, while watching dance shows and consuming cheap booze. That sounds terrible, and it's actually much worse than that. Walking around, it's impossible not to be accosted by door girls, mama-sans, freelance "masseuses," and other purveyors of the dark arts of Asia. I don't need to be told how handsome I am every twenty feet; I just want to drink. There is also considerable ladyboy risk—the Philippines is no different from Thailand or much of Southeast Asia in that there are so few opportunities for many destitute people in the rural districts that they send their kids (boys or girls) into the cities to serve as prostitutes.

Parading down Burgos with our group presents a hilarious education for a few of the guys who, having flown in from distant lands, are still somewhat unfamiliar with Asia. They certainly hadn't expected to be led around by a few Burgos Street celebrities. "Hey-lo, Henry, where you been?" "Bobby, you back so soon. Your favorite girl inside tonight." That's like going from New York to a strip club in Tampa and being so memorable that they recognize you six months later.

However, with names like High Heels, Rascals, or Ivory's Jungle Room, any further education for our newbies is no longer required. I have no recollection of which particular bar we ended up choosing, other than that it was one that came highly recommended by our fearless ringleaders.

The place is heaving with disgusting, degenerate white men ranging in age from backpacking teenagers to Liverpudlian pensioners who've chosen to wind down their mediocre existence on this planet living in nihilistic self-indulgence and relative comfort, instead of in some miserable British council estate. Of course, it's also swarming with love monkeys, all 9s and 10s by Makati standards.

Relying on his experience and expertise, this is where Varun, the head of syndicate at ████████████, takes over. "How much will it cost for you to kick out every single customer?"

The mama-san thinks for just a few seconds; she's clearly better at understanding risk (and math) than all of us. "You give me seven thousand US dollar, okay?" In another life, she'd probably make a good bond trader.

"Done. Do you take Amex?" He then turns to the groom. "Congratulations, buddy. This is my wedding present to you."

They shoo out all the riffraff, without allowing any "take-out," and then lock the doors so that it's just the twelve of us and thirty or forty girls. It's an open bar, with clothing optional and the "dibs" rule in effect.

My first move is to send one of the girls out to buy some plastic cups and Ping-Pong balls, which are unsurprisingly easy to find in Makati. I make sure she knows to invite our jitney driver back with her to come in and help himself. The Philippines is 98.5% Catholic, but he doesn't seem to require much convincing.

After Beer Pong slowly descends into stakes that are too punitive and sordid to recount, we move on to Liar's Dice. But we play that every weekend in Hong Kong, and it's too hard to stop the girls from signaling to each other. I don't blame them for cheating. After Beer Pong, they're petrified of the consequences of losing.

Next up is Love Monkey Bowling, which doesn't require much explanation, other than to say that we slick down the bar with a layer of cooking oil, and then take turns sliding the naked girls down it, aiming them at impromptu bowling pins in the form of ketchup bottles.

As the "dibs" start to kick into effect, it becomes harder for us to maintain the focus of the group, and therefore impossible to complete any more games without teammates or competitors sneaking off to dark corners for their own game of Doctors Without Borders.

This is where I take charge of a small group, mostly the out-of-towners, who seem less disposed to channel their inner Colonel Kurtz. They haven't been off the plane for five hours yet and this is how day one has started.

I'm going to dial things back a notch or two and take them to the Casino Royale. "Yes, of course it's just like the James Bond movie." As we are leaving the bar, we each grab a love monkey to take with us for good luck. Might as well—they're already paid for, and altruistically speaking, they'll be safer with us.

By the exit, we see Varun, having not bothered to search for a dark corner, with a wide grin on his face. He's got a drink in each hand, a girl under each arm, and another on his lap. "T.I.A., baby. T.I.A." The acronym from the movie *Blood Diamond*—"This Is Africa"—had long since been appropriated as "This Is Asia."

As I knew it would be, the casino is disgusting. "Sorry, chaps. It's not Monte Carlo, but tonight, it'll have to do." I can tell that they don't really want to be there, but I just want to gamble. We start off together at the baccarat table and then gradually jump around in search of blackjack, more drinks, and better luck.

One by one, my compatriots pull the Fenwick Exit and slink away unnoticed. The Fenwick Exit is like the Irish Exit but with a love monkey clinging to your arm.

I end up hitting it big, relatively speaking, considering that I started with about US$1,000 in peso equivalent. Here I am walking away with US$10,000. My only problem at this point is that the payout is all in pesos; it's such a shitty casino that the government-issued gaming license stipulates that they must operate entirely in local currency. My problem is exacerbated by the fact that the highest-denomination banknote is only ₱1,000, or approximately US$20, leaving me with stacks of tired, dirty, well-circulated bills.

Pockets bulging, I head back to the hotel with my lucky charm in tow. Given my success at the tables, calling her a love monkey at this point would almost be degrading. Almost.

I have no concept of time (I had gambled until nearly 8 A.M.), so walking back into the hotel, I run into a few of our group already convening for breakfast and Bloody Marys in the lobby bar.

Feeling charitable once again, I drop my lucky charm off upstairs in my room so that she can at least enjoy the amenities. She's absolutely shocked that I have no interest in fucking her but is quickly distracted by the Frette bathrobe and the rain shower. With that, I lock my valuables in the safe (rookie move—I should have done it when I first checked in) and then head back downstairs, pockets still bulging. After all, I'll need the bricks of cash as props to explain my early disappearance the previous night.

We spend an hour or so drinking in the lobby bar, waiting for the full group to emerge in time for our scheduled brunch. A few wake-up calls, a few more Bloody Marys, and a trip to the bathroom for a quick bump, and we are off through an interconnected series of walkways and office building atriums to the nearby Greenbelt, Manila's version of an upscale shopping mall.

Brunch is remarkably civilized, complete with pitchers of mimosas and bottles of good wine. Relief washes over the newbies; this weekend isn't going to be a complete descent into Hell.

Three hours and one crazy game of credit card roulette later, we are walking back through the mall contemplating our next move. Standing on the top floor overlooking the expansive atrium below, we stop and admire the hordes of locals schlepping across the ground level. We openly compare this view to that of the throngs of admirable and selflessly hard-working Filipina helpers who crowd the sidewalks of Hong Kong every Sunday, sitting in their cardboard box forts while playing cards and giving each other manicures on their only day off. In the context of this fleeting, drunken, yet philosophical discussion about income inequality, I am reminded of the fact that I have roughly five hundred ₱1,000 notes casually weighing my cargo shorts halfway down my ass.

I decide to unbundle one of the stacks and nonchalantly drop a bill over the edge of the third-level railing, against which we are all leaning. The bill flutters around magnificently as it makes its way slowly down, catching the invisible currents that push it ever so gently one way or the other. No one notices until it's about twenty feet off the ground, at which point it catches the attention of just one guy. He watches very hesitantly, clearly discounting the likelihood of this falling object being anything other than a worthless piece of paper, but also hedging his bets by tracking its final movements such that it comes to rest at his feet.

"Well, that was too subtle." This time, I take three banknotes and discreetly let them slip out of my hand. Once again, the slow and unpredictable flutter is a joy to watch. The first guy spots them right away. Unfortunately for him, he's unable to mask his excitement, and a couple of other people immediately stop to see what he is staring up at. He continues with determination, stumbling around, tracking the erratic movement of the falling bills, trying to decide which one he should home in on.

Now, we're getting somewhere. The three lucky recipients thus far, still somewhat confused and unable to ascertain the money's source, are now fixated on the heavens above. This time, I decide to drop five banknotes, once again discreetly enough as to not provide any proof of my existence.

At this point, I've only managed to get the attention of about a dozen people, all of whom have their eyes glued to the sky as real money inexplicably continues to rain down. With them entranced by the fluttering movement of the bills and battling the blinding sun that is shooting through the atrium's glass roof, I drop a few more bills. And then a few more. Finally, I have managed to get the undivided attention of a meaningfully sized crowd, all while remaining undetected.

There are whistles, claps, and cheers. People in all directions, having attempted to figure out what the hell is going on, are beginning to descend and gather below us. Money continues to rain down with a slow but increasing frequency. The security guard working the door at the Adidas shop abandons his post and sprints across, making a leaping grab over the outstretched arms of a meek woman. A few of the retail employees, at the risk of losing what is by their standards a great job, come charging out of their respective stores and join the growing fray.

I respond to the crowd, now more than fifty strong, this time with a cluster bomb of bills in short bursts. Things are starting to get crazy. Hands and eyes to the sky, people are running around chaotically as the breeze pushes the money back and forth, up and down, in all directions. Angst and frustration grow as they contend with the overwhelming task of choosing where to place their focus, not to mention the agony of repeatedly coming up just short. The stakes are high. One rather large, overzealous woman fails to see a bench that takes her out at the knees, sending her tumbling headfirst onto the unforgiving granite floor. "Fuck. I wish I had a camera" rings out from the Wall Street peanut gallery. A young girl, no older than six or seven, having spotted an outlier, patiently tracks the lone bill as it drifts away from the crowd. We're rooting for her; it's now within mere feet of her small hands. Boom! A huge brute broadsides her at full speed with a hit that would cost him fifteen yards in the NFL. Instead, he's rewarded with a day's pay.

To me, this is a social experiment or maybe some kind of performance art. But I can't help it if a dozen drunk white guys in polo shirts, khakis, and Havaiana flip-flops are laughing their asses off. A few of them have now decided to join in on the action. I hand out bills by the handful; it's like we're feeding pigeons in the park, and I'm the only kid who brought birdseed.

All discretion and subtlety on our part is now gone; we're laughing, pointing, and gesticulating wildly in full view of the crowd below. The crowd goes wild; there are now well over a hundred people who have gathered below us. I decide to cap things off with a bang, throwing out thirty or forty ₱1,000 bills at once—a finale of Fourth of July proportions.

Perfect timing to wrap it up. In my periphery, I can see three cops and two security guards running toward us. Were they coming direct to the source for a handout? No. They were coming to arrest us for "inciting a riot."

After a short conversation, we're able to help them understand how and why arresting any of us is just not an option. So they "decide," with our help, that the best course of action is for them to escort us back to our hotel "for our own safety." It makes sense now that a large crowd of people has made its way up to our level, and my pockets are still visibly full.

No sweat; my plan had been to do some more hotel drinking and then take a nap or hit the spa ahead of yet another big night. We return to the hotel lobby with a police escort.

After a few more hours of drinking within the safe confines of our hotel, it's my bedtime. "I'm calling it. It's three P.M. right now; I'll see you back here in four hours."

████████, the head of sales at ████████████, flags down the head concierge and waves him over. "Excuse me, good sir. I'd like to go up to my room to lie down, but I believe there might still be a love monkey in my bed. Is there any way you could have security check for me and remove her as required? Room 1408."

"But of course, sir. That is not a problem."

"The lone Yank on the trip is amazed. "What? They do that? That's fucking genius."

Never to be outdone, Varun pipes, "Room 1202 also, please. But you might want to bring some help. There were two of them, and they were pretty feisty."

This completed the "Day One: Steak Dinner" portion of our itinerary.

Most of us are totally unfazed by the antics thus far; it had long since become our reality. Even the first timers who had, just hours prior, been terrified at the prospect of the Burgos Street love monkey lock-in, are now leading the charge. "Come on, boys. Naps are for pussies."

I'm not sure if we had lost our equilibrium, or found it. But I did know that resistance was futile.

Fuck the nap.

Up next: "Day Two: Dancing Girls."

Epilogue

These are a few of my stories. All bankers have stories just like them, with some variation of degree. Although I am happy to have retired from banking and am now focused on my family, I certainly enjoyed the years I spent on Wall Street, and remain unapologetic for all that I saw and did. I enjoyed the fuck out of it.

I didn't write this book to brag about or glorify any of my experiences. Rather, I wanted to illuminate a culture of systemic corruption and pervasive deviance. After all, the premise of the Twitter account has always been to satirize and criticize Wall Street culture. Industry apologists like to pretend that any stain on the character or reputation of the industry is a function of a few rotten apples. That, unequivocally, was not my experience. And I saw it all, from an indisputably omniscient vantage point.

Most of the people mentioned in this book have moved on to more senior positions at the biggest and most prestigious firms in the world. They're held in high esteem by a society that values wealth and success. They're wielding influence in Washington. They're sitting on the boards of Fortune 500 companies. They're taking Communion. They're leading philanthropic initiatives. They're married to your daughters.

I will certainly concede that the industry has changed in the time since many of these stories took place. Balance sheets are smaller. Risk appetite is diminished. Compensation and incentive structures have changed. That has undoubtedly impacted the culture. Many of the colorful, big swinging dick characters have left the trading floor for the buy side, entrepreneurial initiatives, or just the beach.

But I know that if I'm on a plane to Hell, the first-class cabin will be full.